DATE DUE

			PRINTED IN U.S.A.

NOV 3 0 2012

Marronnage and Arts

Marronnage and Arts:
Revolts in Bodies and Voices

Edited by

Stéphanie Melyon-Reinette

CAMBRIDGE
SCHOLARS

P U B L I S H I N G

Marronnage and Arts:
Revolts in Bodies and Voices,
Edited by Stéphanie Melyon-Reinette

This book first published 2012

Cambridge Scholars Publishing

12 Back Chapman Street, Newcastle upon Tyne, NE6 2XX, UK

British Library Cataloguing in Publication Data
A catalogue record for this book is available from the British Library

ISBN (10): 1-4438-4142-0, ISBN (13): 978-1-4438-4142-9

TABLE OF CONTENTS

LIST OF ILLUSTRATIONS

LIST OF TABLES

FOREWORD

Originating from a conference organized for the Africaphonie Festival in Paris, on May 10, 2011, "Marronnage: Music, Dance and Politics" was intended to be a crossroad of visions, viewpoints and overlapping discourses. In fact, this crossroad was to be a junction between science and the senses, between objectivity and subjectivity, between reflection and emotion, an encounter which would join scholarly analyses and researches with artists' testimonies.

Why choose to mix two spheres which seem to be antithetical antipodes? Why the combination of arts and sciences? The simplest response is as follows: most of the time, we would probably think that people interested in studying music and/or dance have the soul of an artist. It is, therefore, thoroughly interesting to meld the worlds of art and science which are seen as opposed and contradictory, because, in fact, they are not. They are complementary and together can provide perspectives and substance in analyzing a phenomenon. Because the objects of the conference were music and dance, we invited various kinds of artists and scholars: ethnomusicologists, musicologists, art-therapists, musicians, dancers and choreographers. We wanted to see ideas, theories and experiences confronted, and to have them complement one another. The belief in the richness of human experience led us to ask artists to offer testimonies of their own musical grounds and construction, of their musical inspirations and political motivations (if any). It is likely that some artists have produced musical and dance trends which were the result of the social and political circumstances from which they have emerged and developed. The artists are people who allow, through the reappropriation of their roots, or through the fusion of the remnant parts of their native and imposed cultures, the emergence of new traditions and new observances of their cults and rites.

The conference was therefore concerned with the cultures of postcolonial countries and societies, in a period from slavery to the contemporary era, in order to shed light on the various music and dance trends that have appeared. Thus, studying the notion and the expressions of revolt through these artistic trends, we decided to consider the idea of "marronnage" as intrinsically linked with slavery, abolition and the post-slavery period through three distinct axes (which are also interdependent):

Bodily marronnage (traditional music and dances, drumming and skin instruments). Slaves were oppressed and kept in bondage, their bodies used as instruments to increase the economic richness of their masters. They would therefore find relief and freedom in their late-night dances and circles.

Cultural marronnage ("urban roots," music and dances of the twenty-first century): During decolonization, music and dance were also vectors of speeches of freedom, of revolt (during the civil-rights movement), and of the claiming of black identity.

Intellectual marronnage (contemporaneous music and dance of the twenty-first century): It is "intellectual" because many cultural movements in the 1990s, for example, were clearly thought out and philosophically built to counteract the effects of "assimilation" by permitting the emergence of counter-cultures (inheritances of the founding fathers of the black, Panafrican and Afrocentrist movements of the previous period considered).

Consequently, art expressions might be interwoven with our determinations, stances and involvements. The point of this book is to highlight the similarities and the differences which exist between all those trends which have developed in different postcolonial societies with a common starting point, slavery, and with the same colonizers: the French, Spanish and English. The enslaved men and women delivered on the coasts of the Caribbean islands came from various ethnic tribes, thus, their characteristics intermingled and evolved into distinguished cultural and traditional forms with common traits. In fact, this book's purpose is to reveal the codes and the meanings behind the dance and music whose images often are misunderstood, unknown, denied or disparaged, especially when it comes to traditional dances, too often misused or reduced to folklore when there is in fact a depth of meaning behind it. Modern and contemporary black music trends are too often criticized and denigrated because, most of the time, their origins are also ignored.

Here is the summary of the three axes defined before the conference:

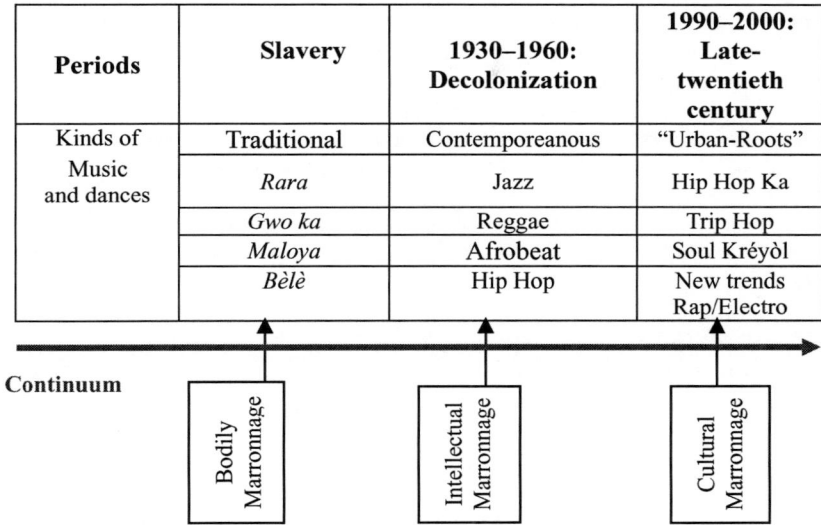

Periods	Slavery	1930–1960: Decolonization	1990–2000: Late-twentieth century
Kinds of Music and dances	Traditional	Contemporeanous	"Urban-Roots"
	Rara	Jazz	Hip Hop Ka
	Gwo ka	Reggae	Trip Hop
	Maloya	Afrobeat	Soul Kréyòl
	Bèlè	Hip Hop	New trends Rap/Electro

Continuum

| Bodily Marronnage | Intellectual Marronnage | Cultural Marronnage |

This book will appeal to a large range of readers: scholars as much as music lovers, professional dancers, dance fans, cultural protagonists, and so on and so forth. Its vocation—as was the conference—is to make this knowledge available to anyone interested in black, postcolonial and politicized dance, music and cultures. In addition, the contributors vow a real passion to their subjects, as most of them are both scholars and artists. They conciliate the worlds of analysis and experience in both living and deciphering the cultural form. Do we need to be immersed in some cultural phenomenon in order to understand it better? Does neutrality count here? Can we rely on a scientific judgement when he or she is immersed in their subject? Isn't that participating observation?

Marronnage will be addressed with questions like: How has this music and these dances of revolt appeared? Can music or dance really be seen as a lever of revolt? What is the musical or instrumental discourse (e.g. ethnomusicology, musicology, musicians, dancers, dance anthropology etc.)? What is a Maroon? What did it mean half and a century ago, in the late twentieth century, and what does it mean today? Is the body of the "Maroon" a discursive process in opposition with the established order, or a body in opposition? Is "Marooning" becoming a "nigger," claiming one's blackness? What are the great periods of identity, racial and cultural acknowledgement and recognition? Do the musicians of those periods consider themselves as Maroons, as rebels, as revolutionary thinkers? Are music and dance outlets for social discrepancies and historical frustrations and/or tools of struggle? What is the link between dance and music in Maroon art expression? To which extent do artists take part into the political process, and is there any such involvement from the artistic field? Are there artists involved in the democratic, political and community processes? Are there forethinkers, pioneers, political leaders among them?

Consequently, the call for papers was the starting point of this project. The scholars and artists who submitted proposals—which were accepted and presented in May 2011 in Paris—appear in this collection. Though a few gave up the project, I solicited others to submit proposals after the conference. Thus, this is a rich cultural piece of which I am really proud to share with readers, researchers and art lovers. It gathers professionals, scholars and artists, depicting and analyzing cultural and artistic forms inherited from the slavery era such as traditional practices in the French West Indies (*Gwo ka* in Guadeloupe, *Bèlè* in Martinique, *Maloya* in Réunion, etc.), and modern music trends like Reggae, Dancehall, Hip Hop and Rap, born from the 1960s and developing up to the present, through the concept of marronnage (whose meaning differs from one place to another). The chapters will enable readers to experience a trip through the Caribbean islands as well as the Indian Ocean (because we often forget that slavery also existed elsewhere in the world, and not only in the Caribbean), and the countries of South America such as Brazil. They will discover the great diversity of the black cultures and of the Black diaspora, meant here in Paul Gilroy's sense, the Afro-descendants.

In the first part entitled "Traditional Drums and Original Marronnage," various approaches are delivered through the artists' lenses, experiences, histories and analyses. They look at traditions as fundamentals of resistance both of themselves and of their native people. Because the drum was an instrument and an arm in liberation during slavery, it is today a symbol of resistance, of inheritance—from the Maroons, the niggers or the *kaf*, or any other group defined in accordance with its African origins— and of communication with the metaphysical and societal spirits.

The second part, "Allegorical Marronnage," reveals how the concept of marronnage, this process of freeing oneself by fleeing from bondage and the dehumanizing treatments the slaves suffered in those islands and countries, is played out socially via customs and traditional practices. Thus, carnival is a projection of marronnage through the reincarnation of historical, legendary and political figures into the artists' and carnival followers' bodies. The body turns into a sociopolitical flag, transfiguring anticolonial standpoints. Elsewhere, the allegory is expressed through the reappropriation or the reusing of public spaces, clearly and primarily seen as oppressive and thoroughly involved in the assimilating project of the societies they live in. Therefore, they reuse these public spaces, turning them into arenas or safe milieus for the positive processes they are involved in. Furthermore, it can be read in a third manner; that music becomes in certain cases a metaphor for marronnage.

The third and last part, "Symbolic Marronnage," exemplifies the fact that marronnage, seen as an inheritance from the past, is a prism of rebellion and anticonformism that artists draw from in order to shape their own forms of expression, their own speech, and direct their political claims through.

Consequently, marronnage is a stance, an attitude, a mentality. This book provides a wide span of shapes, ideologies or demonstrations of marronnage and shows how the quest of freedom expressed during slavery has infiltrated the social relationships and the arts to develop approaches and expressions of identity specific to postcolonial societies, conditioned by the interracial and phenotypico-social interactions, the aftermath of slavery, and undoubtedly the social-economic structures which rank the black communities at the lowest levels. Those music and dances have been, and remain, new cosmogonies with particular codes, new spheres where black slaves, freed men and their descendants could and still can express, scream, cry or enjoy their freedom. All the contributors here shed new light on those phenomena and unveil the preconceived stereotypical, folkloric, sensualized and heavy ideological blanket that conceals the Caribbean, African and Indian Oceanic cultures.

ACKNOWLEDGEMENTS

First and foremost, my acknowledgements will be addressed to all the contributors who willingly participated in this project and provided both their investigations and their passion: scholars Nathalie Montlouis, Dr. Steve Gadet, Marie Cousin, Klara Boyer-Rossol, Dr. William "Lez" Henry, Dr. Michelle Bermiss-Smith and artists Edmond Mondésir, Florence Latappy, Ashaman Jahlawa, Asaliah Gad, Tiwony and Nèg Lyrical. Interestingly, those who participated in the project are, in the most part, both scholars and artists, and consequently they have presented the side of their coin they preferred to be recognized by. Thank you for the richness of your contributions, and for a better knowledge and understanding of those music trends rooted in revolt and rebellion.

The conference which took place in Paris in May 2011 aimed at celebrating the abolition of slavery by broaching a topic which is more and more important in the Caribbean and which encompasses its whole meaning in metropolitan France and in the African diaspora. Consequently, I am really honoured to be able to have this conference published thanks to Cambridge Scholars Publishing, and I am adamant in thanking France as well, since it is a constant struggle to have those subjects broached in that country, even though they must be seen, accepted and inherently incorporated into *l'Histoire de France*.

Two women must also be thanked: Nathalie Montlouis, who is now one of my dearest friends and an accomplice in conferences, and who contributed in the translations and reading of certain articles; and Dr. Michelle Bermiss Smith, who helped in reading those pages as well.

Finally, I address my acknowledgements to history and all the men and women who have built ours. To the freedom fighters and those human beings who struggled, died and survived to make the music that is still vivid and bright today, for us to pass over to new generations and other peoples and cultures.

Dr. Stéphanie Melyon-Reinette

PART I

TRADITIONAL DRUMS
AND ORIGINAL MARRONNAGE

THE EVOLUTION OF *GWO KA* FROM THE TWENTIETH CENTURY TO THE PRESENT DAY

MARIE-LINE DAHOMAY

Nowadays, many details and specificities of the genesis of *Gwo ka* still remain unknown. This work is an attempt to summarise the main phases of the evolution of *Gwo ka* in Guadeloupe[1] throughout the twentieth century, the period wherein the sources are the most numerous. Nevertheless, it is important to insist that the analysis of the complex journey of *Gwo ka* music would require more than a short article.

Born from the encounter between contrasting musical, social and ritual practices from the enslaved African-Diasporic populations, *Gwo ka* music comes from a Caribbean island called Guadeloupe. Guadeloupe is a French overseas department, a true melting pot where Amerindian, African, European and Indian cultural influences have interacted for centuries.

The few historical sources available designate the music of the enslaved under various terms such as *Calenda* (Labat 1704), or *Bamboula* (Merovil 1918) after the emancipation. Nevertheless, the descriptions they give, especially that of the *Bamboula*, present common characteristics with *Gwo ka*, corroborating the theory of its common roots with the music of the enslaved.

Oral tradition bounds *Gwo ka* with a survival instinct, the spirit of resistance, marronnage, the cry for freedom, the distress of exile and the drive for transcendence and creation. *Gwo ka* music is itself a creation of transcendence (Uri 1991, 39), most likely elaborated through various processes of appropriation, imitation and borrowing of cultural features which are almost unidentifiable today, as they have influenced this music for centuries. However, if the ritual function no longer exists, *Gwo ka* remains greatly influenced by African features (La fontaine 1983). A new instrument of percussion emerged from this musical practice: the *Tanbou-Ka*. However, the first photographic evidence of the existence of such an instrument, dating back to the end of the nineteenth and beginning of the twentieth centuries,[2] identified it by the name of *tam-tam*. In the 1950s and 1960s the popular word *gwotanbou* ("big drum") was used interchangeably for the drum and its music.[3] Napoleon Magloire, a prominent *Gwo ka* singer from Mare-Gaillard in Gosier,[4] along with other traditional musicians from the Ste Rose village, testify to having always heard the appellation *ka* from their boyhood. Therefore, the question is: when did the Guadeloupean population used the word *Gwo ka* to designate this music? Could it be a recent circumstance?

This issue is less controversial in the traditional milieu than the significance and the origin of the word *Gwo ka*, for which three theories were coined:

- A mystical approach: the word *ka* allegedly has the same significance as the symbol *ka* in Egyptian mythology.
- An Afro-centric approach: *Gwo ka* could be a corrupted form of the word *N'goka* which designates a drum in North Dahomay and Angola.
- A Linguistic approach: *Gwo ka* could be the translation in Creole (*Kréyol*) for the French expression *gros quart de baril*—"big quarter of a barrel" (barrels used to transport and store salted meat were then used as the body and resonance chamber of the instrument).

Although anchored in the suburbs of larger cities, at least since the end of the nineteenth century, *Gwo ka* comes from the world of the plantation, from the Guadeloupean rural context. This musical genre associates dances, song repertoires and percussion according to the following pattern:

- The audience assembled in a circle (called *la ronde*)
- Two drums are used for the *boula* rhythms
- A solo drum called *make* is used
- A singer and a chorus perform the call and response songs
- Smaller percussions such as *cha cha* are used
- Only one person dances at a time in the midst of *la ronde*.

In the Caribbean, there are music, dances and even drums similar to *Gwo ka*. One can recognize words such as *ka, boula,* and "big drum."[5] However, *Gwo ka* music has specific characteristics and codes exclusive to its Guadeloupean base which are:

- Seven fundamental rhythms, each with specific repertoires of songs and dance steps.
- A *santimanka*,[6] a particular musical colour inherent to this music.

- The *lokans*, the stamp of a good singer, comprises improvisation skills, variations and modulation of the voice, the ability to narrate and eloquence. It also includes the resonance and the sonority of the voice.
- *La rèpriz*, a medium used by the singer, the dancer and the drummer (the *tambouyé)*, to position themselves on the rhythm and the measure. *La rèpriz* resets the dynamic of the musical ensemble. It is also a beat used by the dancer and the *makè*[7] to transition the dance steps.
- Codes, precise phrases of percussion allowing, for instance, the transition from one rhythm to another, or to move to the coda.
- Particular foot work for the dance; the heel and the mid-foot are used as contact points to reach the *bigidi*,[8] which is the state where the dancer is no longer stable on the ground and is on the verge of falling.
- The creation of a special context or space beneficial to its diffusion, such as *la swaré léwòz*[9] and the *kout'tanbou*. *Swaré léwòz* is the name given to the open air parties organized near the factories or the plantations on the workers' pay day or every fortnight (also called *kenzen*). The *kout' tanbou*[10] exists outside of the Léwòz context. The former can be improvised or organized with events such as *la bamboula anba mawché*[11] during local fairs.
- *Gwo ka* is simultaneously regarded as a catharsis and entertainment medium, and even a means of earning a living.
- The lyrics of the songs, often anecdotal, usually narrate the everyday lives of the common people.

At the beginning of the twentieth century, *Gwo ka* was considered to be a music genre practiced by *vyé-nèg*. The songs, dance and percussion distinctiveness were transmitted orally and informally, either by imitation or osmosis. Throughout the 1950s and 1960s numerous folk ballets[12] were performed on local, Caribbean and even international scenes. Although they vectored a *doudouistic*[13] and folk image of the tradition, these groups played a great part in the preservation of *Gwo ka* and in the alteration of mentalities (Leauva 2008).

As early as 1946, the year of the *Départementalisation*,[14] Guadeloupe had become the scene of a major social crisis in which most factories had to shut down causing the rural population to flock to the city. It was a time during which the Bumidom[15] scheme created massive migration to France. A branch of *Gwo ka* would therefore migrate to other lands,[16] where the French dominant culture would reinforce the disgust of the Guadeloupeans and their ancestral traditions.

In 1963, the Guadeloupean Marcel Mavounzy made the first audio recording[17] of *Gwo ka*. Other producers such as Henry Debs and Raymond Célini would follow. Traditional *Gwo ka* from the countryside would henceforth become accessible to all Guadeloupeans. The diffusion of the song repertoire, the rhythms, the *boulagèl*[18] and the *makè* percussion phrases were promoted by this new audio support, making it easy for people to learn. Key *Gwo ka* figures such as the illustrious drummers Vélo, Brabant, Loyson, Chaben, Sergius Geoffroy, Anzala, Dolor and Guy Conquette[19] were brought into the limelight. The latter would conquer the youth of the 1970s with his innovative and modern approach to *Gwo ka*, characterised by his singing and improvised style. He was the forerunner of *Gwo ka* teaching, and the very first *Gwo ka* classes were held in his house at Jabrun in Baie Mahault.

The 1970s and 1980s witnessed a radical time in *Gwo ka* history. Due to the growing nationalistic and cultural awareness fuelling various identity struggles, *Gwo ka* was defined as the only "authentic" music of the Guadeloupean people (AGEG 1977; Lockel 1978). This social movement was encouraged by political parties, trade unions and students alike. In the midst of this Guadeloupean identity quest, *Gwo ka* was to play a major role, which was probably amplified by the aforementioned propaganda throughout the entire island (Cyrille 174). The Radio Station "Radio Tanbou" broadcasted *Gwo ka* music on a permanent basis and the "*Gwo ka* Festival" was created during the same period. This new cultural conscience generated deep changes in the *Gwo ka* world, which was to face increasing influence from modernity and globalisation.

Gwo ka influence exceeded its traditional domain. From then on, it was concerned with socio-political problems, the economy, spirituality, education, the diffusion of information, the creation of slogans or the transmission of messages. Since most of the factories had shut down, the occasions and context for the *kout' tanbou* and *Swaré Léwòz* took over the streets, the churches, the strikes, the political meetings, cultural gatherings, family events, the schools, local fairs and diverse commemorations. The basic configuration was modified, showing an increasing number of *boula*, *makè* and *chacha*. From this period, traditional groups were commissioned to coordinate the *Swaré léwòz*. Proper sound systems were used to optimise the musical experience. The *Léwòz* became increasingly popular as *grands léwòz* could attract around a thousand visitors. All modern means of communication from banners, the internet, flyers, TV advertisements and the media in general became commonly used. The production of recorded music increased, from vinyl to compact discs and sometimes complemented by music videos, and many documentaries have already been produced on the topic.

The transmission of *Gwo ka* was gradually formalised through the proliferation of workshops, classes or music and dance methods. In each district, schools[20] were opened, securing the preparation of the younger generation and producing numerous talented artists of whom many were invited to perform on international scenes.[21] Genuine pillars of this cultural movement,[22] these schools were able to convey to their students legitimate cultural values in addition to the music and dance legacy.

Drum making became a recognized line of work. Each artisan enhanced their research around the sounds, the norms, the method of stretching goat skin[23] and the use of new materials. Consequently, the modern *tanbouka*— of differing craftsmanship with regard to its size and shape—has a higher pitch compared to the originals. The *djembéka* became prominent in the twentieth century and came in the form of a *djembe*,[24] with the same skin tension as the *tanbouka*. The occupation of drum maker was officially recognised in 2011 by the French Ministry of Culture, which presented Yves Tholes with the title *Maître d'Art*.[25]

The notion of folk groups, popular in the 1960s, gave way to choreographic groups[26] and dance companies in the late the twentieth century. These groups allied tradition and modernity in their performances. The choreographer Léna Blou, initiated to *Gwo ka* by Jacqueline Cachemire,[27] founded in 2010 a training centre called *Techni'ka*[28] for professional dancers.

This evolution in *Gwo ka* added meaning to the artistic creation. Every year, the compositions of both the elders and the younger generation[29] have enhanced its repertoire. Polyrythmic[30] innovations resulted from new conceptions of the rhythmic approach, and a new rhythm, the *takout* from the group *takouta,* was created. New talented groups, drummers, dancers and singers have come forward, each one presenting their personal or singular styles and even techniques typical to specific Guadeloupean localities. Nowadays, there are professional traditional artists registered at the SACEM.[31] If the singers are traditionally male, the past twenty years have witnessed an increasing number of female[32] singers, especially in performances or in Women's *Léwòz* (*Léwòz a Fanm*). These women bring to *Gwo ka* a more harmonious *santimanka*. The *Les femmes chantent les classiques du Ka*[33] event allows female singers from all musical backgrounds to experience the particular *Gwo ka* style of singing. *Gwo ka* has also infiltrated carnival through the repertoires of *group a po*[34] such as Akiyo, Voukoum, Mas Ka Klè (Laumuno, 2011), which often have their own *Gwo ka* factions and organise *Swaré léwòz*. During the carnival procession, the *Gwo ka* songs are complemented by an adapted or *senjan*[35] rhythm played on carnival drums.

A modern form of *Gwo ka* emerged from these years of *Gwo ka* "emancipation." Supported by the musician Gerard Lockel since the 1970s, this new liberated approach of *Gwo ka* proclaimed its legitimacy as a true musical genre deserving to be written and played on musical instruments. Nationalist and activist, Gerard Lockel released the first work of his musical group in a box set of three vinyl discs in 1977, then published his *Gwo ka* method titled: *Gwo Ka Modèn*. During the same period, other musicians attempted to associate other musical instruments to *Gwo ka*, such as Patrick Jean Marie and his group Atika, Guy Conquette, Gilbert Coco, Christian Dahomay, Georges Troupe, and Kafé among many others. However, the expression and concept *Gwo Ka Modèn*, which is protected terminology developed by Gerard Lockel, has nowadays entered informal language as the expression *Gwo ka moderne* (modern *Gwo ka*).

Many other groups[36] would later join this quest for a modern expression of *Gwo ka*, from the most "purist" to the most "diluted" forms open to various musical genres. New percussive instruments emerged from these endeavours: the *gwadlouka, the yakalok, la batterie Gwo ka* and the *batrika*.

The *Gwo ka moderne* concept erases the basic *Gwo ka* configuration described above. The call and response form is no longer systematic. The triad singer/dancer/*makè* is no longer at the core of the performance. The stage has become the privileged space of *Gwo ka* expression. The music is supported by the performance, its structure, and harmonisation. Some creations have the ambition to remain authentic in the traditional repertoire. Others, essentially inspired by the *santimanka* and the rhythms, have elaborated a particular sense of harmony. This can be seen in the work of Christian Laviso, who created the *guitareka* concept, a genuine mutation of the *makè* and the *Gwo ka* expression on a guitar, and today he is recognized as a highly talented French guitarist (Laviso 2008), Laviso has embraced jazz influences while remaining anchored to his *Gwo ka* heritage.

Throughout its evolution, *Gwo ka moderne* contributed to the reconciliation of traditional musicians with the Jazz world and vice versa. This concord came after many "hostile" years when *Gwo ka* was not considered a true musical genre. At the end of the 1990s and the beginning of the 2000s, numerous Jazz and *Gwo ka* fusions were made possible through the collaboration of artists such as the American saxophonist David Murray, Gerard Lockel and the *Gwo ka* Masters,[37] or the alliance of the group Akiyo Ka and a Breton group called Carre Manchot.[38] Along with these initiatives and musical innovations, the general interest shown by international musicians[39] greatly helped to effect a change of mentalities as far as *Gwo ka* legitimacy was concerned. The Jazz/*Gwo ka* marriage was consummated through the young generation of Guadeloupean jazzmen, which has borne new concepts and spaces of expression to the international scene through such artists as Franck Nicolas, Jacques Schwarz-Barth,[40] and the Castry brothers. Other musicians would come back to the country, bringing with them their musical experience and incorporating it in the *Gwo ka moderne* concept.[41]

The musical path opened by *Gwo ka moderne* presented a contemporaneous instrumental expression of the traditional frame, which has increasingly inspired other non-traditional musical ensembles.[42] These ensembles are known for using the *Gwo ka* repertoire on other rhythmic forms such as Zouk, Funk and Combo Jazz. There again, the traditional structure is altered, with the pieces performed often aimed at favouring partner dancing. In nightclubs and balls, the *lokans* and the drums are adapted to the rhythm played. There are many interpretations of these traditional songs, performed by zouk[43] singers,[44] however, this phenomenon creates confusion as the younger generation regard them as being the original pieces. Some of these groups complement the *santimanka* with an additional Caribbean touch, as perfected by the group Soft,[45] whose success has spread from Guadeloupe to Caribbean and European shores, while the group Kriyolio experiments with the *santimanka* through the *guadajazz* combination.

Urban music, Hip Hop, Dancehall, Ragga, and Slam[46] have also came into the heritage of the *Gwo ka* rhythms, dance steps and *tanbouka*. The encounter of these different musical genres occurred during two performances: Dub N'Ka in 2003 and Urban'ka in 2007 in which the masters of *Gwo ka* shared their musical experience with urban music celebrities.

Finally, at present two ideologically and musically opposed spheres are attempting to interact: *Gwo ka* and opera. Indeed, some lyrical singers have tried their voices within the classical *Gwo ka* repertoire and vice versa.[47] In 2006, Akiyoka experimented with Mozart during the *Journées Internationales de la Harpe* (International Days of the Harp). Christian Dahomay,[48] composer, author and researcher in *Gwo ka*, is currently writing musical pieces for large ensembles. Two of his *Pieces pour Gwo ka et Cordes* (Music for *Gwo ka* and strings), performed by the Chevalier St Georges' orchestra, were played in various classical concerts in Guadeloupe and in France.

Is There a Rupture Between Tradition
and Contemporaneous Creation?

While originally confined to villages or the countryside in general, *Gwo ka* nowadays occupies the entire Guadeloupean territory. It is present in all the strata of the Guadeloupean population. In its traditional form, it could preserve most of its fundamental codes and its primary configuration despite some apparent mutations. Becoming more accessible through a more modern and open form, *Gwo ka* has exploded into a multitude of new styles available to a wider audience. As such, it has a universal propensity as Klod Kiavué, the *tanbou makè* of David Murray's[49] group, explained: "I think that my own compositions are not *Gwo ka* and that those of Murray are likewise open. I would define it as *Mizik a Nèg*,[50] yes; this is how we like to call it, a universal music of the black people." Jacques Schwarz-Bart also sensed the universal propensity of *Gwo ka*:

> I find that there is something bubbling in *Gwo ka* music that favours improvisation. It is a path open to many people. And many will explore it. Similarly to Dizzy, who brought the Latin Jazz form to the Unites States. When he first started, people thought that he had lost his mind. Fifteen years later, Latin Jazz had entered the universal language. In a few years, it will be normal to invite *Gwo ka* jazz ensembles in Jazz festivals. Well, at the moment, the purists do not understand what I do. Sometimes, I use some effects on my sax, and this offends them. If we are able to offend the purists, we must be on the right path (laughs). Because nothing is pure. There is no such thing as pure music. Music equates to movement, so let's make it move.[51]

Nevertheless, modernity needs the experience of these "purists" as they cultivate the *santimanka*. The latter is indeed the foundation and the characteristic feature of *Gwo ka*, sustaining the roots of ancestral inspiration. As long as this *santimanka* reamins identifiable at different levels through both modern and traditional pieces, *Gwo ka* will resist the phenomenon of globalisation. In fact, even when borrowing various characteristics from the culture of the "other," globalisation never ceases to standardize other styles and genres.

At this stage of evolution, one can wonder if the appellation "traditional" is still suited to *Gwo ka*, as oral transmission, typical to traditional music form, tends to disappear in favour of formalised teachings and as its artistic creation, incontestably modern, opens it to the world: "It is better to identify *Gwo ka* as a contemporaneous music, meaning that it is a music that is not fixed in its original period but a music that lives throughout time that it is played and danced while accepting the constraints imposed by modern world" (Laumuno 2011).

In the twenty-first century, *Gwo ka* has become an ethos, a way of life. It epitomises the spiritual strength which helped the people throughout the long nights of negotiation during the LKP[52] movement in 2009. *Gwo ka* is also present in some Guadeloupean churches, whether they be Catholic or Pentecostal, and some use it for therapeutic purposes. The omnipresent symbol of the Guadeloupean identity, the *tanbouka*, is an inspiration for clothes, jewels, craft making, tattoos, architecture, furniture, and brands. The various utilisations of this symbol express the Guadeloupeans' need to introduce themselves as heirs of an original culture and their eagerness to define their territory.

Nowadays, the challenge for *Gwo ka* is to enter the Representative List of the Intangible Cultural Heritage of Humanity for the year 2012. As such, it would therefore be regarded as intangible cultural heritage among other endangered cultural specificities. "Saving" it would mean to ensure "the sustainability, the identification, the documentation, research, the protection, the promotion, the enhancement, the transmission essentially through formal and informal means, as well as the revitalisation of its various aspects."[53] As demonstrated in this chapter, *Gwo ka* continues to develop, multiplying its styles and its spaces. Therefore, it manages its own "sustainability," even its "substance," through formal education in numerous schools and the publication of methods, music scores, the production of CDs and movies as well as the manufacturing of its instruments. Academically speaking, there are numerous researchers and students of various origins who come to Guadeloupe each year to study and write articles on the manifold aspects of *Gwo ka*.

To what extent will such recognition affect Guadeloupean *Gwo ka*? How will France, supposedly concerned with the protection of this heritage among others things, "strive"[54] to enforce the various measures and policies of which the inventory is the only mandatory aspect according to the convention's wording? What will be both the triggering factors of this endeavour and its manifestation in the cultural life? These are current issues still to be discussed in the *Gwo ka* world.

BÈLÈ IN MARTINIQUE:
THE FOUNDATION OF RESISTANCE
AND EXISTENCE

EDMOND MONDÉSIR*

(*) Translated from French by Nathalie Montlouis

In my childhood, I was never directly involved in *Bèlè*. This disconnection was due to the fact that, at that time, I lived in a village where *Bèlè* was not actually practiced. People who practiced *Bèlè* (the *Bèlè* people) did it very naturally within their homes and families of their neighbourhood. They never travelled to do performances. However, I had heard about one of my grandfathers who was a *Bèlè* drummer from various stories. I had gathered that he was so passionate about drumming that he experienced many problems in his personal life—his wife actually left him because of drumming. It is from there that, in an obscure corner of my conscience, I was persuaded that I was from a lineage of *Bèlè* people. Nevertheless, at that time, I had never directly interacted with *Bèlè*.

However, I used to hum various songs; actually, they were fragments, partial reproductions of various songs that came to me God only knows how. These were tunes that could be heard anywhere, as though floating in the atmosphere. These were a type of song that could have been derived either from *bèlè*, *beguines*, Christmas carols or from the singing part of the tales that were told in wakes.

It was the era of oral transmission. We have to realise that there was no radio and, of course, no television. I have had the opportunity to hear people "make music" in the neighbourhood, especially at one of my uncles or at some of our neighbours or family friends' house. There used to be balls with one or two musical instruments and people would beat on anything at hand—chairs or tables, in a similar fashion to the Christmas Carol or *Chanté Nwel* musical tradition.

I remember that there was a courtyard where we rolled dice in trays placed on trestles. Inside the house, others sang and danced while many ate and drank. The day after, one could find incrusted on the ground the tops of the lemonade bottles drank during the party.

Therefore, we did have a cultural practice linked to singing with some form of drumming that was not *bèlè*, as we were not from a *bèlè* neighbourhood. Yet, the youth of the time was in the habit of beating on anything that could produce a characteristic sound or an interesting rhythm, such as saucepans, pales or boxes. This musical practice was the reproduction of tunes and sounds that we heard among us and it is this atmosphere that influenced me in my childhood. As I was growing up, this musical tradition would gradually create in me a fundamental interest in drumming practices.

Edmond Mondésir and his drum.

This love for the drum, this real passion shared by many Martiniquan youths, celebrated by some artists in various compositions, was actually paradoxical. It happened during a time when these musical practices were scorned by mainstream society as they were regarded as "nigger"[55] practices.

This is perhaps the reason why an effective transmission of *bèlè* practices was so difficult; one must know that even in the *bèlè* milieu, one had to face up to prejudice.

This is how things were, and this was my practice. When I go through my memories, I believe that it is probably later, as a sixth form college student in 1963, that I first heard about Ti Emile and *bèlè*. Back then, I did not really pay much attention to it. Paradoxically, it was in France, when I started tertiary education in 1965, that I really got acquainted with the *bèlè* drum sonorities, and encounter was very emotional for me.

Indeed, sometime earlier, several *bèlè* recordings had been released. There was the AGEM record (General Association of Martiniquan Students), made possible thanks to the recordings of Frank Hubert and his determination and intrepidity, as well as one covering Anca Bertrand and Leon Sainte-Rose's *bèlè* approach.

As a student, I was encouraged to deepen my interest and love for percussion, which was being refined and more focused on *bèlè*. In this multicultural environment provided by the university, I was able to realise the importance of one's musical heritage. Moreover, I had access to multicultural musical productions, allowing me to develop my musical inclinations. Indeed, I had numerous Guadeloupean friends who had a more thorough knowledge of their percussive heritage, *Gwo ka*. I had access to their music and I was struck by two records of the legendary Velo, a mythic character of Guadeloupean *Gwo ka*. My next door neighbour was a French Guyanese who urged me to discover various recordings that valorized the particular Guyanese rhythms. There were also the African students who translated their culture through songs and rhythms very naturally. In addition to all of these influences, I was particularly impressed by the musical productions from Haiti. Before I left Martinique, I had the opportunity to listen to the ensembles of Nemours Jean-Baptiste and Wéber Sicot.

It is during this period that I truly became mesmerised by all these musical styles, and I was always listening to music on record players at the time. I remember that I purchased one and I sang these songs and listened to this rainbow of drum-based music all day long. As a matter of fact, I created a rather strange musical instrument from a tambourine and two metal cooking pots tied together, allowing me to produce percussive music in my student room. I remember that I had truly exalted moments beating my instrument and improvising songs with bits of texts and a lot of onomatopoeic speech.

Around the same time I also encountered Cuban music, with its characteristic and fantastic dimension of percussion. They were complex forms, generally orchestrated, which I discovered thanks to the impressive and ever growing record collection of one of my Guadeloupean friends who was a Jazz aficionado. Listening to music was almost a religious ritual for him and I believe that he was the one who encouraged my taste in listening to music. I began to buy records, clearly not as much as he did, but enough to listen to systematically once back in my student room. When I look back, I realise that listening to music had become an essential part of both our lives.

We could be studying alone or visiting other students in their rooms, but listening to music was a constant. "The main auditorium" was the name for the room of this particular friend, who often invited us to listen to his new musical acquisitions.

I remember that he did not like to listen to a particular song. He believed that the only valid attitude was to listen to the entire album. One had to go from side A to side B. If pressed for time, one could listen to just one side, but it was imperative to listen until the end.

All of these people and musical encounters shaped my approach to music. As my ideas were maturing, it occurred to me that once back at home, I would have to work hard to find another dimension to our percussive practice in Martinique. In fact, during my regular holidays in Martinique, I systematically sought to establish a contact with what I considered to be our "own cultural expression" as far as the dances and songs related to *bèlè* drumming were concerned. I used to reflect on the fact that the Guadeloupeans and Africans had their own cultural expression that they valorized, and I was determined to do whatever was necessary to valorize our own. I was driven by this reflection and it became a need for me to elaborate on. In fact, as I listened to other modes of expression, I came to realise that, as a Martiniquan, I had my own and I could not wait to discover it in all its dimensions, developing and expanding it to present it as it really was to others.

I remember that I was totally fascinated by African music, modern or traditional, as long as they were based on percussion or played by instruments such as the *balafon* or *kora*. Nevertheless, this did not create a need to go back to Africa, but encouraged me to work harder towards the elaboration and development of our own Martiniquan musical expression. From the start, my approach was to elaborate a dimension that would be specific to Martinique. This dimension was to take into account our historical background as the expression of our creational process.

When I settled back in Martinique, I decided to systematically go wherever there was drumming. Strangely enough, drumming was to be found in the folk groups of the time. In spite of the fact that, at that time, the programme of the folk ballets was essentially constituted of traditional dances such as *biguine*s, waltzes and *Mazurkas,* there was always a section dedicated to *bèlè* where drumming and dancing were clearly suitable for this expression.

In the same period, I started to investigate the state of the *bèlè* tradition in Martinique. Indeed, I had the opportunity to join various groups in order to take an active part in the aforementioned *bèlè* sections, and I took the opportunity to conduct several interviews. My investigations also led me to the Martiniquan countryside to visit several elders and spend time with them. These people had been influential figures in the *bèlè* world. My aim was to learn as accurately as possible what was done in the past through unobtrusive questions. Indeed, I had discovered that there was a gap between my theoretical questions and the practical preoccupations of my interlocutors. Moreover, it was evident that there was information or events that they were not willing to talk about for personal reasons, and that I was therefore unable to tackle.

There was an undeniable atmosphere of distrust amongst those who knew the authentic *bèlè*. These people had had conflicting experiences at the time of the development of folk groups after the popularisation of the work of Anca Bertrand. There had been great endeavours to adapt authentic *bèlè* practices for an international audience. Many folk groups had been created with this perspective in mind, causing some friction due to the incomprehension between the folk performers and the true *bèlè* practitioners.

This schism created disaffection and distrust, and I believe that at some points several elders were persuaded that the era had gone. They were persuaded that, similar to the way that cars had supplanted mules and horses as common means of transportation, one had to accept that the original *bèlè* traditions were to give way to modern practices and disappear honourably, as even then very few people were still interested.

This was the period of the rural exodus. Many, who belonged to the *bèlè* world from the districts of Ste Marie, relocated to Fort de France, France or wherever employment and the prospect of a better life seemed possible.

This was the general mentality of the time. Undoubtedly, without a revival of the *bèlè* practices, this state of mind would have led to the collapse or the disappearance of these practices. I was motivated by all these factors. I was determined to create a new practice in this milieu, and this is exactly what I have endeavoured to do.

Indeed, we encouraged the creation of an association called ALCPJ[56] (Another Path for the Youth). One of the main interests of this association, which united many young people, was to practice our traditional and fundamental music together. We were involved in an endeavour to rediscover our Martiniquan values and we translated them through the cultural elements that constitute *bèlè* (*tibwa*, drums, songs, dances). We also decided to relaunch cultural elements such as *koudmen*. A *koudmen* is a form of work in self-help groups that many farmers utilised to accomplish various tiring and time consuming tasks. The person who needed a job completed usually provided food and drinks for the many workers who would finish in very little time what could have taken days of labour for a single person. This practice, which consisted in meeting the other workers at an appointed time and place (usually a Saturday) to help someone in farming tasks or something similar, would sustain an effective interest for the rural world in many young people. Through this interest an attraction could be developed, reinforcing the relation between the youth and the *bèlè* elders. The eagerness of the youth brings the vitality necessary to the elders and is essential to the continuation of the *bèlè* tradition.

From this point on, this revival movement relaunched an interest in the *sware bèlè* (*bèlè* evening), which soon became quite a craze. This was the creation of another *bèlè* world. On one hand, the youth saw in it a source of knowledge even though some elders were reluctant to share it. Nevertheless, after some time, it had become evident to these elders that this new movement was an opportunity for them to be recognised as respectable *bèlè* practitioners, admired culture bearers needed and respected by the younger generation. As this movement grew wider, it began to be more important for Martiniquan society.

To get to know or understand the *bèlè* history, it is necessary to establish parallels between our history and that of the other islands surrounding us, in the various countries which also experienced cohabitation with African slaves and the colonizers. To put it simply, one can say that *bèlè* is from Africa. *Bèlè* is the continuation of the African musical practices as far as the rhythm is concerned (due to their main instrument, the drum). However, it is also regarded as African from the perspective of the feel and melodies (even though on this point, one has to take into consideration the European influences) and the dances. *Bèlè* is not a mere reproduction. Indeed, the conditions specific to the various geographical areas where the Africans were sourced were the true origins of these particular processes.

In the Martiniquan case, it is difficult to establish with accuracy the exact origins of the *bèlè* due to the absence of direct knowledge. Indeed, the transmission process is generally directed by ritual practices connected to religious traditions, or the social stability of a given community. Alas, in Martinique this has not been the case for the Africans who composed, throughout our history, the larger ethnic group of the island.

It is singular that one can talk with enough accuracy about the Caribs' or the Kalinagos' ritual practices, music and dances. The same can be said about the cultural practices of the Tamils or about the ritual characteristic of the celebration of the New Year in Chinese families and even the cultural behaviours specific to the community generally known as Syro-Libanese, while the practices specific to Africans are uncommonly "obscure." These are the reasons why there are no certitudes about African heritage. Our knowledge of our African past is mostly based on educated conjectures and theories.

The difficulty in identifying clear African cultural practices is also connected to the fact that the Africans that were taken from their countries during the slave trade era were definitively severed from their homeland. Their social relationships, religious practices and cultures were destroyed.

The rite of the "tree of forgetfulness," through which one pretended to erase the memory of those who were destined to leave Africa to slavery in unknown countries, illustrates the idea very well. On the other hand, all the measures taken to accommodate the promotion of the Catholic faith in these African populations also aimed at destroying the original African ritual practices.

In specific conditions and in some countries, some original African religious practices were able to re-create themselves as syncretised with the imposed religion of the plantation owners. The most popular examples are those of the Santeria in Cuba, the Cadomble in Brazil and the Voodoo in Haiti. These cultural practices have undeniably played a great part in the maintenance and the transmission of musical and artistic cultural expressions. This could also be applied to the transmission of drumming practices.

However, in general in smaller islands, such as Martinique, the process of alienation has been more efficient, rendering the sustenance of African cultural forms difficult and almost impossible. By this, I mean the effective organisation of rituals and ceremonies.

As such, these cultural forms, generally animist, were unable to impose themselves or even recompose themselves in an explicit manner. One may legitimately argue that they were diluted or implicitly reinvested in various cultural creations elaborated by these uprooted Africans in order to regain their humanity. In fact, the African enslaved were not regarded as human beings. They were the legal property of their masters on the same level as furniture or animals, and they could be bought or sold. This was the legal frame of the slave trade sanctioned by the official authorities. This is the reason why music, dance and songs that are usually regarded as mere entertainment become, in some situations, true manifestations of human spirituality. They translate the process through which humankind rises above animalism (which resides in the satisfaction of the primary material needs) to humanity (which is the fulfilment of the spiritual aspiration).

The crux of the matter was for the slaves to be re-established as humans. In fact, if they were trapped in their servile condition, when they were no longer under the direct authority of their masters, they could regain part of their human dignity through dancing, singing and playing the instrument specific to their original culture: the drum.

There is a great number of testimonies from commentators of the time which confirms the idea that singing, dancing and playing the drum were activities greatly palatable to the African enslaved.

The following is an observation from Granier de Cassagnac[57]:

For white people, the night is synonymous with rest. For the nigger, who
only works against his will, the night is the time for dancing ... He forgets
that he had worked today and that one needs peaceful rest to regenerate
one's strength to start again tomorrow.[58]

In Père Labat's works,[59] one can find a similar observation:

Dancing is their favourite passion; I do not believe that there is a people in
the world more attached to dancing than them. When the masters do not
allow them to dance on the premises of the habitation, they would walk
three to four "lieux" after leaving their work at the sugar factory on
Saturday midnight to find the location of a dance.[60]

And even though this commentary by G. Pinckard does not regard
Martinique, it also describes the aforementioned behaviour:

Sunday is the day of festivities for the slaves. They have a passion for
dancing, and the Sabbath that allows them a break from the labor is
generally dedicated to their favourite games. Therefore, instead of quietly
resting, they experience more tiredness or make more personal efforts
during the festivities of Saturday and Sunday than during any of the four
working days of the week. They gather in throngs on greens or on any
small square or street corner of the city, they form a circle in the midst of
the population and dance to the sound of their very dear music, while
screaming their favourite African songs.[61]

There is an almost identical description by Du Tertre:[62]

They spent in this recreative manner not only the entire afternoon on
Sundays but sometimes, they also continue their amusement for the entire
night, parting from one another to go back to their plantations just in time
to be led to work. While men and women dance and jump with all their
might, the young ones constitute another dance next to the adults, where it
is pleasant to see them imitate the postures of their fathers and mothers
duplicating their moves. Nevertheless, what is surprising in these children
is that, like their parents, they do not get tired of this past time. They sing
and dance until they get surrender to Morpheus.[63]

The masters' attitudes often varied on the question of allowing or
prohibiting the slave's gathering, dances and songs. At times, these dances
were judged beneficial for the production of the plantation. Regarded as
security valves, it allowed the slaves to express themselves. At other times,
there were very strict prohibitions as these dances were considered to be
opportunities for slaves to gather, reinforcing solidarity and connections
between workers from various plantations. These gatherings could
promote the forming of eventual revolts or uprising.

It is very interesting to note that after the abolition of slavery, the areas where these cultural practices and the *bèlè* percussive forms were elaborated were the same zones where small farming strived. This meant that these newly freed and autonomous communities profited from the solidarity basis that they sustained through *bèlè* cultural practices.

Bèlè instruments

This can be observed in various expressions such as working songs, or those dedicated to entertainment and gathering for community festivities. Nevertheless, religious ceremonies that may have helped the transmission of the drumming form in Martinique have not been found. Of course, it can be believed that there were and still are systems of symbols and meanings connected to these practices undetectable to the neophyte's eye, and there are indeed some moves and behaviours which cannot be regarded as random or meaningless. Nevertheless, it is more difficult to trace and identify these moves and to get explicit information on them. What one usually gathers are allusions, reminiscences, but not sufficiently accurate descriptions.

Nevertheless, in this "small" country it is strikingly evident that there were original pockets of development for the practices connected to drumming. There was a time when some practices were particular and unique to their regions and totally oblivious to one another, as exemplified by the practices of the South against those of the North.

It is also important to mention the development of the drumming practices linked to wrestling, a genre called *Danmié* or *Laghia*. One must also point out the use of drums and songs linked to planting in the north-east and north-west, even though they are not similar.

Moreover, one has to admit that many practices must have disappeared without a proper system of transmission. For instance, Lafcadio Hearn, a meticulous social observer, when visiting Martinique between 1889 and 1891 referred to a dance that was popular at the time, but has since totally disappeared. To sum up, one may say that research work continues around the *bèlè* world, increasing the knowledge about its practices.

We have more accurate information and knowledge about *bèlè* from the 1940s onwards. In these cases, the elders can testify with more accuracy about the *bèlè* forms that they encountered and that existed before them.

The word "*bèlè*" points to a specific dance, but it is used to describe the drumming dances in their entirety. It is through *bèlè* that Martiniquans express their percussive practices; it is the reason why *bèlè* indicates both the music and the dance.

When used as a rhythm for wrestling, the word *danmié* is used. This "war" rhythm is not similar to the dance and this is the reason why one must make the distinction between *bèlè* and *danmié* when referring to Martiniquan drumming. Yet, within the latter, there is yet another word.

Indeed, the word *Kalenda* is the product of a rich historical background, and as such it is the hotbed of many interpretations. In the *Bèlè* form practiced in the Ste-Marie region (in the north-east), it is the only dance that is performed alone. The other dances accommodate four to eight dancers.

One may often wonder if there are "rituals" in *bèlè*. This means that one has to be clear about the meaning given to this word. The notion of "ritual" refers to a wider frame, the frame of worship, the frame of a cultural practice that implies a particular behaviour defined by codes and precepts. As far as *bèlè* is concerned, it becomes difficult to talk about rituals from this particular perspective since the religious element does not exist in a similar fashion to the Kadomblé or Santeria in the neighburing islands.

Nevertheless, it is evident that *bèlè* also has its own codes, references and modes of expression. Because these practices were not wilfully transmitted in a precise and determined manner, it appears that only a part of these rituals were identified. To understand them further, thorough research requiring minute observational listening and analytical skills needs to be done. This would allow the unveiling of the meaning behind many of these practices, whenever possible.

As far as *Danmié* is concerned, the situation is slightly different. Because it is a martial art, one often encounters references to mysterious "preparations" to render the fighter invincible. It is suggested that "invocations," prayers with magical proprieties, exist. Testimonies and anecdotes on the topic are numerous, yet there remains the question of the "secret of preparations" that remain individual (and secretive) practices. Therefore, this limits the scope of the notion of ritual in this particular context.

Practices such as the sprinkling of rum over the drum appear in the Martiniquan context to be more like reminiscences of systematic ritual practices present elsewhere. For instance, in Voodoo or Santeria, there is an officiating person, recognised by the community, who is able to define with accuracy the rules, appropriate behaviour and taboos. This is also the case in Indian festival ceremonies and rituals where procedures have been defined, learnt and mastered. These rituals can therefore be observed as they are. In *bèlè* practices, one may say that rituals do not exist in the same way. There are underground principles, which are not even scrupulously and systematically respected. Often, practitioners must be reminded of these principles when they have violated them, but the problem is that many do not even know them. This does not mean that codes are non-existent. One can only infer that perhaps these codes lack the power, the strength and the sustainability of those that can be observed elsewhere. This is where the principle of comparison becomes interesting.

If one focuses only on *bèlè* as it is practiced in the Ste-Marie region, one would be able to say that the fundamental rhythmms are *gran bèlè, bèlè,* and *bélia.* From these three principal rhythms sprout several variations: *bèlè kourant, bèlè dous, bèlè pitjé marin bèlè* and *kalenda.* There are also the rhythms particular to the dances performed in rows within the group *lalin klè* including: *bénézwel, kanigwé, mabélo* and *ting bang.*

Bèlè drum

Connected to the three aforementioned fundamental rhythms are three dance patterns specific to each rhythm. Two couples of dancers form a *carré,* or square. Because there are four couples of dancers, the dance is usually composed of eight dancers. The first *carré* or square of couples face each other and begin the dance. The female dancers (called *danm*) and the male dancers (called *kavalie*) dance in shifting positions. There are side and frontal shifts of positions causing the dancers to execute several crossover moves, one being a turn and the other a shuffle. The dancers keep on shifting positions until the first *kavalié* who opened the dance gets back to his initial position. This implies that the women only execute lateral crossovers. When the two couples who formed the first *carré* stop, the second takes their turn and dances according to the same structure mentioned above. When the second square finishes its session, each couple executes the *monté au tambour.* The *monté au tambour* is a section of the dance where the first couple of the first square, followed by the first couple of the second square, then the second couple of the first, and then the last couple, dance towards the drum. Each couple dance face to face in a parade where the *kavalié* demonstrates their skills and the mastery of their art in a communion between their partner and the drum.

This particular structure is found in the other three forms of *bèlè* that were mentioned above. Nevertheless, in *Gran Bèlè*, the dancers never cease to move. No breaks can be observed in the position changing described earlier; the dancers keep on moving in a way that though the dance has a square structure, it looks like a circle.

In the *bélia* dance, things get a bit more complex because the basic step takes the dancer in a back and forth movement. Keeping the pace of the basic step, the dancer still has to effect the changes typical to the *bèlè carré.* Therefore, the changes must be extremely precise for each dancer to maintain their positions and for the dance to look coherent. There is another difference in the section where each couple dance alone. In the case of the *bélia*, it is no longer the vertical move of the *monté au tambour* but a circular motion as the dancers execute the basic step while moving counter-clockwise in the space.

The characteristic move of the *bèlè pitjé* is an accentuation of the fourth beat in the triple in a sharp step called *markaje.* In the group of *lalin klè* rhythms, the dance is accordingly structured in two rows or in a circle and there are no restrictions in the number of dancers. If one is to consider the year 1940 as a landmark, one may say that this era could be regarded as the *bèlè*'s "golden age." All verified testimonies concord in the fact that the *bèlè* is evolving on its own, consolidating its constituting elements.

These testimonies come from families involved in the *bèlè* world. They did not merely give an external description of *bèlè*; they often talked about it as a legitimate social, cultural and artistic activity. In these connected memories, *bèlè* was the expression of a local culture relevant to the villages and the neighbourhoods throughout the 1940s and 1960s. One must mention the pleasure and the total commitment of the *bèlè* practitioners of the time contrasting with the negative image that the society had of them. One must understand that the *bèlè* practitioners were almost excluded from "respectable" society. Even if the village of Ste Marie is often referred to, the memories of *bèlè* practitioners from other localities remain the same.

From the 1960s, one may speak of a second wave. It is the period when Martiniquan society was rocked by a major identity and conscience crisis as the values of the Martiniquan culture came under scrutiny. This period comes just after the events of December 1959[64] linked to the OJAM[65] (The Organisation of the Martiniquan Anti-colonial Youth). It is interesting to note that among the people arrested, many were closely connected to the *bèlè* world.

During the same period, *bèlè* began to appear in the mainstream. This phenomenon was triggered by the Romanian Anca Bertrand, wife of the painter Alexandre Bertrand. Indeed, she was one of the first people from "respectable" society to admire this music that had long been ignored and existed only in its native neighbourhoods. Therefore, she endeavoured to promote this practice, making recordings and having it played on national radio ORTF. *Bèlè*, having been restricted to its rural world, received more and more attention from the urban and well-to-do Martiniquan spheres.

Loulou Boislaville, in the same era, created the Martiniquan Folkloric Group. The concept of the group was to gather in the same performance a mixture of Martiniquan cultural forms. A performance would be composed of *biguines, waltzes* and *makurka*,[66] often complemented by skits representing typical segments of life in Martinique. Loulou Boislaville was also very interested by *bèlè*, and that is the reason why Ti-Emile[67] and his entourage would train dancers who would later be able to join the group.

From there, *bèlè* expanded remarkably well on the international scene. Many folk groups managed to constitute a repertoire of carefully choreographed *bèlè* dances. Nevertheless, this recognition has created a gap between the authentic transmission of the *bèlè* practice and the codified *bèlè* performances of the folk groups. The latter would thrive while the former would significantly diminish.

It is only from the 1980s that cultural activism was linked to *bèlè*. This new dimension brought back the importance of the *bèlè* practice as a cultural movement, a meaningful practice rather than a mere performance.

This is now the time for identity and cultural assertion through *bèlè*, and very different from the folkloric/performance approach.

Various associations were born encouraging the transmission, acquisition and practice of *bèlè* fundamentals as a tradition rather than a folk dance performed for the entertainment of tourists. Many young people joined the movement, becoming acquainted with the *bèlè* practice in all its forms, from singing, dancing to drumming. These associations revived the notion of pleasure in *bèlè*: the pleasure to meet other practitioners in an environment dedicated to the dance aesthetic. We were so concerned to make a demarcation between folk and authentic *bèlè* that we often refused to dance on stage, preferring to dance on the ground, in front of the podium, at the level of the audience. The concept of *swaré bèlè* was revived as a popular dance practice rather than a paid performance. The *moman bèlè*, shorter than the *sware bèlè* that lasts until dawn, also became popular during this period. Nowadays the *swaré bèlè* has turned into a perfectly regulated event, advertised on radio and present on calendars, and it is important to mention a similar development with Martiniquans living in France. *Bèlè* is clearly a dynamic movement.

Bèlè, as a drumming practice, has always been linked to resistance. Drums have always been connected to uprisings and revolts. An example can be found in the events leading to the abolition of slavery in Martinique. In 1848, playing drums was prohibited on the island. A slave called Romain was arrested because he refused to comply; his arrest and the riots that followed forced the governor of the time to publicly decree the abolition of slavery. The drum as a symbol of contestation can be found everywhere. The slave masters' efforts to diminish the subversive aspect of the drum never ceased. They either used straightforward prohibition or sly misappropriation. For instance, the slaves who had any musical talent would be asked to play European instruments in the house, in the hope that it would prevent them from playing the drums.

The process we were involved in was really addressed to the exploration of our selves and was the reason that we were completely fascinated with what we found in the drums, the voice and the dancing. I consider my relationship to *bèlè* to be an effective achievement of an identity quest.

From the beginning it was about affirming, at a time when it was not so easy and obvious, that we had a particular culture of our own. We were wary of other musical forms that we felt were imposed upon us and that we had to refuse them.

I learnt that I had a great-uncle who practiced the *tanbou-dibass*, a thing that I had recently seen practiced by one of my father's big brothers.

I had the opportunity to go to his home and spend a day recording in which I played the *bèlè* drum while he played *tanbou dibass* and one of my friends played bamboo flute melodies.

What also characterized my approach was the need to value and glorify this music in my texts and lyrics. This is very typical. I didn't look specifically at writing a way to express my soul-searching thoughts, but an approach which was, of course, deeply linked to a process of awakening of identity which consisted in standing for the recognition of *bèlè* value, expressing the idea that there was something really essential to us here.

I set up three kinds of approaches. The first was to develop *swaré bèlè* in which the youths could participate actively, through relationships with the elders from whom they had to learn it all. The second was to walk the path toward the writing and production of new texts that expressed the new prospects to which I wanted to contribute. The third (while I had no prior musical training) was the idea that this *bèlè* expression, with its primary rhythms and melodies, and which had to be the matrix for the production of a new musical expression.

Bèlè is alive. It is evolving. But this also means that this development has to be done carefully for the fundamental bases not to be lost in the process, as the conditions in which *bèlè* is practiced today are somehwat different. *La Kay Bèlè* was something very peculiar to a specific period; there were less people than today, and the voice was not amplified. The *swaré bèlè* also happens in very different places today. The sound and voices are amplified, and there are so many *tanbouyé* (drummers), dancers and singers that we have to rotate them. These are problems we have to work on. There is a necessity to develop a reflection on the languages of the body, to determine what is essential and fundamental in that very expression, because the craze for it is so huge that this phenomenon has to be consolidated; a mode of deepening and relation which calls for control.

THE TAMBOR-DE-CRIOULA AND THE ISSUES OF AFRO-DESCENDANTS

MARIE COUSIN

Introduction

In the city of São Luis, the capital of the Brazilian state of Maranhão in the north-eastern region of Brazil, there is a ritual called the *tambor-de-crioula*. This musical and choreographic manifestation has become a symbol of regional identity. Indeed, there is no other place in Brazil where this practice can be found. The *tambor-de-crioula*, or "Creole drum," is practiced traditionally by the afro-descendant people.

The "Creole drum" takes the shape of a popular manifestation during which the participants get together in a circle around female dancers who compete through creativity in front of the drummer. The orchestra contains three "uni-membranophone" crescent shaped cylindrical drums and an idiophone containing a couple of wood blocks knocked against the body of the bigger drum. People accompany the polyrhythmic pattern created by the different rhythms by clapping their hands in time. In the "Creole drum" manifestation, only men can play drums: women dance. However, both men and women can sing together. The songs are "responsorial" (the lead singer and chorus alternate), and a large part of them is dedicated to poetical improvisation by the lead singer.

This musical and choreographic practice, according to history, was created by the Maroon slaves for entertainment. It enabled, until the middle of the twentieth century, the concealment of some martial arts techniques developed by Afro-descendant people to fight the slavery system. Locally, the "Creole drum" is associated with the Maroons and the communities that followed the fugitives' pattern. Nowadays, this practice varies in a local way; there are different styles of dance and drumming according to their communities of origin. These subtle variations of interpretations are called "accents" (*sotaques*): men can dance or fight for example, but in the city of São Luis, the tradition is that women dance and men play drums.

Maranhão State History

The state of Maranhão is located in the north-eastern region of Brazil, between Para, Piaui and Goiás states. The climate is pre-Amazonian, oceanic, and specific vegetation can be found here, for example *sertao*[68] and *cerrado*.[69]

The state of Maranhão inherited its name from the French colonizers who, in 1612, called the island after Maragnan, and founded the bases of Saint Louis city (São Luís), a name which refers to Saint Louis (Daher 2002, 91), symbol of the French Royalty in homage to the King of France, Louis XIII. This French colony was named "France Équinoxiale." It was re-conquered in 1615 by the Portuguese and in 1641 by the Dutch, but the memory of French presence is strong in local souvenirs.

Black slavery, according to Da Costa, began in 1761, "more than two centuries after the first introduction of black slaves in the other regions of the country" (Costa Eduardo 1948, 13). Black slaves formed most of the population of the region. The development of the first sugar plantations in the Maranhão started at the beginning of the seventeenth century, and the island's economy depended on the cotton plantations from the end of the eighteenth to the middle of the nineteenth century, and the cotton culture was progressively replaced by sugar thereafter.

The African origin of the main population of *São Luís* city results from the economic colonial system and from the geographical isolation of the city and his periphery, compared to the rest of the country; this isolation enabled the development of original local practices. However, it was also one of the main Brazilian ports on the maritime road binding the Caribbean to South America.

In 1819, there were about 133,332 slaves and 66,668 free people in the region (Costa Eduardo 1948). The Maroons were used to meeting in the *mocambos*, villages of black fugitives in the forest zones, in Maranhão and in other parts of the country. The local papers gave daily news on fugitives or captured slaves. The region obtained independence on July 28, 1823; the working class was then constituted by the slaves. The state of Maranhão was then characterized by an economic system adapted to the geographical specificities and to the slavery system: inside the state there were rice and cotton plantations (*fazendas*), and on the littoral and river banks there were sugar mills (*engenhos*) and sugar cane fields (*canaviais*), which gradually imposed a social model based on a patriarchal domination system.

In the middle of an agitated nineteenth century, the largest slave revolt faced by Maranhão was the "Balaiada revolt," also named the "Balaios revolt." Between 1838 and 1841, it gathered numerous black slave groups which rose up against the economic system of exploitation and against the oppression that was taking place. The abolition of slavery in 1888 led to the fall of this society, whose economic system had been destabilized by other events: population migrations to the south of Brazil where industrial expansion was occurring (the first wave of migration before the abolition of slavery was due to the selling of slaves of the rural parts by the north-east land owners to Rio de Janeiro land owners), and the arrival of a new European working class, which questioned the necessity of black workers. Two new industries were then established: the textile industry in São Luis city, which has disappeared, and *babaçu* oil trade (a kind of palm tree) in the cities of Caxias and Codo, both of which lasted up to the 1950s.

Tambor-de-Crioula, from Slavery to Afro-Descendants

The Brazilian colonial society was based on slave work, exploitation, repression and domination of the cultural expressions of the dominated class. In the Brazilian *fazenda* system, the social life of the enslaved was organized in the evening after work. Firstly, the "Creole drum," associated with the black Maroon villages, was a means of communication in the forest for the communities constituted by slaves who had fled the plantations.

Nevertheless, this use was stopped because it also signaled the presence of black people. In a context where special police units (*capitão do mato*) tracked down and destroyed the black Maroons' villages, the use of the drum to communicate was abandoned. This means of communication evolved into a means of entertainment; the "Creole drum" circle was a typical party of the black communities. Still currently associated with black maroons, its practice is also a communal and familial manner of expression. Moreover, the fugitive slaves brought a Catholic influence into the communities. The saints were also associated to the drums, and this will be explained later.

In this slavery society, the church represented the centralization of religious authority, which was mainly prohibitive in nature, but which could also allow some freedom. As popular Catholicism developed, the "Creole drum" was shortly associated with syncretic Catholic cults. In particular, there is the cult of São Benedito, the Saint Patron of Maranhão's black people, who is still the patron saint who welcomes in the celebrations of the "Creole drum" to this day. In fact, we can speak about syncretism as a manipulation of Catholic symbols by the slaves; symbols which mean integration within the slavery society, and which allow greater liberty. The body is the only means of communication of the slave authorized by the system. Through the use of the body, freedom is expressed in dancing.

The church imposed new rituals, such as days of rest, feasting and freedom, as well as saint days, Sunday and Christmas. The most important Catholic ceremonies during slavery are the Our Lady of the Rosary ceremony (Nossa Senhora do Rosario) and the São Benedito ceremony. They are accompanied by dances, processions and games. The other important ceremonies are São Gonçalo Garcia, Santo Elesbão, Santa Ifigênia, and Nossa Senhora das Mercês. São Benedito represents the black people's lawyer, and Our Lady of the Rosary, who carries the crown of the Queen of Sky, is associated with Ifa, the Yoruban deity of destiny wherein people consult destiny with cola nuts, stones or rosaries. This Catholic influence was also found in Maroon villages, and even in the *quilombos*[70] there was a priest and a religious office.

In the seventeenth century the religious brotherhoods appeared, and would be consolidated during the eighteenth century. These religious organizations developed particular community characteristics: solidarity between coloured people, and the organization of rituals, ceremonies and work. There were half-caste brotherhoods (coloured free people) and white people brotherhoods. The rivalries between the different groups enabled the development of luxurious and sumptuous ceremonies.

However, this momentary freedom vanished progressively. Many ceremonies, considered scandalous, were soon forbidden. The Congo's ceremony was one of them, which took place in January, and which was assimilated into the Our Lady of the Rosary ceremony.

Slave Revolts and Abolition of Slavery in Brazil

Slavery was abolished in Brazil in 1888, thanks to the "Lei Auréa" law drawn up by Princess Isabel, and voted in on May 13, 1888. However, in 1890 the destruction of the national archives relative to slavery by arson makes it impossible to access sources concerning the origins and the quantity of deported populations. Before this official abolition (followed by illegal trafficking, called "smuggling" until the beginning of the twentieth century) a great abolitionist movement appeared during the nineteenth century.

In 1850, a law prohibiting slave traffic was voted in. From 1870, the South of Brazil employed more and more foreign workers (immigrants) and fewer Brazilian workers. The worker's status issue was addressed, and on September 28, 1871 the "free belly" law was voted in, and the children of slaves were born free. In 1885, the "Saraiva-Cotegipe" law, also called the "Sexagenarians" law, stated that slaves over sixty-five could obtain freedom. Following the abolition of slavery on May 13, 1888, Brazil was still under Portuguese rule. It was declared a republic on November 15, 1889, well known as the "Old Republic" by historians. The first Brazilian Republican Constitution appeared in 1891. On December 14, 1890, Rui Barbosa, an abolitionist, decided to burn, under the Fazenda Government, all the archives relative to "servile elements, to slave matriculation, to free children born under the 'free-belly' law and to slaves over sixty-five years-old freed under the Saraiva-Cotegipe law" in order to spare former slaves from their previous owners' attempts for compensation. This first Republic ended in 1930, due to the "*coup d'état*" organized by Getulio Vargas, who established a military government.

What about slavery in Maranhão? This was a late slavery society which grew considerably from 1750, and especially at the end of the eighteenth century, with slave workers (services, urban work) and farm slavery (rice, sugar, cotton plantations). Fugitive slaves are the origin of Maroon communities (the *quilombos*). Their inhabitants are called *quilombolas*. These communities appeared in the dense forests around the plantations situated on the riversides. It is said that in Maranhão there was no plantation (*fazenda*) without a *quilombo* in the neighborhood and also some *quilombos* inhabitants working in the plantations. A great network of solidarity developed between the *quilombolas* and the indigenous communities, but it was eventually cracked down upon by the state government. Military leaders were sent on missions to the forest in order to put an end to these communities. They were known as *capitões do mato*, the "forest captains."

In the present day, there is a process of recognition, of registration of *quilombola* communities, and of attribution of land ownership according to the lands their ancestors lived on by a specific ministerial department in São Paulo. This point will be discussed later on.

The merchant company which first developed slavery in Maranhão was the Companhia do Comércio do Grão-Pará e Maranhão, governed by Portugal. In 1755, three thousand slaves arrived in Maranhão. Between 1755 and 1777 (the duration of the company's existence), twelve thousand slaves were brought to Maranhão (Santos 1983, 14–15).

The purchase of slaves was funded by this company in exchange for trade monopoly in the port of São Luis. The slaves were mainly from Guinea Bissau (in particular Cacheu) and Angola, which were then Portuguese colonies.

Forty-one thousand slaves arrived in Maranhão between 1812 and 1820. On the eve of state independence, fifty-five percent of the inhabitants of Maranhão were slaves. The population was grouped on the coastal *fazendas* (the western *baixada*) and on the borders of the rivers of Itapecuru, Mearim and Pindaré. This region was covered with a great number of forests and rivers, allowing numerous *quilombos* to grow. Indeed, the inhabitants of the quilombos were protected by the complex geographical characteristics of these almost inaccessible micro-areas and, therefore, could not remain under state control.

The first *quilombos* appeared at the beginning of 1700, becoming an endemic phenomenon of the slavery society (Assunção 1996, 436). Little groups would escape from the *fazendas* (especially in the nineteenth century) and go to live in the forest, and Alcântara, Viana, Vitória do Mearim, Itapecuru-Mirim, Rosário and Manga do Iguará are villages founded by the *quilombos* which still exist today.

A great repression came about, and police investigations were organized by the aforementionned *capitões-do-mato* to dismantle this network, but in vain. Some of the *mocambos* inhabitants, who would then work in the plantations, constituted an information network. Agriculture was practiced in the *quilombos*, as well as cotton plantation, fishing, hunting, cattle farming, and there were even gold sales. These networks enabled revolutionary organizations such as the Viana insurrection or the famous Balaiada to form. The Viana slave insurrection (*quilombolas* people from São Benedito do Céu) occurred between 1867 and 1870, and was repressed.

Balaiada is one of the most important slave revolts that Brazil has encountered. Taking place from 1830 to 1840, it was a revolt led by the poor and the slaves against the elite and the increase of flour and meat prices. It was also a reaction to a national campaign: in 1838, the country organized the recruitment of poor men to serve the troops of the Portuguese Empire. The rebels, called *Balaios*, were not slaves but they would bear revolutionary western ideas.

In 1839, a slave, Cosme Bento das Chagas, became the insurrection leader in the *fazendas* of the Itapecuru-Mirim region. The black people took arms, proclaimed their freedom and fled the plantations. Two hundred slaves were released, and these people joined the Balaios movement. However, the movement was suppressed: in 1842 its leader was sentenced to death and the two hundred freed slaves were killed.

The *Quilombolas* Communities

Today, in Brazil, the ACONERUQ is an organization defending the communities founded by the descendants of the *quilombolas* Maroons.

The Quilombola Rural Black Communities of Maranhão Organisation, founded in 1997, also seeks to represent all the Maroon communities of the state (Associação das Comunidades Negras Rurais Quilombolas do Maranhão). As of September 2007, 423 of Maranhão's communities were counted and connected with this institution. The organization aims at fortifying the organization of the *quilombola* movements and at fighting alongside the communities to regulate the ownership of their ancestors' lands, that is to say the attribution of their owner rights. The *quilombolas* also receive the support of the Maranhão Black Culture Center (Centro de Cultura Negra do Maranhão, CCN-MA) and the support of Maranhão society of Human Rights (Sociedade Maranhense de Direitos Humanos, SMDH). The avant-gardist action of these two organizations began with the Black Life Project (Vida de Negro, PVN) in the 1980s. Today, more than 600 communities are listed.

The departmental organ concered with *quilombola* rights is the Comissão Pro-Idio based in São Paulo, focussing on the recognition of the *quilombola* communities (legislation, judicial action and lands regularization). It applies *quilombolas* rights to their land ownership and to protect their way of life. This right is insured by the Federal Constitution (Constituição Federal), specified by articles 215 and 216, and article 68 of the Constitutional Act and Transitory Dispositions (Ato das Disposições Constitucionais Transitórias). The process of identification and official attribution of land depends on the federal legislation, and is specific to each state. In December 2009, seven states had particular laws: Espírito Santo, Pará, Paraíba, Piauí, Rio Grande do Norte, Rio Grande do Sul and São Paulo.

The Tambor de Crioula in Quilombolas Communities

The "Creole drum" is nowadays a manifest identity fully associated with the *quilombolas* communities. Through its practice, the communities maintain the link with their ancestors' history and assert their identity. The "Creole drum" is the main form of immaterial legacy of the afro-descendants' culture, associated with the African identity. The *tambor-de-crioula* is practiced not only as an entertainment itself or during ceremonies, but it also accompanies the religious cults which stem from popular Catholicism. In the Piqui da rampa community, a ceremony honouring Santa Maria is carried out with culinary offerings and *tambor-de-crioula* circles. In Alcantara, the São Benedito celebration takes place in August. It lasts three days and consists of drummers sitting in circles and playing from twilight to dawn, singing processions during which people carry the statue of the saint and the drums, and a mass celebrated in the main church in front of the Pilori place. In the Bom Sucesso quilombo, a territory formed by thirty smaller communities, peoplealso play the "Creole drum." In Jamary Dos Pretos, the "Creole drum" accompanies religious celebrations honouring Nossa senhora das graças, São Lazaro, and São Benedito.

The *tambor-de-crioula* is really an important expression for the *quilombolas*. It is, above all, the symbol commemorating the abolition of slavery, and sure enough, the "Creole drum" is considered as originating from the time of slavery. It is said that on the day of abolition, drums were played until dawn.

The *Tambor-de-Crioula*: A Definition

The "Creole drum" is a musical and choreographical manifestation organized to honour São Benedito, patron saint of the Afro-descendants since the eighteenth century. It is a ritual which includes both sacred and entertainment aspects. The ritual takes place in a circle of participants, in which female dancers, and sometimes male dancers, will vie with each other in virtuosity in front of the drummers.

The "Creole drum" represents the existence of fraternization among black people, either freed or enslaved, and over a long period of time. These groups once worshipped São Benedito, an expression of freedom. The São Benedito cult was developed in both churches and houses, and was celebrated through prayers during many ceremonial days, and many drum circles took place in his honour. Indeed, the sung poems evoking São Benedito took a very important place in the song repertory. Nowadays, the drum is played for various events such as anniversaries, weekly ceremonies, celebrations of the patron saints, or local Afro-Brazilian religious cults.

To learn how to beat the drum, people imitate the actions from childhood. Innovation and strong personalities are characteristics which are greatly sought within these drum group entertainers, both in female *coreiras* and male *coreiros*. The name "Creole drum" refers to the Brazilian conception of Creole identity: the Creole (*crioula/crioulo*) is a coloured person born on Brazilian ground. The word "Creole" is opposed to the word "Mina" which refers, by extension, to anybody born on the African continent.

During slavery, the *tambor-de-crioula* grew as a fighting style accompanied by drums, practiced by men using foot kicking (*pernadas*) and disequilibria, as can be found in the *capoeira* manifestation. The aim was to knock down the opponent by unbalancing him. The dance for the woman, characterized by the *punga*, a pelvis move, appeared after abolition, while the transformation of the fighting style into a dance occurred in the middle of the twentieth century. In Rosario and other cities, men still practice the fight-dance. The aim is still to put down the opponent by giving him violent kicks in the thighs. In Axixa, men use wood blocks to support themselves so as not to fall too easily and to reinforce balance to make it more challenging. Some of them even attach wood to their legs to make it harder to fall (seen in São João Batista city). In Madre Deus (in the São Luis area), this fight was well practiced by men until 1930 when women started to dance in the circles.

For a long time, the shipping traffic between the Caribbean along the coast toward the city of Rio was the only way into São Luis. This maritime communication may have also permitted the spreading of musical expressions. As moving and sailing slaves between the islands was the custom in the Caribbean, it is likely that people coming from the Caribbean or from Central America would have been brought to Maranhão through slavery. The immigration of the slave population happened just like the immigration of the Garifunas, or that of the French West Indians who immigrated to Cuba (the Tumba Francesa). Therefore, this idea could explain why some of the "Creole drum" characteristics are shared with other Caribbean expressions, such as the use of three drums made out of wood trunk (*bois fouillé* in French West Indies), the coupling of wood blocks (*ti-bois* in Martinique, *Laudes* in Venezuela), the ritual of men who dance-fight (*Ladja* in Martinique), and the way Creole women dress and the dance steps.

According to public events, the "Creole drum" is really appreciated during the Holy Jean celebrations in June. Yet, in the past the drum was associated with public ceremonies, being played during the carnival at the beginning of the twentieth century. Today, however, it is obvious that tourism policies use the "Creole drum" in order to create some strong local identity. At last, the Creole culture and identity are progressively being recognized.

Music and Dance

The "Creole drum" music is composed with a percussion set made of three cylindrical membranophones. The names given to the drums, decreasing in sizes, are: *tambor grande* ("big drum"), *meião* ("the medium one") and *crivador* or *querêrê* in the central towns (*pererengue* in the villages). These drums are made of wood trunks, on which deer skin is spread. The big drum body is beaten using a couple of wooden sticks, the *matracas* (like the Cuban *claves* or French Caribbean *ti-bois*).

The medium drum has the role of the pulse. The little drum develops a rich rhythmic pattern by the use of slap hits, in the high-pitched register. The big drum is the soloist. It is the drum on which the player will develop their personality, especially depending on the importance of the beat of the fist, also called *punga*, that must be correlated with the female pelvis move. The big drum is 1.20 meters high and attached around the pelvis by a belt. The two smallest drums are played on the ground, laid down, put on a beam, and the drummers overlap them. The *matracas* are played on the big drum body, at the back of the lead drummer.

The polyrhythmic is accompanied by a responsorial singing, alternating between the lead singer and the chorus. Here, the singer is generally a man (though it can be a woman), and the chorus is constituted by the group of drummers, men playing the music and women dancing. Regarding the dance, it is improvisation-based, performed in front of the big drum and marked by the typical move, the *punga* or *pungada*. To enter and dance, after greeting the drums, the female dancer must knock her pelvis against that of the woman dancing before her, allowing the new dancer to take up the soloist role.

To dance, people use particular clothes: men wear a straw hat and a coloured shirt, women wear a fabric on their heads, a long, pleated coloured skirt, numerous coloured necklaces and a white lace blouse. It is important to note the actual clothing homogenization, as it must be emphasized that everybody was able to participate without clothing obligations in the past.

The important dancing moves are those of the shoulder (subtle), the pelvis, the feet (discreet variations) and especially the skirt (amplified by the rotations). In the past, the dancer's virtuosity was characterized by personal style. Nowadays, the dance turns define one's virtuosity: fast, spectacular, and impressive for the audience.

During the rituals, drinks (rum with spices) are also significant. Drinks are a ritual obligation, to warm the voices, the hands, the drum skins, and the spirits; to bring together the participants.

The singing soloist has a particular role because they improvise verses according to the context, events which happened on that day, and their personal inspiration. Everybody can be soloist, but generally the leader is the oldest person of the group (man or woman).

Sometimes, several soloists engage in a true singing battle. The most common themes are actuality, social criticisms, feelings, women, events, and very often São Benedito. The most beautiful songs are considered to be the São Benedito songs, because they are seen to be the most emotional poems.

The Position of the "Creole Drum" in the Emancipation of Creole Identity in São Luis

The *tambor de crioula* has been constantly developing in São Luis since the 1960s. It was prohibited for a long time in the centre of the city by dominant social and political groups, because it was a symbol of local "blackness" and a practice which had a disruptive influence on the economic and social system. Free to be practiced in the suburbs, it was forbidden in the centre of the town because it was also considered to be opposed to the morals of the dominant class. Numerous interdictions, arrests and confiscations used to occur, and oppression and domination were supported by articles of propaganda in the newspapers.

There were prohibitions of practices considered as going against public morality, such as meetings of black people, a traditional Amerindian medicine called *pajelança*, or even some of the popular Catholic rituals not recognized by the church. The *terreiros*, Afro-Brazilian ritual places, were invaded by the police, with those practicing the rites were arrested and put in jail. Some of the ceremonies such as the *bumba-meu-boi*, the cattle ritual organized to pay homage to Saint Jean, were seen as "immoral and stupid." This prohibition which forbade ceremonies in the centre of the town lasted until the 1950s; all manifestations from popular culture were relegated to the peripheral suburban areas.

The revival of popular culture begun in the 1950s with a *Bumba-meu-boi* competition organized in the João Paulo area by the municipal prefecture. In 1962, to celebrate the three hundred and fiftieth anniversary of the city, a great folk festival took place, including the presence of *tambor-de-mina* groups (an Afro-Brazilian religion based on the *voduns* cult). The Newton Bello government developed a tourism policy which used popular culture to attract tourists. Under the Sarney mandate (the Governor of Maranhão in 1965 and President of Brazil from 1985 to 1990) the Tourism Department was created.

Developing this type of tourism enabled the "Creole drum" to be recognized; however, the protagonists of the "Creole drum" movement and the communities who practice it are still suffering numerous prejudices from the upper-class of the town. On the one hand, it can be stated that preserving the popular culture of a certain layer of society allows for the preservation of this class system. On the other, the joy conveyed by this ritual, which is the purpose of the "Creole drum," is due to its profound symbolisation of freedom, expressed through music and dance. Likewise, new ways of life, cooperation and solidarity organizations are developing.

The Patrimonial Future of the "Creole Drum"

The Creole drum was recognized as "Brazilian immaterial heritage" in 2007. It was integrated into the current list of twenty-two registered immaterial items, including Samba de Roda and Wayãpi culture, which are the only two items also recognized by UNESCO's immaterial heritage program. The "Creole drum" is the eleventh item on the Brazilian list, and this recognition allows for the development of back up, education and valorization programs. Regarding the density of Brazilian culture (practices being specific to villages), the list is poor: a few manifestations are recognized, whereas, in fact, many should be. The institute responsible for the immaterial heritage of Brazil is the IPHAN (The National Historic and Artistic Heritage Institute), created in 1937 during Getulio Vargas' mandate (1930–1954).

Other institutes support the "Creole drum" and afro-descendant culture, such as the Centro de Cultura Negra do Maranhão (Maranhão's Black Culture Centre), created on September 19, 1979 to defend the Afro-descendants' actions and rights, and the Commissão Maranhense de Direitos Humanos (Maranhão's Human Rights Commission).

Importance of the Folklorist Movement in the Recognition Process of Popular culture

The first researchers to examine the "Creole drum" were the folklorists in the 1930s. They were interested in its "original" or social aspects. *Tambor de Mina e Tambor de Crioula*,[71] written by Oneyda Alvarenga in 1948, is the first work published on the subject. This book is based on the Andrade's folk research mission in 1938, which aimed at collecting material of Brazilian popular music.

Among other works, *Maranhão, Folclore brasileiro* by Domingos Vieira Filho (1977), or *Folclore do Maranhão* by José Figueiredo (2003), illustrate the Brazilian folklorists' movement. But this movement, which aims at studying the popular traditions in the 1930s, is very different from the European conception of "folklore." The folkloric research tradition gave birth to the researchers' infatuation for popular music. As a link between this research movement and others, the Maranhão folklore commission, created by Sergio Ferretti and Mundicarmo Ferretti, keeps this researching tradition up-to-date by regularly including new views.

The *Tambor-de-Crioula* in the Present Day

The "Creole drum" is now practiced by Afro-descendant people, the *quilombolas*, as a village and community practice, and in the urban frame as a local practice through friends and family networks. In the city of São Luis, a lot of people are still ignorant and afraid, because for a long time drums were associated with evil practices. Therefore, people who practice it in the centre of town come from Maranhão's interior cities or from the suburbs.

Currently, the spread and development of the *tambor-de-crioula*'s practice is organized in various ways. First, practice occurs in the city as local parties, where the presence of recognized and esteemed drum masters or dancers brings with it a dynamic. We can also point out the organization of master classes in some areas where popular culture is no longer practiced by Afro-descendant people. These include drum classes in the centre of the town, and dance, *capoeira*, theatre or popular culture courses in academies.

The municipality also organizes festivals regularly (Rufou Tambor in 2004), and documentary film showings in popular culture centres. The "Creole drum" circles are organized during Saint Jean (June and July) on public scenes and places (*palcos* and *arraias*). The "Creole drum" is also played during celebrations of the patron saints (Sao josé Ribamar, Alcantara), in particular for São Benedito ceremonies, and several records were edited and supported by the municipality. The "Creole drum" is also presented in museums (Casa do Maranhão, Casa da Festa, Centro de Cultura Popular Domingo Vieira Filho), and in educational and didactic exhibitions as well.

Since its official recognition in 2007, the *tambor-de-crioula* has become Maranhão cultural symbol supported by politics and tourism. It is practiced in the centre of town in a free manner during some days of the week. A new urban public is made up of the intellectuals and artistic *intelligencia*. In present day São Luis, there are more than eighty "Creole drum" groups, either regrouped in organisations or independent. In 2009, the Casa do Tambor de Crioula (House of the Creole drum) was opened. However, beyond this institutionalization, the "Creole drum" preserves its spirit of freedom. There is still no special place or specific moment to practice it, and it remains the symbol of the resistance of the black people of Maranhão.

MALOYA AND DANCE

FLORENCE LATAPPY

My goal is here to give my own definition and vision of *maloya* and to explain the reasons why I have decided to practice this traditional dance, an inspiration in the development of my choreographic work and therefore a difficult path to walk. I will also explain how I perceive this music, how I interpret this dance and its place in Réunion.

Some Postulates

As an artist, I can only claim my own truth. I do not seek to impose my views, and I only seek to say what I feel and think through my artistic work. I only wish to assert my generosity and my sincerity and I try to respect as much as possible the work of all artists and everybody's opinion. It is important for me to assert this subjectivity as my work is based on sensitivity and not on rational analysis. I take from my long experience as well as the knowledge and the different approaches I have acquired over the years. I have no pretension to exhaustivity or exclusivity, and even less to perfect objectivity. Many people claim that they are not subjective because they use a strict methodology and written documents. The question is: do all these things make them totally objective?

The advantage of the artist is that they should not pretend to hold all the key elements of their art and culture in their hands, even after years of study and practice. I say this because of the many defenders of the so-called cultures of the world (aren't all cultures of this world?). I present here my vision as an artist. I am neither an ethnologist nor a scientist, though I had the chance to study languages at university and, in my opinion, everything is useful everywhere. Dancing allows me an approach based on feelings; without it I cannot investigate, reflect or choose any other approach. I usually combine various approaches and leave the rest to time. In my artistic work, I realize that reflection and sensibility end up meeting in a natural way. When one is ready, when things are due to happen, they just happen. Dancers learn to listen to themselves, their bodies, and so listen to their whole being, because our bodies do not function on their own, independently from our souls, like some kind of mechanical toy.

I insist on these postulates because they might not seem so obvious to some people. In fact, I have noticed that many people make judgements based on clichés such as "dancers work with their bodies" (meaning, "they don't have a brain"). But dancers are like anybody else; there is an infinite range of quality of people. Another thing we hear is that "Réunion traditional dance is some 'islandish' kind of thing," meaning, "it must look like some tribal African or Vahine dancing." Of course, when you do not know anything about Africa or Tahiti or the island evoked, it is easy to fall into prejudices, and everybody has plenty of prejudices! Nothing reflects a culture better than its prejudices. For example, when I am in metropolitan France, people ask me if I am really from Réunion because I am a white-skinned woman. When I go to Réunion, people ask me if I am Creole[72] because I can speak French perfectly. I could go on and on. Up until now I would say that what has affected me the most in my discovery of *maloya* is prejudice. Prejudice often reflects a lack of knowledge, curiosity, communication, and open-mindedness. At the same time, I have had wonderful moments with the very people that had the greatest prejudices about me and the themes I worked on. I realised that those who say they do not know anything often have apparently less prejudices (since they do not know, they do not expect anything specific from me) than those who pretend they know it all better than anybody else.

Who am I?

I was born to a Réunionese mother and a metropolitan French father. I spent the first seven years of my life in Réunion. Following this, I grew up in suburban Paris surrounded by my mother's family, more specifically with my grandmother, whom I would question a lot about our family's history. I was deeply marked by all this. I lived in the nostalgic atmosphere of the exiles who literally pounced on everything that had something to do with their motherland. Later, I went to Réunion for holidays, and the bond was strengthened in a completely different way.

Inheritance

When I was a child, my mother used to sing many *segas*.[73] From what I can remember, these songs that my mother sang, and that my sister and I sang with her, were my first encounter with island music and dance. We would often dance, the three of us or with the family, and many times we would get together and listen to the singles of Loulou Pitou and the other hits from Réunion. My discovery of *quadrille* and other dances, including *maloya*, is anecdotal. It is during one of these family reunions that I discovered the first *maloya* LP by Firmin Viry released in Réunion. I knew nothing about *moring*, a traditional dance that my grandfather used to practice, as far as I know. One day, my mother told me that, as a child, she had never had the opportunity to listen to *maloya*, but that she had been nourished by the *segas* on the radio or the ones that street singers like Madoré used to sing. She discovered *maloya* as an adult with a *Zorey* (the name given by the people of Réunion to those from metropolitan France) who had taken her to a *servis kabaré* (this will be explained later) at the house of a family that lived in the middle of a sugarcane field. Why this ignorance? Why could *Maloya* not be heard on the radio? I wondered. *Maloya* was forbidden.

Definitions

What is *maloya*? We could describe it in musical terms as a set of binary and tertiary rhythms with regional variations (east, west, north, south) and the dances that accompany them. First and foremost, we could also say that this is a family tradition and that its origin is found in the slave population of the island. Therefore it is syncretic music and dances where African and Malagasy influences are significant (because of the history of the origins of the Réunionese people), but where we can also find the traces of other slaves, such as Indians called *Malbars* in Réunion.

The *Servis Malgas* or *Servis Kabaré*

Maloya can also be bound to an animist ritual practiced by some families on the island and called *servis kabaré* or *malgas*. Generally, it consists in honouring the dead or one particular dead person by "calling" them through a master of ceremonies (the queen or king) who embodies the spirit of the dead to speak to the living. This person possesses a particular gift, making this phenomenon possible. This ritual usually follows this sequence: the formal ritual part with sacrifices and offerings, a meal shared with everybody (friends, family and neighbours) followed by a party where everyone dances and sings *maloya* and where anyone who so wishes can play traditional instruments. During the ritual part, only the designated people, usually the family, can play music and only certain songs are sung on the order of the king or the queen.

Transmission

According to some elders and, in fact, in some families, people would dance *maloya* in more isolated ways for fun during neighbourhood parties or in their homes. It is important to underline the importance of orality in the Creole culture. *Maloya* is transmitted orally and all the traditions related to it are communicated that way. Therefore, we cannot count on films or writings to help us. The very few writings from the slavery era come from rich and literate colonials or European clergymen whose perception is very much influenced by the prejudicial ideology of that time.

Maloya Characteristics: Dance

Generally speaking, rhythm and music are the main elements of this traditional Réunionese dance. The dancer marks strong and weak beats, dances according to the rhythm of an instrument played or answers a beat in a sort of call-and-response game. Another fundamental element is the mobility of the spine, and more particularly of the hips, but also of the shoulders, sternum, feet and knees. The Creole dancer does not create straight lines, instead they work with curves, because our bodies do not have right angles and are not symmetrical. Another characteristic is the presence of the circle and spiral (movement and space). Even when they dance in pairs, dancers spin around a circle or around their partners: the dance becomes an instrument for communication symbolised by the circle where a whole assembly can see and be seen and participate. Both partners come towards each other, nearer and nearer, and as soon as they meet they dance away once again, spinning quicker and quicker as if to escape, only to come back once again towards each other and repeat this game over and over.

Meetings and Discovery

In the 2000s I decided to take the plunge in a choreographic adventure and became more and more interested in my Creole origins. After a few years of university studies and various jobs, during which I also spent some time reading about the history of Réunion, I widened my field of investigation, became interested in so-called "world" dances and followed the intellectual and cultural situation of the island. I also started frequenting Réunionese associations and dancing in a folk group as it was the only way for me to combine my passion and my work as a dancer with the quest for my origins. I met musicians and cultural activists, and in particular Guy Valiamé who has since passed away. With his small group of *maloya* lovers, I participated in *kabars* (parties where *maloya* is played) and in other events related to *maloya*, but my dance was totally separated from these activities and occasions with the amateur folk groups remained only a few. I became interested in choreographers such as Chantal Loial, Norma Claire, Irène Tassembedo, and George Momboye; Africans, Caribbeans, but also Brazilians who, in my opinion, showed us the way. They value their cultures, all the aspects of which are still unknown or prejudiced in the Western world. They work in the traditional and modern aspects.

Foundation of the Maloya Métiss Company

Florence Latappy in "I'm Coming From the Umgosi" by Company Maloya Métiss.

After many unsuccessful investigations to find a Réunionese company which works on *maloya* and the culture of Réunion, I came to the conclusion that I had to start on my own if I wanted to work on *maloya* as a dance. Thanks to Guy and other professional dancers who encouraged me, I decided to keep on working, without knowing exactly where I was going, to finally create the Maloya Métiss Company in November 2004. I was surprised to be the only one interested in what enthrals many musicians from my island. I was also surprised that my mother and my family did not know more about this culture. They sometimes told me about *Kaf* (or "black") music with, more or less, contempt. I understood this was a taboo because of racism. But with time, I found it went further and that this rejection was a way for some Creoles to forget the misery of slavery their ancestors suffered, not such a long time ago. I also discovered that very few Réunionese people do not have enslaved ancestors. This is due to the fact that, during the time of slavery, there were very few women and the only ones available were slaves. We are, then, all children of colonials and slaves.

My Definition

Therefore, it is obvious that this tradition can hardly be understood without taking into account its human and ritualistic dimensions. *Maloya* is all at once an instrument of communication, improvisation and expression. As traditional musician *Tiloun* very rightly said in an RFO interview during the 2010 Sakifo Festival, it is also a philosophy. In my opinion, it is impossible to approach the *maloya* culture if it is not through sensitivity, although it is also possible to do it through a more rational way. *Maloya* is not rational, however. It has a very peculiar groove that very few foreigners have been able to reproduce. When you dance to this music, the main work is about feeling the groove without which you simply cannot dance! That is why I have approached *maloya* by immersing myself progressively in it, to feel the music and the groove as best as I could. The main rhythm comes from the bass of the *rouler*. The sound is extremely grave and vibrates very much. It is the vibration that will transport the dancer and the assembly; it will literally anchor the body of the dancer in the ground and penetrate deep inside them to make them move and vibrate. The other instruments give additional colour to the music while the *rouler* replaces the dancer's heart; it resonates as much as the human heart, and that is why sound technicians have to adjust it so it always dominates over the other instruments.

Maloya, A Secular and Sacred Dance

Just like any other dance, *maloya* is at the same time profoundly organic and eminently spiritual. It is through *maloya* that some participants of the *servis kabaré* will go into a trance. Even though, regarding its origins, *maloya* takes a festive aspect and authorises all sorts of improvisations, thereby allowing free expression of one's feelings, for me it is linked to *servis kabaré*. It is, at the same time, a very secular and a very sacred tradition.

Maloya is at the heart of the fundamental contradiction of humankind: it is made of flesh and blood, of soul and spirit. It reminds us that we are made as much of flesh and blood as of deep spirituality.

For me, my discipline, dancing, also takes on these two fundamental aspects. It happens through the body, but the body cannot exist without the spirit, otherwise there will be disembodiment, that is, death. Only the dead are disembodied. The living are at once the body and spirit. One doesn't exist without the other. It is cartesianism and rationalism that separate the body from the spirit, or is a bad interpretation of incarnation, because the human being is not God, and only God, or the dead, can be disembodied. We see here why it is possible to believe in a God and practice *servis kabaré*: many Catholics and Hindus participate in this ritual in Réunion.

I strongly believe in the strength of the human spirit and body, and I never separate them, especially in my work as a choreographer. On the contrary, I look for a balance between the two, without really investigating. That is, I let things happen. I search; that is, my work consists in experimenting, it is a game of multiple trials, with or without success, to find what is going to make this body-spirit balance a reality and what is going to include my whole being, without forgetting the intellectual part of me. For as long as I do not reach that balance, I keep on searching. This search becomes a game that never ends because human beings are always changing. Life is change, alteration, and movement.

My Approach

I became interested in *maloya* thanks to some musicians who participated in *servis kabaré*. For them, *maloya* is a passion and a way of living. I realised that the idea that I had of my own culture did not correspond with reality. It was a cliché.

I also had the impression that I was not myself in the society I was living in. Human societies rarely encourage this body/spirit balance: we often have to play roles to work, to exist in a group, a family. We have ready-made images imposed upon us to which we cling without really ever knowing why. Often, even when we think we are matched more or less with the representation we were attributed, that same representation turns into an empty shell because it does not correspond to what we really are.

At that time, I realised that the education I had received from my mother and her family came in part from a culture totally different from the one that surrounded me in metropolitan France. I wanted to understand this, and at the same time I met those musicians and discovered *maloya*. I had also found dancing a long time before that. Everything came together regarding a search for identity, depth (adequacy between an image and the meaning it carries) and the realisation that part of the culture of Réunion is sullied, despised, unrecognised and hidden.

From left to right, up to down: the *kayamb*, the *rouler* and the *sati*.

That curiosity came with an interest awakened by the real depth of this dance composed of feelings and vibrations, and that sets free the imagination. When you dance in pairs, you look for each other, you get closer yet never touch: it is a parade that gets lost in an infinite game. The *rouler*, which is the basis of *maloya*, the *piker*, that marks the beat and the counter beat, the *aigu* that is used to underline the rhythm and the *kayamb*, the instrument that literally dances in the hands of the musicians, are all protagonists of a drama or a comedy. The singing is often improvised by a leader and repeated by the assembly forming a choir: it can take on all the colours of emotions and human spirituality.

Even if, like all traditional dances and music, *maloya* may seem repetitive, it can become an infinite basis to work upon because you can express everything through it and embellish it with all kinds of influences in an infinite variety, since *maloya*, like the people of Réunion, is mixed and syncretic. Mixing is at the very heart of *maloya* and it is possible to add to it because it leaves so much space for improvisation.

For me, the difficult part was to choreograph it, to isolate some steps while retaining that special groove. I am still working on this and I think that future generations will also have to work on that process. However, we will have to avoid the mistake of codifying it, a process that would open the way to an academic code which would not correspond at all with the spirit of freedom that is at the core of *maloya*!

A Commitment

In my choreographic work, I wanted to come closer to a part of myself that had been forgotten in the teachings I had received in metropolitan France. The history of my family and the places where they lived and everything that had to do with them—all that is a part of me, of my inheritance. I have practiced a lot of Western dances (classical, jazz, modern, contemporary) where the outside influences can be felt: Africa in the case of jazz, and Asia for modern and contemporary. However, the point of view taken to write about these dances is obviously Western. Creole culture is based on orality, human relationships and a global approach that is not rational and is not cartesian, just like *maloya*.

I received a Creole education, therefore, in the Réunionese sense of Creole identity, an education with strong African and Asian influences, although the French imprint is also very deep because we come from as much Malagasy, African and Asian slaves as from French colonials and mixed Creoles. Anyone who lives for some time with a Réunionese family or comes from Réunion and lives in metropolitan France realises that even the way we see the world is different. This is logical since our realities are totally different. The history, geography and even the language are different because Réunionese Creole has a grammatical structure that is totally distinct from French.[74]

I first wanted to come closer to my Réunionese origins: Madagascar, Africa, and the most despised influences more particularly. I also took an interest in Indian dance (especially *baratha natyam*) and Tai Chi, for example. I wanted to work on the syncretism that is one of the most essential aspect of our mixed culture with strong Afro-Malagasy influences: *maloya* and moring.[75] I am also very interested in contemporary African dance and follow it very closely.

Since the foundation of my company, I have claimed this attachment through my way of dealing with traditional dances that can only be approached through practice, since there are no (or almost no) written sources or films. These Afro-Malagasy traditions, very vivacious and enduring thanks to the commitment of Réunionese musicians and artists, are symbols of our culture, as far as we are concerned.

In these practices, improvisation and free expression have also influenced my choices. The slaves who invented these traditions were not allowed to get together to practice them. This music-dance nonetheless imposed itself, and not without trouble. For a long time, it was an underground art, relegated to the status of a *kaf* ("black" or "nigger") dance; that is, the poor, the slaves, which bound it to the extreme misery of those people, our ancestors.

My approach was preceded by musicians, linguists and writers that have worked to make *maloya* recognized as intangible heritage by UNESCO, after many years of struggle. Today, old fighters such as Danyel Waro or the groups Baster and Ziskakan, storytellers like Danyel Honoré, or writers such as Axel Gauvin still have to fight, because the extremely violent system of colonialism persists in people's mentalities. But whether we like it or not, we are what we are: children of sailors and prostitutes, of French, Portuguese, and English (the island was occupied by England for a few years); of slave traders and of slaves; of *Gran Blan* ("big whites" or "big landowners"), of *Petit Blan* ("small whites" from "the High," poor farmers who arrived at the later part of colonialism and were sent to the higher grounds of the island to farm, as this was the only free land there was); of mixed Creoles. Our culture reflects all that. Like Danyel Waro says: "*anou mèm zanfan batar*" ["we are all bastards"].

Western ethnocentrism is now being questioned in many areas and scientists recognise that everything is relative, depending on which perspective you watch: there are thousands of ways of viewing reality, there are many different truths, and often all points of view converge or complement themselves.

My work is about these differences and more especially those we do not want to see because they remind us of so much misery and violence, and of slavery. What I wish to transmit is that everybody must look for what they are and want to become according to their own reality, their own truth. In my company, my approach is that I want to find my dance and help others find theirs according to what they are and without denying any part of themselves on the pretext that it does not correspond with societal norms. When you want to become an artist, you have to give yourself the permission to be yourself, otherwise nothing makes sense.

This work on memory is essential if I want to find in myself that forgotten part that is present in many other Réunionese families. For now, I have not worked much on Asian influences, because, socially speaking, it seems less problematical to have Chinese and Indian origins (in my experience). I feel that these influences are in me and I have to listen to them. The slave system ended, creating a specific fragmented culture: on one side, the white culture that has been creolised with *sega* and *kroche*,[76] for example, and, on the other side a multifaceted culture such as Hinduism (with a practice specific to the island, walking in the fire) and Afro-Malagasy with *maloya* or *moring*. These worlds often meet and sometimes mingle. And there are also other influences such as Chinese, or Swahili, and a mingling of cultures occurs. For example, we use Indian musical instruments for *maloya*, while some people observe Catholic,

Hindu and Afro-Malagasy rituals simultaneously. There is still a great deal of investigation to be done in this area.

The Importance of *Maloya* and Dance in Réunion

Nowadays in Réunion, it is normal for any musician to play some *maloya* and to use traditional instruments, no matter what the style of music played. As for dance, it is unbelievable to note that *maloya*, *sega* and *quadrille* have only a touristic value. Music groups put dance in the background and the dancers are often women of the family. As in family traditions, the women's importance in *maloya* is secondary. Often, women form the choir dance with a pretty dress to enhance the group. Even when a woman is the queen in a *servis kabaré*, she never plays an instrument. In fact, women rarely play an instrument on stage, and it seldom happens in a group that the leader is a woman, although things are beginning to change. Professional dancers never, or almost never, officially travel with a group. In Réunion, the professionalization of popular dances has yet to happen the way it has with musicians playing popular music. Dance is practiced, on the one hand, in its Western style and, on the other, in its popular, or traditional, style. Moreover, there is a separation between what is traditional (amateur folk groups) and hip hop (amateur teams or, more rarely, professional companies). However, anyone observing people dancing in the *kabars* (concerts where *maloya* is played) or in dance classes can see that the Réunionese are very often talented and show a great sensitivity to the shows offered to them.

Prospects

I hope other choreographers will work on these traditions and that the testimony of the elders will be numerous and constitute a field of exploration for future generations. The musicians have shown us the way and have accumulated treasures from which dancers can draw. Let us anticipate that others will take over. I hope that the talents that are being lost will no longer be so and will enable, at last, an expansion that Réunion deserves. It is up to us, the Réunionese, to give everyone a place. We represent only one percent of the French population. It is up to us to take the place that is ours.

PART II

ALLEGORICAL MARRONNAGE

FREEDOM IN THE MAS:
MARRONNAGE IN TRINIDAD'S CARNIVAL

MICHELLE BERMISS-SMITH

The literal, historical instruments of the past form what Caribbean philosopher-novelist-artist Wilson Harris calls[77] the "prison of the object." These narratives—Victorian travelogues, for example—became established and remain at the heart of discourse on the Caribbean. As Derek Walcott observed in his 1992 Nobel Lecture,[78] these are largely self- and empire-serving unsympathetic accounts, meant to arrest the higher aspirations of those designated the empire's lesser subjects. In the diaspora created by the enslavement and colonization of Africans, the black body was itself made an almost inescapable prison.[79] A variety of resistance strategies evolved, from the fields[80] to JJ Thomas' *Froudacity*. Under legal slavery, marronnage was one of the few desirable and permanent bodily escapes. Whether in the swamplands of Florida[81] or the mountains of Jamaica,[82] a hardy contingent would create and defend a way of life, apart from the constricted roles enforced within others' grand narratives of history. This form of escape, however, was for the few rather than the many. The majority, for a variety of reasons, would not practice literal marronnage.[83]

Speaking (only somewhat) more theoretically, another, cultural form of marronnage is, in Harris' assertion, that "a philosophy of history may well lie buried in the arts of the imagination." One version of that alternative "philosophy" animates Walcott's *Fragments of Epic Memory*, leading him away from the "prison" of criteria, by which the Caribbean[84] is bound to fail, toward an increased emphasis on self-definition: "To be told you are not yet a city or a culture requires this response. I am not your city or your culture. There might be less of *Tristes Tropiques* after that." More importantly, these arts of the imagination are themselves truly alive, with "a delight of conviction, not loss" in the performance of community rituals. We feel Walcott's struggle to free himself (and the Caribbean) in the deliberate reframing of the previously-misread "evocations of a lost India" in more appropriately meaningful terms: "Why not 'celebrations of a real presence'? … Why not the perpetuation of joy … Why was I not letting my pleasure open its windows wide?" Walcott uses faith, religion, joy and celebration to reframe and redirect perceptions established "in the wrong light and with the wrong eye"; his Nobel lecture is a literary monument to a specific and important function of cultural marronnage.

However, despite important literary and historiographic interventions, relatively few had or have access to Thomas' or Walcott's cultural marronnage, just as relatively few could be actual maroons. Instead, following Robert Fariss Thompson's model, my analysis is focused on adaptation(s) of cultural artifacts, and seeks popular expression(s) of the "alternative philosophy of history" we may find "buried in the arts of the imagination." Given its centuries-long tradition in Trinidad and its continuous evolution in response to social and political (as well as artistic and technological) developments, I identify carnival as one of the key "epic stratagems available to Caribbean man in the dilemmas of history which surrounded him" (18). From the use of colour as "a poetic and liberating device" (33), to instances of oral/aural and visual coincidence, carnival enables an epic "Caribbean architecture of consciousness" which supports:

> a range of variables—**variables of community** in the cross-cultural tie of dispossessed tribes or families—**variables of art** and a consciousness of links between poetry and drama, image and novel, architecture and sculpture and painting—which need to be explored in the Caribbean complex situation of apparent history less ... until an active imagination **opens gateways between civilizations**, between technological and spiritual apprehensions (29) [emphasis mine].

In articulating such a "gateway complex," we may therefore establish a continuum rather than a contrast between Thomas' era and ours; as well as between Walcott's contemporary literary defence of Caribbean identity and subjectivity, and the popular practice thereof in the streets and other venues of carnival. The valorization of this "range of variables" is evident in the carnival tropes of beauty and energy embodied by the celebrants, and set forth as the heart of their *identity* (in both senses of the word[85]). This broadened "architecture of consciousness" translates into greater accommodation for the fullness of the human spirit: the gateway means much more than just escaping the "prison." We struggle with life, but we survive *for* joy.

> Dance! There is dancing in the calypso. Dance! If the words mourn the death of a neighbor, the music insists that you dance; if it tells the troubles of a brother, the music says dance. Dance to the hurt! Dance! If you catching hell, dance, and the government don't care, dance! Your woman take your money and run away with another man, dance!

> Dance! Dance! Dance! It is in dancing that you ward off evil. Dancing
> is a chant that cuts off power from the devil. Dance! Dance! Dance!
> Carnival brings this dancing to every crevice on this hill.
> —Earl Lovelace, *The Dragon Can't Dance* (1997, 13–14).

Carnival reinforces an African-derived, diaspora-reinvented, spiritually sustaining tradition; in this it is like many of the cultural artifacts examined in Robert Farris Thompson's *Flash of the Spirit*. One key characteristic of carnival is that it is, of course, celebratory. I argue that this focus on joy is an important and political point. Carnival is explicitly opposed to "Froudacity," an overwhelmingly pessimistic and externalized perspective on black/colonial inadequacies and shortcomings. Carnival also dispenses, however temporarily, with what Walcott called the "sigh of History": the sense that the Caribbean landscape, and thus heritage and narrative, is to be read principally in the ruins of plantation slavery. Carnival refocuses participants (including spectators, as I will discuss below) on the extraordinary joys of their reality as opposed to quotidian pessimism. Carnival periodically reads them into a space of joyous living in history rather than sulking or raging as its victims. As Wilson Harris has observed, even militant and anti-imperialist critics may "fall victim to the very imperialism they appear to denounce [because they] have no criteria for arts of originality... and the history they write is without an inner time" (1995, 22).

Originality and inner direction find few more compelling expressions in the Trinidadian context than carnival. In the Commonwealth Award-winning novel *Salt* (1997), Earl Lovelace's Trinidadian protagonist aborts his planned "escape" from the island in confronting the question of what he means to save his students, not from, but *for*. From his first post-epiphany project through to the narrative's conclusion, the teacher-turned-politician attempts to build an inclusive, national community, not in the vividly tangled thicket of historical grievance, but in the (intermittent) living freedom of carnival celebration.

I would like to focus particularly on two of the most visible aspects of carnival joy: its celebration of beauty and energy. There is an important, physical dimension to the joy expressed in the (stolen? temporary?) freedom of the body. Employing a narrow definition of beauty, and particularly excluding blackness and black characteristics, was and is key to fortifying the prison.[86] Although (neo)colonial attitudes about race, colour, class, gender etc. still maintain, the key aspects of carnival—the music and the masquerades—continually bring forth an increasing range of both "community and art." The bodies, fabrics, feathers and paint illustrate all kinds of aesthetics. The seemingly trivial focus on beauty in carnival collectively brings to life the Trinidadian saying: "All of we is one."

This diversity-identity is reinforced by Soca songs which are explicitly descriptive of diverse kinds of beauty which are all Trinidadian, or all Caribbean, or even all women. These lyrics do not often share Jamaican roots reggae's consistent focus on the hardships of poor, usually unseen ghetto people. Taking the joy of survival as its jumping off point, postmillennial Caribbean Soca more often valorizes women as metaphorically and visually admirable, independent, actively and successfully engaged in modern life. When Alison Hinds sings "Roll It Gyal," there is an explicit dual message: the woman addressed is encouraged to "roll" her body to the music, but all of that beauty and energy isn't just for show. It is these same qualities that enable her to "go to school girl and get your degree/ nurture and take care of your pickney/ show it off now and let the world see/ roll it gyal, roll it gyal." This woman is empowered not despite her body, but, at moments like these, comfortably and joyfully within it.

When carnival music changed from more traditional calypso to Soca in the 1980s,[87] there were complaints about the losses to and destruction of the art form through this faster, electronic sound. Despite the grumbling of those who "needed no instructions" in their music, contemporary Soca artists have remained focused on this paradigm shift in energy: listeners expect to be commanded to jump, wave, *move*! This popular culture expression corresponds well with the literary trope of motion within Caribbean lives.[88] Increasing globalization and more capable technologies have meant new "motions," new sets of possibilities for transnational diasporic lifestyles. The tempo with which we have to keep pace, the work and energy demanded, continually increases. Decades ago, innovations like the VCR meant that within a month or so after carnival someone would return to New York with a tape that my whole family would watch. This was amazing: to watch Trinidad at home on one's own television! By 2010 however, those once-treasured tapes were themselves obsolete: I was live-streaming events over the internet. The high energy of Soca music reflects the joy of surviving this reality, in demanding bodily demonstrations of fitness, flexibility, endurance, balance[89] etc.

Carnival's focus on beauty and energy is more than a "reversal" of the assigned role(s)[90] of victim and/or bystander, and more than a fun, short escape. The "epic stratagem," in the Harrisonian sense, is that the masquerade(r) is the truer self. This necessary bit of illogic, predicated on the heightened focus on their beauty and energy, leads participants into self-affirmation beyond "reason." It is harder for history, politics, etc. to make one feel imprisoned when what we see and hear reinforces the feeling that our shared humanity makes us beautiful, energetic and joyous. Songs like David Rudder's "High Mas(s)" and Machel Montano's "Higher Than High" explain this shared carnival feeling in more overtly (and appropriately) spiritual terms. In his Soca, Rudder prays: "Our Father who has given us this art/ So that we can all feel a part/ Of this earthly (lesser) heaven ... amen!" Montano's song presents two sides of the same coin: an uptempo "power Soca" version, and a sparser kettledrum remix which emphasizes paired Rastafarian-style *Nyabinghi* drumming and the choir's background vocals. Both artists point to the same carnival intersection of the sacred and the secular; participants are witness to their own beauty and humanity, and the masqueraders' jumping up becomes a leap of faith.

As in the previous quotation from Lovelace's *Salt*, Bob Marley's song "Them Belly Full" exhorts listeners experiencing tribulation:

> You're gonna dance to jah music, dance/ We're gonna dance to jah music, dance
> Forget your troubles and dance/ Forget your sorrows and dance
> Forget your sickness and dance/ Forget your weakness and dance.[91]

Dancehall artist Mr. Vegas makes the same point, albeit in more secular terms,[92] when he urges: "When you see wicked people, take 'way yourself ... spin with it and take 'way yourself." The festivity these Caribbean men are promoting is neither mindless nor casual; seen in these contexts, dancing is an essential element in the struggle to preserve one's sense of humanity. When animated with beauty and energy in the sacred-secular-spectacular matrix of the carnival, the masqueraders are moved. The spiritual experience is one of reconnection; but not (only or simply) to Africa, but to the diasporic experience of creative, performative survival in motion. Trinidad's carnival operates in exactly this way, celebrating the freedom and energy of the body in (cultural) marronnage: self-liberated, in public and on an epic scale

In 2008, when Fay Ann Lyons (now Lyons-Alvarez) failed to become the first woman to win a Soca Monarch title, even her now-husband Bunji Garlin, a repeat Soca Monarch himself, agreed with the widespread public opinion that she had been "robbed." The highlight of her competitive performance had been her masquerade as the Silver Surfer. This was much more than just a costume based on a recent Hollywood film: The character is "one of the noblest and most tormented cosmic entities in the [comic book] universe," she said, adding, tellingly, that "the Silver Surfer treasures freedom above all else." Many black fans were also convinced that the ethnically indeterminate Silver Surfer was black, a reading aided by Laurence Fishburne's voicing of the character in the 2007 film. According to the Marvel [Comic Books] Universe Wiki:[93]

> The Silver Surfer wields 'the power cosmic,' absorbing and manipulating the universe's ambient cosmic energies. He can augment his strength to incalculable levels, and is almost totally indestructible. He can navigate space, hyperspace and dimensional barriers, and can fly at near-limitless speeds on his board, entering hyperspace when he exceeds light speed … The Surfer does not require food, drink, air or sleep, sustained entirely by converting matter into energy … The Surfer has demonstrated limited telepathic ability on occasion, and has proven able to influence human emotion and sensation.

Ms. Lyons-Alvarez demonstrated her Trinidad Carnival version of "the power cosmic" for and with her audience: they not only jumped and waved to the music as ordered, but she was in such control of the hyped up crowd that she was able to stand on a surfboard and have them pass her over their heads, "surfing" on their carnival energy! Her performance exemplified the sacred-secular-spectacular, adopting an unexpected mas(k) and playing it with beauty and energy; moving and being moved by the "cosmic" power of their collective joy. Competing again in 2009, she unleashed the power, this time sweeping the three categories in Soca Monarch (Power, Groovy and People's Choice awards) as well as taking the Road March title for most popular song for masquerading carnival bands. Her groovy Soca song celebrated the build of the "Heavy-T Bumper," her own slang for a large-bottomed woman (she happened to be in late pregnancy herself). Her power Soca song strongly asserted both her individual identity, saying that "who doh like mi could bite mi." But she also placed equal emphasis on her place in the continuum, claiming she was "musically bad from since I born, legacy fuh generations." Her stage performance played out those ideas by including both her former Soca star father, to whom the song's title "Meet Super Blue" refers, and her in-utero baby daughter (she held the microphone to her stomach as a child's voice performed a verse). She broke the gender barrier to become the undisputed Soca Monarch not despite her body, but because of the beauty, energy and joy she encourages in fans who co-create the cosmic power they feel during carnival. Fay Ann Lyons-Alvarez won while squarely self-located as a daughter, wife and mother-to-be who would continue to represent, as she always has, for a new generation that is reconfiguring independence on its own terms, for a new century.

This reconfiguration is as essential to the sacred-secular-spectacular matrix of carnival as it is to individual participants. Lovelace's novel *Salt* illustrates that neither the abolition of slavery nor independence from colonization brought about a fully realized, free, and cohesive national community. Beyond the political party and the nation-state, new and remixed narratives of identity and freedom are being played in songs and masquerades, interwoven in tropes of physical beauty and bodily energy. The impracticality of marronnage as self-alienation or escape from the known world's ills is reconfigured as joyful self-reclamation and demonstration of public presence. The Trinidad Carnival enables this complex, self-renewing and contemporary sense of "freedom in the mas."

JAZZ MUSIC AND AMIRI BARAKA'S CONTINUUM: A PERPETUAL MARRONNAGE?

STÉPHANIE MELYON-REINETTE

"As I began to get into the history of the music, I found that thus was impossible without, at the same time, getting deeper into the history of the people. That it was the history of the Afro-American people as text, as tale, as story, as exposition, narrative... that the music was the score, the actually expressed creative orchestration, reflection of Afro-American life, our words, the libretto, to those actual, lived lives. That the music was an orchestrated, vocalized, hummed, chanted, blown, beaten, scatted, corollary confirmation of the history ... That the music was explaining the history as the history was explaining the music. And that both were expressions of and reflections of the people!"
—Amiri Baraka

Introduction

Within the whole range of music we know or we may have heard, perhaps only once in our life, is Jazz. Exceptional Jazz; the only music which is genuinely polymorphous. Jazz is the only music which avoids any kind of monolithic crystallization. Unlike Rap or Soul, which are fully recognizable by their forms and rhythms, by the phrasing of its interpreters, Jazz has different shapes, different faces, different minds and souls. Even though we cannott deny that there are many influences within Rap (west or east coast for instance), the beats, the saccades, the codes are specific to this very music. Rap is both glorified and despised for its counter culture and materialistic values. Robert J. Lewis depicts this ghettoic music as such:

> The repetition in Rap might be the rap of someone banging his head against a wall over and over again, protesting against the life he can't get out of that he doesn't want to lead that doesn't let him live, that doesn't allow him dignity, self-esteem, a place in a community. Rap ... is someone's confession about how it feels to be trapped in a "no exit" life.
>
> (Lewis 2001)

Another example: Stanley Crouch, jazz music critic for *Jazztime* among other magazines, seems to have much less esteem for this music category:

> One can always be sure, deep down, that one is far superior to those jungle bunnies hip-hopping along. For at least a hundred years, there have always been whites willing to pay Negroes top dollar if they dedicated their careers to proving the inferiority of black to white ...What Rap most importantly proves is that Negro American youth culture—just like every other youth culture suffering from the pop entertainment pressure to shock, to outrage, to scandalize—is as vulnerable to decadence and hollow materialism as anything else.
>
> (Crouch 2002)

By asserting such sentiments, Crouch demonstrates how controversial he can be as Rap music is considered worldwide, alongside Jazz music and Rhythm and Blues (amongst others), paradigmatic of African-American culture. And as for diffusion, Rap music, like Reggae or Hip Hop culture, is almost universal given that they have spread all over the world and transformed and mixed in various countries and are part of the "blackstream," a term coined in my personal researches for the "black mainstream." To be accurate, the objective of this article is to speak of marronnage through the spectrum of Jazz styles.

Two keywords are used here: "controversialism" and "marronnage." They will be at the core of this study; the latter is seen as the process, whereas the former is the trigger for this dynamic. By quoting Crouch on Rap, I wanted to emphasize how Jazz could be seen through one of his most virulent "Negro-aesthetics" advocates by presenting another quote of his: "That very quality, that maturity, had always separated Jazz from the boyish and girlish inclinations of popular culture. One went to Jazz wishing to learn how to become an adult, not seeking justification for one's teenage limitations." So, by reading Stanley Crouch, we reach the conclusion that Jazz is synonymous with maturity, excellence, achievement, creativity—in other words, perfection (at least when played by the rule book).

Approaching the issue of marronnage through Jazz music is ideal, though the exercise might be more hazardous than with any other kind of music. To understand where we want to lead the reader's reflection, it is necessary to define this concept, being the centre of our reasoning. Marronnage refers to the fleeing of slaves from their masters' plantations in order to find shelter in the heights of the islands they had been carried to on slave boats. Those slaves, sometimes Creolized and very often freshly arrived in the New World, hid in the mountains (*mornes* or *mòn* in Creole) or in the forest. This phenomenon was common in all the colonized areas of the Caribbean or American. Some "tribal" societies have emerged from those marginalized people and continue today in certain postcolonial countries. Consequently, those Maroon communities (they were called *Neg Marron*, *Cimarron* and *Neg Mawon*) were both marginalized, self-ostracized and were the result of escape. They demonstrate the ideas of freedom, of freeing oneself, of fleeing from something with either survival and the maintaining of ancestral and deep-embedded mores, cultures and practices, or the shaping of brand new kinds of cultures resulting from syncretism as a consequence. In the modern Caribbean, the word "marronnage" is largely used to describe similar realities. Men hiding on nearby islands during the 1960s to 1970s nationalist movements in the French Caribbean was a significant example of the practice of "marronnage."

Now, transferring this concept over to arts or music allows for an observation of the flows, trends and various expressions that have emerged during the previous decades and centuries during the birth of black music. As this book aims at shedding light on codes, meanings and expressions as vectors and receptacles of political discourses, political commitment, or politicization, Rap might seem to be the most tangible expression of black politicization and controversialism. Yet this writing will deal with the birth and development of Jazz through two interwoven prisms: Amiri Baraka's continuum, and our own ideas derived from field research and interviews with Jazz artists. This will show that, more than Rap or any other kind of black music, Jazz is the very paradigm of antagonism and the counter culture. Jazz doesn't respond to any fixed representation or form, hence, the new concept of "world music," covering a very large range of music. Jazz has spread all over the world and has been translated through multiple dimensions.

In *Blues People: Negro Music in White America*, Amiri Baraka (formerly known as LeRoi Jones) writes about Jazz, demonstrating how this universal music evolved and mutated, between, by turns, European-wise (allegedly created by white American musicians, as Miles Davis falls in this category) and African-wise trends (created by black Americans), between re-appropriation and alienation, and between action and reaction. From Smooth Jazz to Free Jazz, Swing to Bebop, Work Songs to Gospel, and so on and so forth, he described a continuum made of breaks and fusions for a bright, organic, reactive and vivid music genre and range. Roughly speaking, we can reasonably state that Jazz is the result of a multitude of marronnages, since there is always an A point, a starting point of a process which consists in going further, in deepening the research of newness to reach a B point, which stands for an innovative vibration. I do not write here as musician or musicologist, but as a simple Jazz listener and sociologist. Consequently, it is about analyzing a very specific process, marronnage, through the social phenomenon of Jazz to understand how its declensions can be understood as demonstrations of human renewal and revolt against (so-called) imposed models. To do so, an exploration of white and black definitions will first be made in order to contrast those community viewpoints and how they have evolved so far, in order to analyze the birth of black music through Amiri Baraka's continuum as action or reaction. Secondly, we will look at how Jazz is marooned or being marooned from its emergence and broadcast system. Finally, the revolutionary trends and the political circumstances related to the development of Jazz will be examined in relation with the topic of politicization.

White Definition Versus Black Definition: What Is Jazz?

First of all, it is essential to define what Jazz is by looking at the various criteria it has been attributed. This is something like an identity of Jazz that we will try to establish by pointing at some important historical features. Stanley Crouch wrote in *Jazztimes* that:

> Jazz has always been a hybrid. A mix of African, European, Caribbean and Afro-Hispanic elements. But the disctrict results of that mix, which distinguished jazz as one of the new arts of the 20th century, are now under assault by those who would love to make jazz no more than an "imrovised music" free of definition. They would like to remove those elements that are essential to jazz and that came from the Negro. Troublesom person, that Negro …
>
> (Crouch 2002)

Crouch, as stated earlier, is definitely a controversialist.

The Early White Definition

In the beginning, when Jazz was still an unknown musical genre, or at least when it wasn't recognized worldwide, it was completely depreciated by the mainstream culture: white people. As a matter of fact, they considered Jazz as low quality music, the black person still being defamed and vilified as an inferior being. From the late nineteenth century, segregation was rampant and forced the black person into bondage anew.

Black people suffered a disrepute so that everything linked to black experience and black creation was dismissed as primitive.

Jazz was also seen as the music of the poor quarters, of dirtiness, and of sex. "Jass" was meant to define a music of ejaculation, a word linked with sexuality and decadence. Jazz was also rightly linked with gangsterism: as a matter of fact, from the 1920s to the 1940s the mafia were involved in "arts sponsorship," producing black musicians so as to invest their money. The crossbred, the "mulattoes," agreed with the white men's opinion so as to resemble them more, and they rejected Jazz because it represented everything they wanted to escape: black poverty and the past they couldn't stand.

It was only after years of evolution, and after whites began to play Jazz and allowed its marketing (the first men to be produced were the Original Dixieland Jass band [ODJB] in 1917) that this music was finally recognized as genuinely creative, melodic, listenable or else "musical." After its full development, Jazz is now seen as the "American classical music." However, we must emphasize that, at the beginning, Jazz aesthetics were completely rejected by the the all-white mainstream. In fact, European aesthetics were the standard to which all the other kinds of music were compared: "Culture was Eurocentric—convinced that the best and noblest were the products of the Old World which the United States had to learn to emulate." These criticisms were essentially linked to racism. The *New York Times* insisted that Jazz "is merely a return to the humming, hand-clapping, or tom-tom beating of savages" ("His Opinion Will Not Be Accepted," November 13, 1924).

As a consequence, to conclude this first part, Jazz was scorned by mainstream opinion, by most white people, until it actually became "mainstream." I met a young white musician named Gavin Fallow who said: "I see Jazz in any kind of tune in the 'Jazz idiom.' There is a certain vocabulary that belongs to Jazz." This is an idea celebrated by many African American musicians.

African American Definitions:
As Many Paths as Visions

There is no single and unique definition of Jazz, even amongst black people, though there are some rules that characterize it, improvisation being one of them. However, the sense musicians give their artistic expression varies and depends on many more criteria, and we can distinguish as many opinions as experiences regarding how black people might have lived. These definitions are very personal because they match their political convictions, their life experiences, their objectives and their expectancies.

I met and interviewed different African-American Jazz musicians in New York City as I was doing my field work, and I collected their words, impressions and definitions of Jazz. This enables us to offer a rather wide range of descriptions and meanings. Below are the responses of Randy Weston and the members of his African Rhythm Quartet in answering the question: "How would you define Jazz Music?"

Randy Weston who considers himself to be an African, and who has moved to Morocco, firstly gives an historical definition of Jazz. But as a fervent believer and spiritual man, he feels that Jazz is the result of the African slaves that "put their spirituality into European instruments, to create Blues." Regarding Jazz, he states that improvisation is inherent to it: "Music is nature. This is the same thing. Consequently, as nature changes with the seasons, music must always be improvisation, change. This is in African traditional music very close to nature." Morever being inspired by Africa, he doesn't call his music "Jazz" but "African Rhythms."

Talib Kibwe Blue, the saxophonist of the quartet, emphasizes the fact that this music is common to the whole world: "Yes, Jazz is universal, and this is the only universal music for it's played everywhere. Classical music, Reggae, Salsa, and so on, are not played in every country. Only Jazz is played everywhere." His own definition of Jazz is more poetic: "Jazz is Emotion, Spontaneity, this is a deep-inspired music. Jazz doesn't belong to us. This is a gift to the world."

Born in New Orleans, **Benny Powell**, the trombonist of the band, stated: "'Jazz' is an economic word; Jazz is the expression of a people with African origins. This is a celebrating of all life, of the simplest things of life (birth, death, christenings …). This is a spiritual celebration. When you are not educated, it's more natural." He added: "Music makes work easier, daily life easier. During slavery, the labour was very hard. The Negro Spirituals are the basis of Jazz, and they narrated what the African slaves had been through: "Nobody knows the trouble I've seen." Through music they could relieve themselves. The key of Jazz is personal expression. Certain musicians imitate a formula; this is a mere remake of what they have heard before."

Drummer **Neil Clark**: "Jazz is an art of improvisation; this is the highest form of improvisation, developed by Africans in America, which translate the various dimension of the African Americans' experience (history, culture, politics, economics …). Jazz can be sensual. Many black musics are sensual: Bossa Novas, Sambas, Boleros … for they are expressive. Jazz is expressive but not necessarily sensual. Sensuality is the way blacks express themselves. Their musics are very organic, and deal with very organic themes. But Jazz isn't as abstract as other forms of music. Sensuality isn't limited to Jazz."

Reggie Workman said: "For me, Jazz music shouldn't be coined 'Jazz.' It's the music of the African-American experience. 'Jazz' is a bastard word. This was the industry that created this word to make something positive of it. But this is completely negative, in fact, because it involves musics that don't have anything to do with Jazz. The word to use is 'World Music'."

I asked then: "Does colour still matter?" He answered: "Colour has always mattered. "Jazz" has been shut in a caste system, because it is [part of] an economic area that includes that. But you see my wife is from Slovenia ... But the most important thing isn't colour but music. We must keep in mind that quality is the essence of Jazz, is the most important. We must go beyond this caste thing, we must forget about ethnicity and seek what's important for us, to the art form."

The definitions are quite different, but they demonstrate the heart of the matter. Jazz is all of these things: improvisation, the art of expression, nature, universality, sensuality, even though improvisation is seen as the main and most important trait distinguishing jazz from other repertories. John F. Swed, professor of African American studies, anthropology, music and American studies at Yale University wrote:

> Improvisation—the art of composing in the moment, in the act of performance, without a written score—has always been seen as what sets jazz part from other musics. It may or may not be true that no othe rmusic counts so much on instant creativity, expecting every musicians to rise to a certain level, but jazz musicians and their followers talk and act as though it is. They speak of going beyond the limitations of the precomposed, beyond the simply interpretive, to a more deeply inspired and more instantaneous creativity, to a level that may put the improviser much more in touch with his or her conscious and unsconscious states.
>
> (2002, 65)

Where the matter differs is on the level of identity: How do they consider themselves? They are African Americans for us, but each of them privileges one aspect of their identity: some are Africans, others accept both sides. To quote Neil Clarke from the African Rhythm Quartet:

> I feel I'm an African in America. I consider all things that can be positive for me in both. I want to emphasize the African side, for America wants you to forget where you are from, to forget your roots. America is synonymous with unfairness; pain and I don't want to participate in. Yet

America give sopportunities—he pointed out that he owes much to
America as a musician—So I'm conscious that it's a very delicate balance.

Jazz in Amiri Baraka's Continuum:
A Music of Reaction

As for many black and Afrocentrist musicians, critics and music lovers,
Jazz music has often been "colonized" by white musicians, in that it was
invaded so many times by European cultural elements and values that it
was almost unrecognizable. These forms were based on melody and
harmony, whereas African music was characterized by improvisation,
spontaneity, call-and-repsonse, percussiveness and vocalizations. They
tried to cast Jazz into a rigid mould: because many black musicians were
uneducated and illiterate, Jazz was spontaneous and heartfelt. Now it is
written and composed according to rules because it has been in touch with
white musical classicism.

The Colonization of Jazz by the European Tradition

Among these so-called colonized styles, we can distinguish landmarks
between Dixieland, New Orleans Jazz, Progressive Jazz and Rock'n'Roll
(three of which appeared at the same time in the 1950s, the third in the late
1960s). We will give more details regarding three kinds, Symphonic Jazz,
Swing Jazz and Cool Jazz, as they are some of the best known in the
present day:

Symphonic Jazz: Paul Whiteman was known as the "King of Jazz."
To many Americans in the 1920s and 1930s, this avuncular, rotund figure,
waving a baton, and with a wry grin under his pencil moustache,
personified Jazz, although everything his band played cannott be
considered as Jazz, encapsulating arrangeemnts of the light classics to
settings for singers. Hughes Panassie said in 1934: "Paul Whiteman, who
once had a band that could really swing, concerns himself with what the
public wants. He specializes in what strikes me as empty pompous
performances—nicknamed 'Symphonic Jazz'." Among the members of
his band were those who have been seen as the best white soloists in the
history of music: Bix Beiderbecke, Jack Teagarden, Frank Trumbauer.[94]

Swing appeared in the second half of the 1930s and coincided with the
era of the big tour. Mainstream Jazz had turned Jazz into variety. They
were great musicians but they played so perfectly that they completely
distorted this music. Among the best-known musicians of that period were
Duke Ellington, Jimmy Lunceford, Art Tatum, Coleman Hawkins, and

Lester Young.

In the fifties, **Cool Jazz** emerged with a big star, Miles Davis (a black man) in New York. But it was on the West Coast of the USA that Jazz had the greatest influence at that time.

Re-appropriation of Jazz by the African Americans

Regarding the Africanizing styles, they were essentially African-American with regard to musical structure. Through them, the African-Americans tried and somehow managed to reclaim their music. Each time it was an awakening. Each time they were aware of the fact that they had been deprived of their dearest, most valuable property: their music. Therefore, they called for their creativity to innovate, to break the rules of mainstream tradition anew by returning to the source, Africa, and its rhythms. They aimed at counterbalancing the sway and the control white people had on Jazz.

In the forties, **Bebop** appeared in reaction to the Swing Era. It was the meandering of the Jazz Phenomenon (due to the war and economic problems[95]) that gave rise to this genre. This initiative was taken by Thelonious Monk, Dizzie Gillespie and Charlie Parker, who needed to renew the musical language. The maintream music, Swing, was too perfect in composition (arrangements, inflexibility of the repertoire etc.), and removed improvisation and solos. Bebop was a first movement of protest.

Rhythm and Blues in the late forties (after the Second World War) resulted from the will of the newly urbanized black population to look forward, wanting to forget the past of their harsh lives (slavery, segregation, poverty etc.). They wanted to enjoy their new lives, to entertain, and this music aimed at pleasing people. This was a mix of Jazz, spirituals and Blues, as well as the Tin Pan Alley romantic style. It was heterogeneous and evolutionary, and the new record labels enjoyed a fruitful and lucrative market, as the blacks had become consumers.

Table 1. Amiri Baraka's Continuum: Major Trends and Events (1600s–1920s)

	World Events	Jazz continuum	US landmarks	
1600s	Slavery/Triangular trade	Work Songs		
1800s		Gospel	Aft. 1830s: *The Great Awakening* Christening of the Slaves **April 8, 1864**: 13th amendment, the Abolition of Slavery **1867**: 15th amendment, voting rights for Black men	
1900s		1900s: **Ragtime New Orleans Jazz (Dixieland Jazz)**		
1910s	**1914–1918:** World War I		**1910** **1917**: Original Dixieland Jazz Band (ODJB), 1st recording	
1920s		**Blues (cities). Symphonic jazz**	**1920**: Volstead Act Alcohol prohibition *Race records*, recordings of vinyles for	**1910–1940** *The Great Migration* Former slaves' exodus to The northern cities

Table 2. Amiri Baraka's Continuum: Major Trends and Events (1930s–2000s)

1930s		**Swing**		
	1939		**World War II**: economics and rationing; the music industry suffers.	
1940s	**1945**: World War II	**Bebop** Jazz musicians begin to travel to Third World Countries	No recordings.	
	1946			
1950s	**1954**: Indochina War	**Cool Jazz / Hard Bop**		
	1954			
	1962: Algerian War			
1960s	**1955**	**Free Jazz**	**1955–1968**: Civil rights Movement	Latin jazz, Brazilian jazz,
	1975: Vietnam War	**Soul Jazz**	Black Power movement	African fusion, Indian fusion
1970s		**Jazz Rock & Fusions**		
1980s to the 2000s		**World Music**		

In the Sixties, **Hard Bop** was a response to Cool Jazz and somewhat a continuation of Bebop. This was an assertion of black identity in the face of the success of West Coast Jazz. It was aggressive, which is why the bop was termed "hard." The protagonists of this period are Max Roach, Clifford Brown, Art Blakey, Charles Mingus and John Coltrane.

Between the Sixties and the Seventies, **Free Jazz** was a new revolution: it was synonymous with revolt, revolution, and resistance, and coincided with the black revolution. As a matter of fact, the free jazzmen wanted to break off from the white tradition that had poisoned their music and wanted to give birth to a music so original and African that whites wouldn't be able to steal it by imitating it. They claimed their African identity through it. Cecil Taylor, Ornette Coleman, Eric Dolphy and Arche Shepp where notable proponents of this music. Some found it completely weird, completely at odds with that they called Jazz initially and that the critics agreed with this.

Marronnage:
Emergence and Defence against the System

Marronnage finds various expressions in the Jazz continuum. The seed of it all can be encountered in Africa, as the germs of this music lie in the first links of the "forced" migratory chains, the result of the triangular trade of slavery. Black people were kidnapped, bought or exchanged and transported to the shores of the New World to feed the flow of energy needed to make the plantations flourish: this is the African diaspora.

Two kinds of marronnage can be explained in the following. First of all, the deportation of the black man to a new world is a kind of disaffection, a distance imposed on the enslaved people, a distance from their origins. And yet, Africa crossed the ocean with them, as a souvenir, as physical reminiscences, as a philosophy and as beliefs. This marronnage made them closer to their sense of culture. The other marronnage deals with Jazz as an antagonism to the music industry in the USA. The way Jazz exists as music is rather unorthodox: this is "marketing marronnage."

Deportation: Africa in America

Many African Americans wanted and still want to see their culture given back to them. In conversation with me, Talib Kibwe Blue was adamant that Africa was the cradle of Jazz, as it is for mankind: "we must be conscious that we all come from Africa." He told me that a journalist once asked him (a very stupid question in his opinion): "What gives you the authority of playing Jazz?" He simply answered "Authority? I can play Jazz because I'm an African-American and Jazz is my heritage."

So, briefly, the story of African-American music begins in Africa, in the frame of the slave trade, when thousands and thousands of West Africans were sold by their peers to the white colonizers to acquire knick-knacks and things that were worthless in comparison to the worth of thousands of lives. They were deported beyond the Atlantic Ocean to enter into bondage, but in their misfortune they brought with them their biggest wealth: music. Everyone knows that music is inherent to African lives. As a matter of fact, singing is a daily celebration. To each moment of their lives, they dedicate a song: cultivation, harvesting, marriages, births, deaths and funerals. Music is functional and circumstantial. This tradition, this trait that characterizes the African population, has also been brought to America.

In *Blues People: Negro Music in White America*, Amiri Baraka showed how similar the West African songs and the Work Songs of the African slaves in American fields were. After their deportation, they began to work in the cotton fields and sugar cane plantations to the benefit of their white masters. To make their condition more acceptable, their lives and their pain bearable, they sang in the fields while working. From then on, Africa entered America to mark, in an indelible way, the musical history of the New World. The Work Songs fulfilled all the criteria their original music did: they were functional and helped the slaves stand the cruelty of bondage.

Through this pattern, it is easy to highlight the reasoning of certain black jazzmen regarding their African, Negro origins which they claim and emphasize in Jazz history. Their songs, after some evolution, even served to mock their white masters or to communicate secretly, such as Gospel, disguising messages which helped the slaves to find the right spiritual path.

Jazz: Art Versus Trade

The rules of commerce do not match up with the rules of art: Jazz abides by the second of these. Usually, Jazz, first and foremost, tries to reach a certain originality and to be sold afterwards, whereas the music industry had already set a term to pigeonhole musical genres. That's to say that if some composer presents a product which doesn't match their definition of "Jazz," it won't be considered as such unless that product is altered to fit the category.

In the late 1940s, this phenomenon had already happened. The term

"Rhythm and Blues"[96] was coined to qualify a new kind of black music and to replace the labels "Race Records" and other "sepias." The music industry, in this way, sells a form, a mould, and not an abstraction. Peter Margasak underscored that Jazz aims at surprise, while commerce aims at suppression of this surprise: "In theory, at least Jazz transforms itself into something new before ever becoming formulaic while business identifies something as a form and attempts to develop a hard and fast definition, it's easier to sell something that's solid than something that's amorphous."

Peter Margasak stated that majors record labels are the face of Jazz to the general public. He wrote : "Too often jazz recordings released by the major labels serve as barometers for the health of the music. The major labels spend the most money on advertising, receive the most record-store shelf space, and garner the most press; to the general public, the major labels are the record industry" (Friedwald et al. 2002, 109).

But concerning the Jazz business, the major labels aren't representative of it at all. The "real thing," that's to say "real Jazz," isn't produced by the few giants of the industry, but by many independent labels, also called "indies."

Most of the time, jazzmen choose indies because they are allowed greater freedom in their choice and in the shaping of their music than through working with majors. They can keep their stance of originality and "off-the-beaten-track" mindset, and focus on quality and creativity instead of concentrating exclusively on the marketable side of the business. In basic terms, this is art and not business, even though they have or wish to make a living out of it.

There was a proliferation of indies as soon as the majors turned their backs on Jazz. Most of them continue to contribute "Jazz buffs" to the business, to help perpetuate it: "In many cases such imprints are labors of love that owners operate as backbreaking hobbies ... labels like Okka Disk in Chicago, Wobbly Rail in Chapel Hill and AUM Fidelity in New York ... (Margasak 2002).

As stated, most jazzmen choose independent labels to commercialize their music because they are freer. Peter Margasak recalled that Ben Allison and his cohorts—pianist Frank Kingbrough, saxophonist Ted Nash, trumpeter Ron Horton—all record for tiny independent labels like Palmetto, Arabesque and Omnitone.

From the 1960s on, there is a meandering of the Jazz business: as a matter of fact, there has been a downsizing process, aimed at saving money or investing money in other more profitable fields. Peter Margasak stated that:

Back in the 1970s and the '80s each of the six major distribution companies handled a number of self-contained, independently operated jazz labels, but in the last few years the landscape has been altered greatly … There are now five companies following the merger of UNI and Polygram—a similar merger between EMI and BMG threatens to reduce the number to four—and they now exert a much greater control over a radically reduced number of Jazz labels. Such consolidation is a cost-cutting measure and it follows that Jazz departments at each label undergo the same downsizing process … The UNI/Polygram merger found the former's jazz department, GRP, combining with the latter's, Verve. To enhance economic efficiency both staff and roster were reduced.

(Friedwald et al. 2002, 110)

Diffusion

The first methods of circulating Jazz were those which primarily allowed the expansion of African-American music (gospel, blues, and jazz) from the southern countryside of the USA to the northern and western urban areas of the country. **Touring** was the main means of diffusion, helped by the waves of migration contributing to the spreading of that music, including Medicine Shows and Minstrels shows. Touring began from the 1920s, and today, it remains one the best ways to circulate music. Ven Vandermark said "Take the music to the people. Bring it to where they feel comfortable hanging out." Nowadays the philosophy is still to get close to the audience, and concerts are still the best way to keep in touch with the public. Proximity is obviously decisive in preserving the intimacy and the complicity that exist between the performers and the audience: African American music creates catharsis through call-and-response, for example. This is art for art's sake.

Recording is the second means. From the 1910s there have been recording societies producing Jazz music (Original Dixieland in 1917) and "race records" with the classical blues and its first professional female performers: Bessie Smith, Billie Holliday and Nina Simone. Third, **broadcasting** is the final means. Black radio stations were the best ways to distribute the music, and to be on air was really significant for the artists. Those means are still useful, however Jazz radio has tended to disappear and black radio stations are not helpful anymore, as they prefer lucrative music and feature mostly rap, soul or R'n'B. Nowadays, radio is still very much in demand as a medium, but it is part of what we call "big business" and is a form of media that submits to certain rules that artists must comply with in order to be broadcast.

Moreover, even though Jazz has a mostly white audience today, it is still difficult for all musicians to advertise through the mainstream media, because most artists don't fall under mainstream labels and codes. McDavid Henderson explains: "Whether they've tried in the past and failed or not, Jazz labels must either continue or begin to advertise in African American periodicals. Such magazines as *Ebony*, *Jet*, *Essence*, even *Savoy*, have sizable constituencies and represent potential untapped fans. The same holds true for African American newspapers, which continue to have a healthy readership, even if journalism surveys and consultants ignore them" (Henderson 2003). Thus, the black press remains a good deal for many esoteric, eclectic and experimental artists.

Now, though residing in a certain cultural and economic space, Jazz continues to evolve with time and socioeconomic circumstances. It turns out that technological progress has affected all kind of music, and Jazz has not escaped this fate. In fact, e-commerce and digital recording are paths that its musicians have and will continue to walk. Because music is more and more dematerialized, it has to follow this tendency to be in tune with the listeners, who are also consumers. In that sense, Jazz has to follow the mainstream, the wave, the conjuncture, because this marooned market has to remain in a sustainable position, to some extent.

1960s Marronnage, Black Revolutionary Jazz and Politicization

The 1960s: Global Upheaval

This last part will deal with the various musical movements that were predominant and characteristic of the 1960s revolutionary era and that coincided with the black movement for Civil Rights, the battle for recognition and recovering of their identity with Afrocentricity. It is possible to see that political circumstances thoroughly impregnated the artistic spheres in the United States in the 1960s, and here we agree fully with Amiri Baraka's thesis: musical styles are influenced and shaped by society. The messages that are passed over to the public, whether negative or positive, whether superficial and childish, as Crouch maintained, or serious and politically-oriented, whether dealing with love, passion and hate or about race or money, are rooted in music, and music is intrinsically rooted in society and mirrors the reality the artists evolve in. Therefore, of course, Jazz has always carried some translation of the society in which it has existed.

In the 1960s, globally speaking, the world was caught in a frenzy, a revolutionary and political trance that overwhelmed all nations and mentalities. Specific events provoked the raising of antagonistic philosophies and perspectives. After the Second World War, the Cold War erupted almost silently. It is possible to think that this war of positioning was not raging everywhere, because, obviously, on the battlefields blood is usually shed. These battlefields gave birth to other kinds of struggle—struggle on the spiritual and philosophical levels. Regarding the US, the war in Vietnam made demands on people's spirit and commitments and, whether against or for the war, people had to take a stance. All over the world, at the same time, riots and upheavals broke out, such as in Indochina, Algeria and Africa as the decolonization of the European and American powers took place. Along with nationalist movements, claims of independence and the internal struggles of many nations, the world appeared to be on fire!

In the USA, the late 1950s and the 1960s were a period of great mobilization for the black community. It was, politically and socially, an extremely tense period for African Americans who tried to flee from the unacceptable living conditions they had to bear daily. Police harassment, segregation, racism, insalubrious housing and menial jobs were their routine. They united to struggle against injustice around political leaders such as Martin Luther King Jr. from 1954, following Rosa Parks' arrest, Malcolm X and the black Muslims in the mid-1960s and after this the Black Panthers, and so on. Organizations such as the National Association for the Advancement of Colored People (NAACP), the Congress of Racial Equality (CORE), the Student Non-Violent Coordinating Committee (SNCC), and the Southern Christian Leadership Conference (SCLC) emerged, allowing them to gather and fight together. So grassroots movements were initiated with different kinds of demonstrations, from sit-ins to the Black Panthers' armed parades, through non-violent manifestations and trials (we know that demonstrations on the streets preceded the trials, since these were the various rights they managed to acquire on social and racial levels). However, in the musical sphere, on stage, artistic expressions became weapons of contestation. The idea was to diverge from mainstream jazz, or what was considered to be a part of it, and to generate new codes, new semiotics, in order to create a new sense of life, new paths toward freedom, the freeing of oneself.

Upheaval, Avant-Garde and Music Action Groups

It was in this climate of unification in the different African American communities that Free Jazz appeared with the creation of organizations of musicians. In fact, John Coltrane's *Ascension* was the starting-point for this avant-garde movement, the freedom of this piece energizing musicians.

In the 1960s, specific community associations, or action groups, aimed at gathering artists and at exhorting a new kind of grassroots movement at the artistic level: the creation of alternative trends and scenes. In Saint Louis, the Black Artists' Group (BAG) initiated by Oliver Lake, Julius Hemphill and Floyd LeFlore, mainly dealt with fundraising and teaching. In New Orleans, the New Orleans Academy of Creative Arts (NOCA), the equivalent of Chicago's AACM, received students like Wynton Marsalis, Alvin Batiste and Kidd Jordan. In Los Angeles, there was the Underground Musicians' Association (UGMA) initiated by pianist Horace Tapscott, whose action was centred in Watts where many riots occurred at that time. Some of them were really committed to grassroots movements against the police through social unrest, typical of the marginalized fringes of the United States metropolises. Steven Louis Isoardi wrote: "In placing themselves and their art in the grassroots centre of African American concerns and life, they also knew that they would be targeted by the police, for whom any critical black movement or organization—cultural, social, or political—was seen as a threat to the existing order" (Isoardi 2006, 89). Yet, the first aim was to open new spaces of reflection and creation to fight against the musical establishment which deprived the black community from its sense of self. Isoardi explains further:

> UGMA's prominence in South Central L.A. and on 103rd Street attracted artists in search of an alternative scene, of an environment that allowed for expansive artistic boundaries and participation in the evolving social consciousness of the community. The wake of the Watts uprising brought an influx of members, mostly in their tewnties, many recently discharged from the military, a few already working in support of various civil rights causes, and some struggling to find their personal and musical identities while submerged in the morass of entertainment industry commercialism.
>
> (Isoardi 2006, 90)

Regarding Chicago's AACM, Joseph Jarman explained to Alyn Shipton that:

> there was tremendous anxiety in the political climate at the time ... So it was a very exciting, nervous period. Of course, within each community it was very calm and relaxed. We had experienced a view of union. And that's how the letter [from Abrams] came about, because we were experiencing unity in the various communities. [The intent of the whole idea was to allow us the opportunity to perform; but to perform with dignity, with pride, without humiliation, without limitation].
>
> (Shypton 2001)

Globally, more than "originality," "unexpectedness" was the pinpoint of the movement. The changes that occurred in instrumentation were also new ways of bringing surprise into in the music. Unusual combinations of instruments could permit the appearance of completely different shades and tones in the musical landscape. Saxophonist Roscoe Mitchell began:

> ... to explore ideas that nobody in the New York School had done, beginning with very small sounds: tinkling bells, shaker and scrapers, unusual cymbals and so on. He found he could use the contrast between these quiet, unusual timbres and the full sound of saxophone, trumpet, and drums to convey a combination of ideas and emotions not always present in jazz: irony, lyricism, and sarcasm.
>
> (Shypton 2001, 811).

Other changes also occurred, but in the structural composition of the band. The instrumentation was influenced by the political climate. In fact, the new Jazz was a protest against the establishment of the society: against racism, against Vietnam and in favour of decolonization. They wanted to avoid staleness and repetition, which is why they entered into projects that linked their music to other cultures: they used traditional Indian, African and Japanese instruments and turntables as well, for they were fascinated by unusual tones and colours. As stated, it was a matter of freedom, and the freeing of onself. Maronnage is manifested here through both the choice of liberty in improvisation, and the rupture with the mainstream mindset and "dictatorship." Free Jazz was somewhat the foundation of what is called World music today.

From Free Jazz to World Music: Intermingling with Other Cultural Spheres

Free Jazz is the trend which initiated the process toward the integration of foreign elements into Jazz music, allowing for more nuanced colours and shades in the music. The introduction of new instruments is a perfect example of their marronnage from the classical codes imposed on the music by the white mainstream conformist practitioners and markets. Thus, their travels abroad and what they learnt there gave birth to new energies. We can emphasize the fact that the 1960s proposed renewals which were definitely directed at valuing the so-called Third World countries' music and instruments. Can this be said to be a "blackening" process?

From Free Jazz instrumental marronnage, we may consider that alongside it emerged various kinds of fusion, such as Latin, African,

Indian, Brazillian or Japanese. Blending Latin music and Jazz wasn't anthing new in the 1970s—we have already given the example of Gillepsie working with Chano Pozo, and who afterwards fueled this crossover, cross-fertilization between Cuba and America, introducing many "cubanos," including trumpeter Arturo Sandoval, to the international scene.

Caribbean and Latin melodies that were "jazzified" resulted in new musical styles: thus Mambo is a "jazzified" Danzón, and the jazzification of traditional Cuban orchestras resulted in Salsa. Latin Jazz is of course the blending of Jazz and Latin rhythms. Among the best-known Latin-American jazzmen are Cubans Candido Camero and Chico O'Farrill. The former is a conga player who worked with Dizzy Gillespie, Saxer Gene Ammons and pianist Randy Weston. He mixed Jazz with Latino-American music, traditional Yoruba culture and Calypso. The latter was hired as an arranger by Benny Goodman, who wanted to enter the world of Bebop. Later, he composed his "Afro-Cuban Suite" in 1950 and his second long-playing piece for Gillespie. The King of Mambo and Latin Jazz, Tito Puente, a great timbalero (he is more famous as an instrumentist) played a major role in the fusion of Jazz and Afro-Cuban rhythms. As a leader he recorded more than a hundred albums and won four Grammy Awards. In the 1950s he recorded "Abariquito," "Babarbatiri," "El Rey del Timbal," and in 1963 "Oye Como Va." Other great musicians of this kind of fusion were Ray Barretto, Eddie and Charlie Palmieri, and Machito.

Regarding African Fusion, we must emphasize the fact that Africa has always been regarded very specifically by the black American community, as they consider this continent to be their motherland. Coltrane's "Africa" in 1961 and Ellington's "Jungle" period are meaningful examples of this infatuation with Africa. African fusion history began in South Africa with a big band known as Chris McGregor's Brotherhood of Breath with McGregor himself, Mongezi Feza, Dudu Pukwana, Harry Miller, Louis Moholo and British players such as Malcolm Griffiths, Nick Evans, Mike Osbornes, John Surnam and Alan Skidmore. This movement was initiated by the climate of protest that overwhelmed the country because of appartheid. The most impressive fact regarding these musicians is that because of the restriction imposed by the regime, censorship was also applied to music, and they had to practice on pennywhistles in training for their first attempts. The Jazz Epistles, featuring Abdullah Ibrahim (piano), Jonas Gwangwa (trombone), Kippie Moeketsie (alto), Johnny Gertze (bass) and Makaya Ntshoko (drums) and Hugh Masekela (trumpet), were the first all-South African band to record, two years before Coltrane recorded "Africa." In the USA, the leading figures of African fusion were

Masekela, who moved to America in 1961 and blended bop and South African township music, and Abdullah Ibrahim who was noticed by Duke Ellington while he was accompanying his wife, singer Sathima Benjamin, with the trio to Zurich. They recorded in 1963 and Ellington made Ibrahim known by getting him booked at the Newport Festival.

In South Africa, musicians like Darius Brubeck and Pops Mohammed, who led the Jazz department at the University of Durban as a multiracial workshop, strove to find new talents. Those who "burgeoned" under apartheid have now blossomed, such as bassist Victor Ntoni, drummer Lulu Gontsana, and sax player Barney Rachabane. Above all was pianist Moses Molelekwa who melded his strinkingly original playing and compositions with the new urban form of Kwaito music.

The Indian subcontinent was very important in the constitution of the "free" instrumentation of the New Jazz bands: sitar, tabla, and other traditional instruments have become consistent ingredients in many Jazz groups in the world today. Like Jazz Rock, Indo-Jazz fusion was initiated in Britain. The reason could be Indian immigration due to the former Commonwealth which linked the United Kingdom and India, and gives them priority regarding entry to British soil. Indian violonist John Mayer and altoist Joe Harriott were the first to experience the fusion of Jazz and Indian music. One or two years later, the Beatles worked with Ravi Shankar. Harriott's free jazz group was made up of trumpeter Kenny Wheeler, bassist Coleridge Goode and pianist Pat Smythe, alongside Indian musicians Diwan Motihar on sitar, Viranu Jagani on Tamboura and Keshau Sathe on tabla. This movement premarturely died with Harriott in 1973 and was reborn in the 1990s when Mayer decided to reform the group. In the USA, the movement began with the band, Oregon, whose most prominent member was Collin Walcott who mastered several Indian instruments (such as the sitar, the tabla and traditional percussion), and worked with American clarinetist Tony Scott in his first attempts to fuse Jazz and Eastern music.

We can also evoke Brazilian Jazz. Concerning this fusion, American musicians experimented with samba and bossa nova (mixing samba and modern jazz). Names such as guitarists Antonio Carlos Jobim, Luis Bonfa and Bader Powell, Joao Gilberto, percussionist Airto Moreira, singers Flora Purim, Astrud Gilberto and Els Regina are notable in this field. Two landmarks that marked this trend are: on March 13, 1962, Jobim recorded "Desafinado" with Stan Getz and the Quartet of Charlie Byrd. In 1963, Stan Getz and Joao Gilberto worked on themes like "Corcovado," "The Girl from Ipanema" and "Desafinado" with Herbie Ellis and Laurindo Almeida on piano, Ramsey Lewis on guitar, Bud Shank and Coleman

Hawkins on saxophone and Herbie Mann on guitar.

One of the best-known Brazilian jazzmen in America was Gato Barbieri, who was famous for his commitment both to music and politics. On the two albums recorded in Buenos Aires, Rio de Janeiro and Los Angeles, he used instruments from Argentina and the countries of the Andin Cordillera that he had discovered: harp, Indian flute, Bandoneon, a small four-string guitar, and the Indian drum as well as more traditional instruments such as guitar, electric bass, drumkit, and percussion. In 1969, he released *The Third World* illustrating his return to his Latin-American culture. The album is a symbol of the struggles of many South American countries: each theme evokes a Third World country. Argentina is recalled by Tango by Astor Piazzola, Brazil by Zelao. With regards to his styles, his religious and mystical context was in the mold of Coltrane, being quite incantatory. It lay between Free Jazz and Fusion, an intermediary path. However, the Brazilian trend was somewhat short-lived because immigration from Brazil was less important than for those from Cuba or Puerto Rico.

For Jan Garbarek, world music "has at least two meanings ... a regular meaning: music composed of ethnic elements from various parts of the world ... [and] American pop music. It's everywhere and everybody listens to it whether they like it or not ....." So, Jazz is a world music since it is a syncretic blending of African or ethnic elements with European influences in the United States that has spread both outward and inward. Jazz has "marrooned" everywhere in the world, and World Music and Jazz festivals can be found all over the planet.

Conclusion

This development signified also that jazz would someday have to contend with the idea of its being an art (since that *was* the white man's only way into it). The emergence of the white player meant that Afro-American culture had already become the expression of a particular kind of American experience, and what is most important, that this experience was available intellectually, that it could be learned.

(Amiri Baraka 1963)

In fact, the right word for all African-Americans today is "World Music." For many of them, Jazz is world music, because it has been a "worldly" music. Nowadays, it is seen as the classical music of the USA and a music that results from a tradition, and an ethnic group, the African Americans that were originally a rural community, have elaborated it. This is what we learn through Amiri Baraka's continuum. For this author, poet and music critic, Jazz originates in Africa and is and remains a Black music which has had to struggle against the "whitening" of its notes and shapes, by reinventing every ten years or so new expressions, new forms, new structures, and is sometimes destructed, as with Free Jazz—a real and true process of marronnage. From the original material of "African wailing," to paraphrase Randy Weston, to a kind of rhizome-like repertory.

As a result, Jazz is a meeting point between different cultures. At the beginning it joined African tradition and European classical music. Now Jazz meets any kind of music: it blends with Third World music, with the classical, let's say "traditional," music of others countries, and so on. Jazz is a crossroads of civilizations echoing many voices. Even though many musicians or critics, such as Stanley Crouch, disparage white Jazz musicians and consider the dominant group's influence as deleterious to Jazz, since it was born black, and will remain so for them, today it is a matter-of-fact that Jazz has spread worldwide and is dyed and coloured with as many shades, nuances and gradations that exist in the world. Jazz was firstly black, and through marronnage and wishing to escape from whiteness or whitening by walking foreign roads and paths, has become more open to the world. Thus, race doesn't matter regarding Jazz aesthetics today. Ben Ratliff wrote that:

> The fact is that race means less and less–both in terms of the acceptability of a composer or musician to the "marketplace" of jazz, such as it is, and in terms of the music actually played. And as the music of Cuba, the Middle East, and Africa is incorporated with more accuracy and rigor into jazz, any divisions you might be able to crowbar between "black" and "white" jazz are looking more fraudulent.
>
> (Friedwald et al. 2002, 24)

Obviously, there are still trends wandering away from mainstream codes. Mainstreams must be understood as " ... the majority truth of art: a few people establish a language, and if they've hit on the right ingredients, it becomes commanding, by a mysterious consensus" (Ratliff 2002, XVII). And so, mainstream being also a dynamic, and with the codes imposed on the society also evolving, marronnage is an incessant and never-ending process and we can bet on the emergence of new trends. Will we have to wait for a political revolution to see this?

MIZIK KONT PWOFITASYON:[97]
THE SOCIOLOGICAL RELEVANCE
OF GUADELOUPEAN MUSIC.

STEVE GADET*

(*) Translated from French by Nathalie Montlouis

"If you want to control the people, control its music."
—Plato, *The Republic*

"Good music never fails. It goes straight to the depth of the soul reaching out to the sadness that consumes us."
—Mozart et Métasbase, from *Lettres sur Haydn*

Music can be said to be both an element and a product of a culture that bares commercial and subjective traits equally. It is because of its commercial nature that music production is regulated by an industry. Music has always been a predominant means to vector ideas. On January 20, 2009, a general strike broke out in Guadeloupe. It was organised by a collective of forty-nine members of trade unions, political parties, citizen and socio-cultural associations. This collective, Lyannaj Kont Pwofitasyon[98] (LKP), was created in December 2008 during the first demonstrations against the high cost of life and the increasing prices of petrol in Guadeloupe. Similar coalitions sprouted in other French overseas territories such as Martinique, St. Martin, French Guyana and Réunion with, sensibly, the same arguments as the LKP. One of the latter's goals, according to its list of claims,[99] was to halt the abusive exploitation of Guadeloupe.

Throughout the protest, the collective was undeniably supported by the population. It is for this reason that this chapter examines the LKP's demands in order to analyse the Guadeloupean musical creation. On April 17, 2009, during an interview on a Guadeloupean radio, the Martiniquan singer Kolo Barst, author of particularly "activist" songs, declared that: "the artist's function is to foresee …"[100]

Through this chapter, I will attempt to capture the relevance of

Guadeloupean music as an indicator of the condition and evolution of the Guadeloupean society. If music can be considered as a mirror of the social environment in which the artist evolves, one can bring forth the following interrogations: Have the Guadeloupean authors/composers grasped the "societal spleen" revealed by the social movement of January 20, 2009? Were the themes developed on their list of claims throughout the crisis present in the lyrics and themes of Guadeloupean music heritage? I will therefore strive to contribute to the debate by analysing Guadeloupean musical production from the 1940s to the 2000s.

Since the invention of musical support, music production fares better with time. As an efficient tool for committing notions to memory, music can inspire new waves of mobilisation. It can, in fact, convey sets of images and ideas from one generation to the next. What could the motivations of these cultural innovators be? Musical compositions (lyrics and music) are grounded within the timeframe in which they are conceived. Nevertheless, it can also foresee circumstances to come. The sociologist Alain Touraine recognised the importance of cultural expression in social movements. Cultural expressions have complex relationships with social movements. Cultural creation can be a support for the diffusion of these social movements as well as a means to sustain them, as it can concretise ideas, emotions and facts.

The LKP's claims can be classified under several headings: the conditions and standards of living, education, training, employment, trade union rights, freedom to enter a trade union, public service, local production, territorial planning and infrastructures, valorization of local culture, and reparation for social and economic injustices.

The exploitation of a category of people by another and the impression of not having enough control over one's destiny are among the first arguments developed by the LKP in 2009. Interestingly, this theme was present as early as 1942 and 1943 in the Guadeloupean musical expression. It has been translated by Victor Vervier, also known as Lebrun, in his song: "sé sémésié ki ni la baw an men, sé maléré ka travay san landemen."[101] On February 13, 2009, the historian Francoise Verges, in an interview for the periodical *Le Monde*, stated that if the Guadeloupean society has not been frozen since 1848, the year of the abolition of slavery in the French Caribbean, then there are *immobilisms* that surface whenever there is a social discontentment. In 2009, many small and medium businesses were owned by the descendants of the enslaved. Nevertheless, the grand majority of the land property and the import trade were and still are controlled by the descendants of the slaves' masters.

From the 1940s, the concern over the unequal distribution of riches appears in the lyrics of popular songs. In 1982 Robert Loyson, one of the most prominent *griots* of the *Gwo ka* world, denounced the economical dangers of the French Caribbean system. According to his analysis, the sugar cane sector, the pillar of local production, must be protected and valorised as a means to create employment and increase riches:

> An mwé papa wo ! la gwadeloup tranglé ! mé zanmi la Gwadeloup tranglé, la Gwadeloup pé ké détranglé … sé kann nou ka planté, sé a lizinn nou ka vann kann la, ou fèmé lizinn Sentmart, an vrè la gwadeloup tranglé, a lè kilé yo fèmé Blanchet, fèmé Darboussier, o la la gwadeloup kalé ? sé ouvriyé la ki té an lwizinn la, dèpi tan yo ka travay a lwizinn, a lè kilé tout lizinn la fèmé, ki koté yo kay travay ? … la Gwadeloup antotyé, fè manèv pou koupé kod la an kou a li. Pa tini richess, sèl koté ki ni richess, sé kann a maléré.[102]

When Robert Loyson reflected on the sugar cane situation in Guadeloupe, he also mentioned the working class that constitutes its manpower. In another song called Ji Kann a la Richèss,[103] Loyson called once more on Guadeloupeans to be mindful of the sugar cane harvest, the same harvest that generates riches and employment: "Gwadeloupéyen jété on koudzyé si la rékolt, si zo pa poté koudzyé, la Gwadeloup ké an faillite."[104]

Lyannaj Kont Pwofitasyon pou Détotyé la Gwadeloup[105] is the self-explanatory name of the LKP collective. The motives and the ethos of the latter are grounded in Loyson's discourse. This Guadeloupe described by Loyson as being *antotyé* (entangled) and trapped, must be *détotyé* (untangled), freed from its shackles.

The LKP also developed the theme of alimentary self-sufficiency and sustainable territorial planning. As early as 1998, a musical formation from the Reggae/Dancehall culture, the Karukera[106] Sound System, challenged this issue in their song "Bato la."[107] Both singers, Brother Jimmy and Oliver Stone, denounced the hyper-consumerist habits of their fellow citizens and the general denigration of the agricultural world. The Karukera Sound System tackled the issue of alimentary self-sufficiency against the politic of territorial planning favouring construction to the detriment of arable land:

> *Mè di mwen ka yo ké fè jou la bato la pé rantré ?*
> *es sé moso batiman ou fwiyapen yo ké manjé ?*
> *mwen diw woy, woy i ja tan pou nou lévé*
> *An nou kontinié lité pou péyi la pa tombé …*
> *Arété pran nou pou tèbè, arété pran nou pou fwansé*
> *Arété fè nou kompran sé richès pou nou adoré*
> *Patrimoine kiltirèl, apa yenki wonm é dansé*

Travay tout la simen é le week-end gade télé
Pandan si tan péyi la li menm ka sombré
Mwen savé maren péché, agrikiltè byen déterminé[108]

The boat, to which Oliver Stone refers, symbolises Guadeloupe's dependence on imported goods. Reacting against politics of territorial planning and social choices that do not favour alimentary self-sufficiency, Stone calls on his audience to realise the importance of local agriculture and fishing. He also entreats the Guadeloupeans and the local institutions to consider the local cultural specificities in the projects included in the development process.

In the second stanza, as pertinent as the first, Brother Jimmy exposes the habits of consumption and the mechanisms that are, according to him, detrimental to the development of the island. One understands that these mechanisms are rooted in the benefit system, which produces a lack of business initiatives, the depreciation of farming activities, the "overconsumption" and the systematic selling of arable lands.

alè la pani pon moun ki vlé planté kann
ni travay la tè pou manjé madè ou ziyanm
la gwadeloup désidé woulé yenki an japan
sé Mitsubishi, Hyundai, Daewoo ka vann

yo vlé pa travay la tè menm si pa ni travay
tout moun vlé vinn medsen avoka sé la pagay
nou ni on bèl péyi, ékonomikman i si la pay
si ou gade situasyon la anyen pa kay
avè on system konsa, pa étonéw kè ini onlo rakay
twop moun assisté yo ka pwan nou pou timanmay
avan nou té ka pwodui, exporté en chay
alè la nou pa ni ayen, nou ka achté yenki Hyundai
ka konsomé twop, sé nou lé rwa du champagn
ka konsomé tèlman, nou pa ka vwè lé fay
yo ka pran tout tè an nou, pou mwen a pa on détay[109]

In 2005, the group Soft released the song "Kadans a Péyi la," announcing the LKP social movement. Their musical style intertwines traditional music with Jazz colours. Fred Dehayes, the lead singer, sang:

Yo pa vlé Sentélwa,[110] *yo pa vlé Marcel Lollia,*[111] *en vérité yo pa enmé lokans a péyi la*
La soufriè pa ka domi, kon vou kon mwen i ka bouyi, nimpot ki jou fo sa pété
Sé li ka chayé mwen, sé li ka brilé mwen, sé li kay méné nou pli wo ...
Nimpot ki jou fo sa pété, soufwans a péyi la ...[112]

The expression "Kadans a péyi la," points to the rhythm, the mores, and the cultural heritage of Guadeloupe. Those who live on the island without adapting to this rhythm or *Kadans* feed a duality, a distress that leads first to implosion, then to explosion. Being a Guadeloupean, adopted or by birth, signifies embracing the cultural, ecological, social and historical inheritance of the island. The social movement started by the LKP can be seen as the result of a "social spleen," a societal anguish which, just like the Guadeloupean volcano Soufrière in 1976, erupted in 2009.

On the same album and with the song "Krim Kont la Gwadloup," Fred Dehayes calls for the prosecution of those that he believes are guilty of crimes against Guadeloupe. The theme of the song is not directly linked to the LKP's platform, but it portrays accurately the debate that occupied all the participants of the social movement. Indeed, the main question was to identify those responsible for the exploitation of the island. This debate divided the people in two groups: "yo"[113] against "nou."[114] The antagonism between "yo" and "nou" actually became the theme for the social movement's signature tune. In the same song, some major companies, local politicians, *békés*,[115] along with the governmental policies are accused of "Krim Kont la Gwadloup." In many respects, it is interesting to note that from the analysis of the group Soft, the "criminals" responsible for the Guadeloupean social problems are first and foremost the internal components of the population.

> *Mwen menm pa méyè ki on dòt, fò zò ban mwen avi a zòt*
> *lè an ka gadé sa ka pasé, ni dé moun fò nou poursuiv pou krim kont la Gwadloup.*[116]

They also criticise the integrity and the efficiency of the local politicians. The political mandate, instead of being approached as a means, a mission, is regarded as an end in itself, slowing down the island's progress:

> *on pakèt moun kenn mò pou mè, menm si kè a yo vinn anmè, monté alyans é vann dé frè pou ganié trofé a rété lontan, pasé dé méri an éritaj é pou lé zot yenki chomaj, on vié ti lajan an ka gannié, an ka gadé lé zòt ka bombansé ...*[117]

> *Politik touné an makakri, intélektièl asi niaj, yo ka domi Ni on pakèt moun ka amizé, zafè a yo bèl lè nou mélé Istwa an nou pa ka vansé ....*[118]

In this instance, music allows one to challenge the authority of the established powers. Scholars and politicians are portrayed as disconnected to the population's reality because of their lifestyles or their functions. Those who have vested in themselves a great capacity of reflection and action are not up to the task.

A section of the Guadeloupean youth is also placed in the dock. The youth, featherheaded and improvident, indulges in self-pity instead of endeavouring to achieve serious objectives:

> *Jénès ka di pa ni ayen pou yo men ka yo menm ka fè ba yo*
> *sé fè ti nat é kritiké pandan yo ka gadé télé ...*[119]

> *On jenn tiré asi on jenn, on nèg tiré asi on nèg*
> *Sa ki pi kriminèl adan tou sa, nou sizé la nou kenn gadé sa.*[120]

It is a fact that this youth is but a branch of a tree that reflects the roots of a society that was certainly not able to pass on an edifying sap. Consequently, one may say that the Guadeloupean society is termitic.

The only theme that has been taken indirectly by the LKP's platform and appears in the song is the concern over unequal distribution of riches, negatively affecting the poorer social classes and the African-Caribbean population. The economical agents are particularly targeted:

> *An ka mandé'w ka ki libèté lé ou pa ni lajan pou manjé*
> *Mwen anvi vrè égalité lè pitit a maléré toujou maléré*
> *Mwen anvi vrè fraternité, an ka vrè a pa aka nèg lajan mété ....*[121]

Closing the song, in an uncompromising address, Soft invites each component of the Guadeloupean society, including themselves as citizens, to acknowledge their responsibilities. Indeed, according to the song, every Guadeloupean is to blame for the backwardness and the underdevelopment of the island. The piece ends with a very pronounced percussion rhythm, and throughout the melodies are particularly fluid and smooth:

> *Mwen menm pa méyè ki on dot, si zo vé zo pé gadé avi a zot lè an ka gadé*
> *sa ka pasé, sé nou menm fo nou poursuiv pou krim kont la Gwadloup.*[122]

In 2001 with the album *l'Indiscipliné*, it was one of Guadeloupe's Rap music voices that denounced the living conditions and the distress of an entire country. Indeed, it is as an observer of the Guadeloupean society that the rapper Fuckly painted an uncompromising but edifying portrait of Guadeloupe with the song An Ni Marre.[123] With this song, he described a Guadeloupean society full of contradictions. The following themes, also taken up by the LKP, are found throughout his analysis: living conditions, quality of life, professional training and employment. The verbal magnifying glass, with which he scrutinises a Guadeloupean youth in need of values and goals, is very pertinent:

> *Lanné la sa ann gadé jan sa ka maché, sé vann lanmò an saché*
> *Tout an jénès gaché /koupé, détayé, anpoché /Diab-la ka ba'w an rikoché*
> *Dé biznès ka rapòté é la police ka kapoté/ kravaté ka profité*
> *Blok-la ka ankésé/ Fè bizness anba fèy vin an sèl moyen de rézisté*
> *... Jénès-la menasé scié canon scié*
> *Pa ni travay tout moun èksité pou an banalité*
> *Sizé a bò sité ka atann le Déluge*
> *Sé boug-la la san anbisyon ka chèché an grabuj*
> *Nou adan on stad ke pou viv fow pran'y malad*
> *Pa rakonté on salad an Gwadeloup fow pran'y malad*

> *Papa'w ja fatigé manman'w ja fè dèyè édikasyon aw dead*

> *An ni "marre" Violans é fizi/ Ja lè pou tou sa fini*
> *An ni "marre"/Magouilles corruption/ Tout moun égri sa ké mal fini.*[124]

The purposeless youth mentioned by Fuckly appear particularly concerned by the demands connected with professional training. Moreover, his analysis foresaw the violent episodes that happened during the LKP's demonstration in 2009. Idleness and desperation, the lack of moral values and latent violence materialised during the night of February 18 to 19, 2009. He also expressed in the chorus the feelings of Guadeloupean youth as overwhelmed, neglected. This generation is under the impression that they are not on the same footing with other components of Guadeloupean society. According to him, this two-tier society offers very few solutions through the agency of its institutional representatives:

> *On minimòn dintégrasyon, on maximòm dekspulsyon, on maksimòm de problèm*
> *On minimum de solisyon, on maksimòm ki pé pa asimé an tan kè papa*
> *O pli tass ka pran kal pou alòk familial, o pi patron volè, magouyè, èksploitè*
> *O pi baré lari sendika, o pi grévist , o pi promès bidon chak fwa i ni élèsksyon*
> *O pi fouré men aw adan kès a La Région ...*
> *Ni an bann irèsponsab sé yo ki rèsponsab /A fòs mété an ba tab lajen kontribuab*
> *Rézilta tout moun diab/ pandan ou ka soufè an silans bak a sé mésyé plen ésans*
> *Sé on sèl sians pou pé kouyoné maléré é tout moun sav lè bayè ba, bèf ka soté*[125]

Fuckly underlines the complicated relationship that the population shares with its elected politicians. He also brought forward several complex themes such as clandestine immigration, the Guadeloupean family crisis, the misuse of public funds, as well as the pungent relationship between the well to do and working class. All of these themes are symptomatic to the social movement promoting a more rigorous control of the economic, social and cultural orientations of the society.

Music is a language, a set of symbols written or spoken, which allows members of a society to communicate among themselves (Macionnis & Plumer 2002, 101). Music defines moral values. It is also a means through which former generations pass on culture and history to others. Music has a preponderant role in the shaping of a collective identity, of the collective memory and of collective action. Music has played an important role in social movements in general but particularly in African American movements.

Throughout history, as discussed by Paul Léo D'Hurville, messages placed in music by Guadeloupean artists certainly have germinated and grown into this unprecedented mass mobilisation.[126] Despite itself, the population has been prepared. Music is able to create a way to achieve what the sociologist Robert Merton calls "the creative prediction."[127] Without a shadow of a doubt, music has contributed to this anti-establishment endeavour. Since the 1940s, Guadeloupean artists have translated into music numerous messages regarding social ills, the core claims of the LKP:

"An konnèt wòl a pawòl pou fè on pèp lévé tèt" Exxos Mèt Kakos[128]

How can one explain that the policies of radio broadcasting do not promote this aspect of Guadeloupean music while privileging "bashment" scenes and popular American music? It is a fact that socio-political and anti-establishment arguments are not always present in music, as it also has a recreational function. Nevertheless, there is an obvious imbalance between clear-sighted and purely entertaining music. After the genesis of the LKP mobilisation, some radio stations started to play socio-political songs, realising the popularity of the genre. Where does this imbalance come from? Is it from the audience failing to express their expectations to the stations? Is it from the programme planners who shape the musical taste of the masses? Is it from the artists who must conciliate artistic independence and financial dependence?

"Sé èvè mizik yo pran nèg"[129]

Music is an active agent for the construction of the ethos of the Guadeloupean society. It is not merely a mirror reflecting the qualities and the flaws of the society. If one looks closely, music can be seen to be a window opening to the future. The analysis of the artist is not always recognised by the scientific and political world; nonetheless, the former offer a pertinent judgement. It would be useful for those in possession of the political, economic and social tools to be mindful of their voices. The artists are immersed in society; their sensibility presses them to express what they see, what they hear and what they perceive. If the sociologist's function is to analyse society's dysfunctions, the Guadeloupean artist stands as a pertinent sociologist, privileging the field work and immersion methods.

REGGAE, RASTA AND THE TRANSCENDENTAL USE OF ALTERNATIVE PUBLIC SPACES IN THE UK BY DANCEHALL DEEJAYS[130]

WILLIAM 'LEZ' HENRY

In this chapter I will present an understanding of the role of Reggae music and Rastafari in the creation of alternative public arenas that were far more than merely spaces of resistance, but were in fact sites of transcendental edification. The approach suggests that wherever there was a high percentage of African Caribbean communities in the UK during the 1970s to late 1980s, sound system[131] deejays used the Reggae Dancehall arena as an alternate site of learning. Significantly, it was the practised usage of "oral skills" in Creolised languages, couched in Rastafarian and Garveyite[132] sensibilities, that underpinned and ensured the perpetuation of these politically driven, vernacular cultures.

I will argue that expressive musical cultures, which operate as alternative sites of racial, social, cultural and political resistance, combat the imposition of an "alien" worldview on an "outernational"[133] level. I will therefore demonstrate how there are certain similarities in the way the hegemonic Eurocentric worldview, which generally depicts the African diaspora as a "lesser race," has been historically challenged and refuted through specific forms of Creolised cultural antagonism.

Introduction

The great white man has succeeded in subduing the world by forcing everyone to think his way, from his God to his fireside. He has given to the world, from his bible to his yellow newspaper sheet, a literature that establishes his right and sovereignty to the disadvantage of the rest of the human race.

(Marcus Garvey, cited in Martin 1986, 89)

When alternative public arenas as a site of belonging are evaluated through the lens of the British deejays, we find that their lyricism offers a practical assessment of what it means to be included or excluded from the wider public arena. It is from this premise that I will present an "insider" account which will more accurately reflect this ongoing need for an autonomous self-representation, using knowledge drawn from within the culture to challenge misrepresentations from without. I am a Reggae-dancehall deejay, Lezlee Lyrix, which means I was one of the pioneering figures in this form of cultural representation, that which gave a potent voice to the "voiceless" black youth who felt alienated in the land of their birth. The relevance of this perspective is highlighted when ascertaining the points of both similarity and difference in the black struggle against European cultural hegemony. This comes into sharp focus when we consider the dilemma one faces as the subject/object of a language, Standard English, that reinforces your perception and position as an "other" in your "mother" country. This is especially true for those deejays whose lyricism is largely reliant on the usage of the "Patwah" Jamaican language, coupled with Rastafarian sensibilities, as the template upon which they engineer their disapproval of a society that does not cater for their blackness. This represents a fundamental problem when endeavouring to understand the efficacy of this musical culture, because the key to unlocking the rationale behind these cultures is often concealed in the manipulation of ordinary language. I argue here that these types of social commentary need to be understood within their own "frames of reference," and not abstracted from the cultural milieu out of which they arise, as they have an "outernational" significance that fills in many gaps in the history of black people in the UK.

In light of the above, I will detail how those who were/are "other" to Europe's "self" regard this as a premier "voice" in our struggles against the myriad manifestations of white supremacist thought and action that psychologically conditions many black people to become anti-self. That is why I will consider concrete examples such as the seminal role of religion as a force for enslavement or liberation, in the Rastafari world view, as well as tackling the incidence of shadism[134] that globally blights black communities and has done so for generations. This means that I will argue from the deejay's perspective for a notion of musical expression that highlights the role black cultural creativity plays in the formation and utilisation of "alternative public spheres" (Gilroy 1987) that represent a direct challenge to forms of whiteness that are often unacknowledged and therefore remain unchallenged. Consequently this will enable me to consider the significant role black music, Rastafari, and "alternative public spheres" have played in the lives of black youth in Britain during the crisis period of Britain in the 1970s and 1980s, as well as their role in shaping and determining contemporary forms of expressive youth cultures where notions of "belonging" are aired and discussed in languages that more accurately reflect their take on social reality.

God, Rastafari and black solidarity

I sing conscious songs. It doesn't make sense I sing songs without meaning. I have to sing to protect my brothers and sisters.

(Admiral Tibet, cited in Foster 1999, 208)

Reggae is not a yes music. It's a militant music and it's a vibes music and it's a love music. And they don't want that because what we will be doing is opening people's eyes to reality and that's not the thing that they want.

(Blacker Dread, author's interview 2010)

Admiral Tibet's sentiments about why he has to sing songs with "meaning" to "protect his brothers and sisters" mirror my own feelings about the role of Reggae music as a vehicle for promoting black solidarity. This perspective runs contrary to the view of Reggae music which, during the 1970s and 1980s, was seen as a "Rasta-rudie black oriented counter-culture" (Pryce 1979, 156) with "decidedly criminal connotations" (Jones 1986, 56). Obviously, this argument meant that any notion of Reggae music promoting positive notions of "solidarity" across the "black Atlantic" (Gilroy 1993) was hardly recognised. For as Blacker Dread suggests, recognition of the significant role of the discursive nature of this cultural form, as disseminated through the medium of Reggae music, cannot be overlooked as its basic function is to "open people's eyes," a perspective endorsed in the following:

Reggae music for me represents the poor. The downtrodden, the oppressed, the impoverished the persecuted individuals. First and foremost black people are Africans on a global scale. And anybody of any colour can look to Reggae music for soul food, for guidance in this time and henceforth throughout them entire life. 'Cause Reggae roots music is the only music that represents them in its entirety and uncompromising and never been sugar coated from Bob time, from Peter Tosh, Bunny Wailer until this time … This music is given to us from the Almighty via Jamaica to the world.

(Junior Kelly, author's interview, 2010)

Junior Kelly makes it quite clear that Reggae is for everyone on the planet who requires this "soul food," but its African roots must be recognised in much the same way as the presence of the Almighty in our lives as human beings. That is why Rastafari, especially during the 1970s and 1980s, made the presence of God more palatable to a black youth who were experiencing rejection in the land of their birth; this was an active God rather than the passive one that seemed to appeal to their parents' generation. Thus, any endeavour to ascertain why black youth in the UK sought solace in Rastafari's message, which meant accepting H.I.M. Emperor Haile Selassie as the Godhead, must take account of the fact that in many black communities "religion is a total involvement ... not a mental exercise" (Barrett 1988, 27). Therefore, recognising an exposure to black Christian styles of worship, especially black Pentecostalism which provided "one of the only safe spaces where black identities were celebrated and perpetuated" (Beckford 1998, 26; Beckford & Henry 2005), coupled with charismatic leadership, explains why the deejays had such appeal, since their role within culture was to move you with the word. This is in much the same way as a good preacher would move the congregation with the word, and this provides a template for rethinking the role of religious belief and practice in counter-cultural spaces. That is why the black youth were ready to receive the libratory message when confronted with the "oral skills" of many advocates of Rastafari on the Reggae recordings that dominated the black communities in Britain during this moment:

> Every time you hear a word it conjures up an image, therefore my mission is to fashion my words in a way that reflects the plight of the African and doesn't reinforce the negativity that is associated with the Motherland. So my lyrics are like a stepping stone to educate the youths and help us get back to where we once were and Reggae music is the vehicle to carry that message.
>
> (Macka B, author's interview, 2001)

Macka B exemplifies how this cultural knowledge, gained from the various types of symbolic (sacred/secular) language we were exposed to as members of black communities, made it easy for the Reggae deejay to embody this alternative self-perception and deliver the message "to educate the youths" on sound systems. Similarly it explains how sound systems became the vehicles for this "intervening medium" and provided the locus for an "adaptive response" to racism by grounding religious beliefs in a most practical way. It was practical because the cultural knowledge base was both familiar and malleable enough to supply the deejays with the ideological ammunition they required to bridge the gap between artist and audience when they performed. Moreover, because the first sound systems were generally owned or controlled by the parental generation, there was an opportunity to ideologically bridge the intergenerational divide that separated many black youths from the older generation by providing a space within which we could share stories and recognise the commonality of our condition as the recipients of white racism. This demonstrates how the alternative worldview made manifest in the marriage of the Rastafari message and Reggae music, as an "organiser" of "consciousness," cannot be separated from a tradition of struggle against oppression, which subsequently promotes black solidarity. In fact:

> Anti-black racism was firmly entrenched in British society before the large-scale migration of African descendants from the former British Caribbean colonies in the 1950s. But coming from countries where social hierarchies based on skin colour existed, it was not only dreams for a better life that some immigrants brought with them, but their own form of prejudice which valued light skin and derided blackness.
>
> (Gabriel 2007, 57)

Gabriel raises a crucial point of discussion, which is that many of those who came from the Caribbean, especially from Jamaica, which is where the majority of migrants hailed from during the post-1948 Windrush[135] period, had a colonial mentality burned into their psyche. One consequence of this was an ingrained terror, fear and distrust of their own African humanity, which is a major factor in the psychological make-up of any politics of representation that speaks to, and from, a "dispersed people." Therefore we must recognise that the mechanism that enables us to strive for a sense of oneness in a global sense is in a constant state of flux, within which notions of time, space and "cultural history" are reworked, reconfigured and adapted to suit the purposes of the present circumstance. That is why decolonisation of the mind is crucial to any understanding of the anti-racist struggle, but not to the exclusion of the continually lived experience of the most disaffected members of society who are invariably judged by their black skin, regardless of what shade of black that skin happens to be. Crucially, this is also the key to understanding the popularity and appeal of the cultural form beyond the black communities, for as suggested by Gilroy the transformation of host communities by their exposure to black forms of popular culture is a consequence of how a "musical culture supplies a great deal of the courage required to go on living in the present" (Gilroy 1993, 36).

Equally it was the "social gospel" of Marcus Mosiah Garvey that underpinned the lyricism of the deejays, who saw in his message an indictment of white racism that made perfect sense wherever they dwelt in the black diaspora:

> I believe with Napoleon. When some one asked him "On what side is God?" he replied "God is on the side of the strongest battalion." Napoleon

was right. He had a true concept of God. God is really on the side of the
strongest peoples because God made all men equal and He never gave
superior power to anyone class or group of people over another, and
anyone who can get the advantage over another is pleasing God, because
that is the servant who has taken care of God's command in exercising
authority over the world.

(Garvey 1986, 44)

Garvey's words make it clear that we cannot overlook the significant
role religious forms play in the formulation and reformulation of the
social, cultural and political sensibilities of the largely disenfranchised
black communities in the UK, especially the youth. To do so simplifies the
role that the Bible and God have played, and still play, in the
psychological make-up of the generations of peoples of the African
diaspora who use their belief in the divine as justification to chant down
Babylon. This means that we must recognise the manner in which the
historical experience of chattel slavery is totally relevant to any
understanding of contemporary black musical expression. For as Alleyne
suggests, the merging of African and European religious forms with music
and dance was a key factor in unifying the slaves in Jamaica, "because
they were major instruments of cohesion and revolt" (Alleyne 1988, 118).
This type of merging is, according to Spencer, not unusual for peoples of
African ancestry as it is akin to an African notion of spreading or
transmitting a "social gospel" (Spencer 1995, 68), dealing with real and
earthly problems. The religious message has to be conveyed in a manner
in which the people can truly recognise their lived reality, and more
importantly actively participate as part of a conscious collective effort to
remedy the negative aspects of this ongoing reality. Hence, irrespective of
age, Africans on the continent and their descendants throughout the
diaspora were, and still are in many cases, expected to partake in
"religious ceremonies," because "African religious traditions take into
consideration not only one's intellect, but also one's emotions, the mental
and the visceral" (Barrett 1988, 27).

To demonstrate how the "spreading" of "their ideologies" in the
context of the deejay manifests in its most practical sense, let us further
consider this notion of the "social gospel" in black music, which draws on
the legacy of chattel slavery in an endeavour to empower black people in
the present. It is part of the deejay's role and purpose as spokesperson for
the community to "release within the people a feeling of power" (Alleyne
1988, 118) over the negative aspects of everyday living during the
cathartic moment that is the deejay performance. This demonstrates how
black music is a vehicle for the dissemination of these "hidden voices," as

it provides a space for the deejays to partake in a diasporic system of intellectual exchange, thereby placing their lyricism in an "outernational" context, because the language of choice, Patwah, and the worldview it represents cannot be geographically bounded. This means that the deejays consciously challenge the notion that they should be expressing themselves in Standard English, because this is the language that they are formally educated in. This point is made by Wong (1986), who argues that black youths resisted their mother tongue's "alphabet of terror" by embracing Rastafari language and symbolism. These types of knowledge are ever-present in Reggae music and are demonstrative of the role and purpose of black music as a site for countering white/European cultural hegemony, since black history is not found "in the standard textbooks" (Ture and Hamilton 1992, 38) of a dominant culture.

Rastafari argue that African people need to be aware of the need to seek out their own history when visiting institutions like a public library or a university, that which they dub the "lie bury" (the library is the place where lies and truth are buried), or the "you never see" (university is the place where you never see or hear your story in the world they are describing, with regard to an African, historical contribution to anything of note). Rastafari teaches us that because our history is generally "hidden," what we experience in places of learning is in essence "head-deacy-shun," based on an over exposure to that which we too often encounter in the "lie-bury." This means that Rastafari has evaluated the notion of what it is to be "educated" by your "enemy" and concluded that what occurs is decadent and something to be shunned, unless you appreciate its role in perpetuating African inferiority. Therefore, "Man must use Men language to carry dis message" (Bongo Jerry, cited in Brathwaite 1984, 37). You will notice how the idea of Rasta as "Man" and Babylon (the enemy) as "Men" is crucial to this argument, because it is based on how to think of an alternative self within the confines of the English language. In this case, "Man" is a metaphor for an enlightened African humanity, which "overstands"[136] why "Men," racist Europeans, continually "downpress"[137] us through entrapment within the confines of Standard English. In much the same way, it allows us to appreciate how much of an epistemological problem cultural interpretation can become, when endeavouring to present an alternative worldview through an analysis of a vernacular culture. This is because the vernacular form contains the means to transmit messages across time and space that allow one generation to speak to another, as well as adding new solutions to age-old problems. Thus, it can offer a type of stability through the retelling of stories of transcendence based on specific types of historical narratives, thereby disrupting our present understanding of the language of formal learning and recognised instruction.

Deejay lyricism is often an exemplar of this thinking in action, as when deejays perform on the sound system they are free to present alternative histories of the African-black presence that are often "hidden" from the wider public gaze. Moreover, those deejays who are proficient in excavating history often demonstrate how "the aftermaths of slavery still endure in the social forms and perceptions of New World peoples" (Mintz 1989, 62), as evidenced in the following extract from "African Slavery" where it is argued that:

> Some people nah go like what me say, but me a go say it anyway, me a go talk about slavery and the effects of it today, some people just don't want to know, about four hundred years ago, but the thing about slavery its affecting people now … what about all the lives that were lost, what about the black holocaust, what about African slavery and what its done to you and me … Oh I can see the effects of slavery still in the community, no identity suffering from amnesia, a case of lost memory, Black man and woman can't you see your history never start on the plantation … Holocaust is a word they use for what the Nazis did to the Jews, compensation was never refused, their own land they even got to choose. So what's wrong with us, was the Black holocaust not so serious?
>
> (Macka B 2000)

Macka B clearly states that as people of African ancestry we are still affected by chattel slavery, especially those who are suffering from a type of "amnesia," who have no awareness that their "history never start on the plantation." This line of argument is the contemporary manifestation of a historical "mode of response/resistance" to, and rejection of, the imposition of European cultural values on African peoples. Thus, Macka B's lyric is designed to counter a Eurocentric/ethnocentric way of presenting a whitewashed "history" with a blackness which is dependent on "making connections with the entire Diaspora" (Back 1996, 145). Making these connections includes a re-linking with a more positive sense of a historical African presence that did not begin "on the plantation." Thus the role of the deejay as educator is exemplified in Macka B's account, as he seeks to promote awareness of how the legacy of chattel slavery impacts on the way we perceive ourselves in the present. Of equal importance, by making connections between the African and the Jewish holocausts, he highlights the manner in which the African has been historically miseducated, as many people have no idea of the true extent of the destruction meted out on the African by racist, slavemaster Europeans.

In the case of Reggae/Dancehall music, these "connections" are maintained because it was/is "protected" by a "language, a colour and by a culture which had been forced to cultivate secrecy against the intrusions of the Master Class" (Hebdige 1979, 434). This is why these cultures often resist the "outsider's" gaze because, as I suggested above, this is one aspect of how black music creates an alternative space for those who view their ongoing oppression as a consequence of white domination. It is prudent to state that those who recognise this reality utilise black music as a conduit for presenting counter ideologies, because "many don't want to know, about four hundred years ago." Moreover, from Macka B's argument it is clear that black people need to take some responsibility in countering this loss "memory loss" and the best way to do so is to use black music. Consequently:

> If you wait for another man to save you will never do anything for yourself. God has given me this gift and the talent to speak and people find it interesting and listen. I cannot therefore abuse that talent ... Reggae music is like a vehicle for me to right certain wrongs cos sometimes you just have to do what you have to do no matter about the consequences, cos people don't care about what they do to us.

> (Macka B, author's interview 2002)

According to Macka B, using his "talent," which for him is a "gift," to document and disseminate his innermost concerns enables him to partake in an autonomous system of knowledge exchange that tackles the issues that impact black people the most, regardless of "consequences." It is crucial to make this aspect of the culture known as many of the issues deejays deal with in the UK are known across the "black Atlantic," and in the next section we will interrogate this aspect by focusing on shadism as a direct consequence of white supremacist thought and action.

Shadism:
Whiteness and the Colouring of Consciousness

> Now we are told that we're all the same, as long as red blood ah run through we vein, but there's one big difference ah the mental strain, of an African body, white man brain, our harmony's gone self-destruction ah reign, that's why we ah dead from crack and cocaine, you think of Afrika, you start feel shame, images of savages that the world can't tame, of our natural looks them start feel shame, and try to disguise our African strain, ah European look them ah try maintain, ah barbecue them hair, again and again!!

> (Lezlee Lyrix, African Body 1991)

The above lyrical extract is taken from a song I used to perform on the Reggae Sound System circuit and it speaks to the manner in which whiteness impacts our everyday realities and manifests as shadism; the worshipping of a white or light skin to the detriment of yourself and other black people. It documents that no matter how we strive to achieve an alternative Africentric[138] worldview (Henry 2006, 12), it seems many are still wittingly, or unwittingly, measured by alien registers that have been normalised as part of the black experience in Europe's New World. I suggest they are normalised points of the historical dimensions that must be considered in such debates as these, where we are seeking to comprehend how to overcome such divisionary tactics. Disjuncture and continuity are often masked by a historical process that was devised, and constantly updated and adapted, by white supremacists to "turn us fool against ourselves." For example, I can clearly recall the furore created by the Reggae performer Buju Banton when he controversially stated: "Me love me car, me love me bike, me love me money and ting, but most of all me love me browning (Buju Banton 1992).

The suggestion is not that Buju's words are revelatory as in they offer new information; what he is telling is that he, as a dark skinned African, found it necessary to say this in a Jamaican context in the 1990s. The fact that he had to quickly record a counter to this song, bigging up the "Black Woman," or that many other Jamaican performers recorded counters to Love me Browning, one of the best being Them ah Bleach by Nardo Ranks (1992), is moot in a country whose primary slogan is "Out of Many, One People." Yet a cursory glance across the social landscape reveals that the "One" of the "One People" seems to always favour the lightest complexioned "One," the whitest or brownest "One." Consequently, we now have the Jamaican performer Vibz "Michael Cake-Soap Jackson" Kartel promoting skin-lightening products and stating "the girls them love out me bleach out face" in his song "Look Pon We" (2011), or the young man, who according to Cooper:

> … knows that bleaching is wrong but he's a Deejay and wants to look good for Christmas. So he's going to continue to bleach and going to put on a cap, put on a long sleeve shirt and when they see him people will think it is a browning coming through. And that whole notion of coming through suggests that there is a colour barrier that he's going to breach and he's going to be somebody else. And to me that notion of seasonal browness[139] was quite remarkable as he knows he isn't brown but it's like a kind of cosmetic, it's an accessory. Light skin colour is a fashion accessory which he is going to have for Christmas, like Christmas tree lights.
>
> (Cooper, author's interview 2010)

The most striking aspect of the above is not the fact that this young man conflates, probably unknowingly, these Eurocentric ideals and the invented tradition of Christmas with the desire to be "light skinned." Rather, it is the hidden aspect that is seldom considered, which is that the organising principle behind this mentality is whiteness, because "whiteness is taken to be a natural fact, beyond the bounds of consideration" (Pickering 2004, 91). This is whiteness as a conceptual framework and not merely a way to describe white people, which is where I think many fail in having the right conversation and thus draw the wrong conclusions as they focus on complexion rather than a system of power. Moreover, as is suggested in Cooper's extract, the Jamaican's desire is for brown and not white skin, which means the psychological dimensions of being embroiled in this system of differentiation has myriad manifestations and differing expectations that are context dependent. Indeed:

> This breakdown can be used to show where the facile assumptions of civilisationism become untenable. It is also necessary to affirm that the peculiar synonymy of the terms "European" and "white" cannot continue. And yet, against a wealth of detailed historical and cultural evidence taken from all across Europe, identity, belonging, and, consequently, the imperiled integrity of nation states are being communicated through the language and symbols of absolute ethnicity and *racialized* difference...Two practical consequences follow: First, that historians of Europe's repressed, denied, and disavowed blackness must become willing to say the same things over and over again in the hope that a climate will eventually develop in which we will be able to find a hearing, and, second that we must be prepared to step back audaciously into the past.
>
> (Gilroy 2004, 155)

The suggestion is that we must ensure that we have meaningful discussions that speak to the nuanced notions of what it means to be black or African in the twenty-first century as part of our mental decolonisation process. More so when we are "audacious" enough to locate the present in a past that has meaning to us, but mindful not to fall foul of the ultimate stumbling block which is the fixation on skin pigmentation as a true marker of difference, as if a conflation of black, white or mixed/dual have an organising principle that makes sense beyond our inherited racialised realties. This speaks to why we must locate the spaces where whiteness is countered and an African or black aesthetic is presented as the norm. Paradoxically, we can locate this in the context of the Jamaican Reggae Dancehall space; the same cultural space within which Buju Banton made his "browning" statement, because:

> One of the beauties of Dancehall culture in Jamaica is it gives black
> women a space to see themselves as sexy and beautiful, because when you
> look at the mainstream media say in Jamaica the images used in
> advertising are the anorexic, light skinned type that is used to advertise the
> up-market products, and the working class body is used to advertise soap
> powder and this type of thing.
>
> (Cooper, author's interview 2010)

Cooper's observation is telling as it highlights how there is a power
dynamic that needs to be considered, because "advertising [has] turned
these domestic servants into icons of generalized servitude" (Pieterse
1992, 155), and these "domestic servants" are the descendents of the
African Chattel slaves. Therefore, where you can have a country like
Jamaica, which is regarded in the outside world as a black country,
supposedly independent, its organising principle is anchored in the
supremacy of white, or light, skinned people. More importantly, Cooper
makes it known that whilst the barriers are in place and do in fact impact
the lives of the majority of black Jamaicans, those said Jamaicans find
modes of expression that embody an aesthetic appreciation of their darker
skin that is often dismissed as fad or fashion. In this instance, "dance
becomes what Pierre Nora terms a *milieu de la mémoire*, a commemorative
site or mnemonic methodology of cultural survival, retention and
transmission" (Benston 2000, 86). To Benston's poignant observation we
must add the transcendental nature of the cultural forms that are used in
this way, as these libratory spaces are those within which we, as African
people, work and rework our identities in ways that make sense to us in
the present, because:

> In many regards, modern Black popular culture can be defined as the
> formation and articulation of public spaces of resistance, reclamation and
> autonomous creativity against and beyond the hegemony of western
> modernity and racism ... In the Ragga dance-hall, clearly, what is being
> celebrated and displayed is the highly eroticised female body; the "Black
> woman's-body" spectacularly revealed—near naked—yet tantalizingly
> "veiled" in garish shocking pinks, yellows and lime greens. Hairstyles in
> contrast emphasize false or processed hair, often elaborately bedecked and
> intricately and rigidly gelled in place, starkly contrasting with the gyrating,
> twitching fluid "flexings" of the body below.
>
> (Noble 2000, 157)

In line with Noble's suggestions I want to consider the way that certain
aspects of "black culture" highlight the importance of understanding that
such usage of artistic or cultural expression are direct challenges to a

white/European aesthetic. The point is that blacks in Britain (and obviously in many other colonised spaces and places) are, from day one, bombarded with "all things white and beautiful" (Henry 1996, 19). This naturally gives rise to negative representations of African ancestry which need to be not only resisted and countered, but trashed and transcended. For instance, to see a "Ragga girl" in a Jamaican or UK Dancehall with blonde hair cannot be read in the same way as you would a black girl in the UK who adorns herself with blonde hair out of the belief that it makes her closer, or more acceptable, to white people. What this means is that even if you are considered to be of brown or mixed or dual heritage, these notions of identity are always consciously or unconsciously performed in response to whatever form of whiteness is used to "measure" our humanity. Therefore, the modes of response to this form of domination generally absorb and synthesise various elements that, once sewn together, became a potent voice in the quest for real social change across the urban landscape. Hence, a more positive notion of identity can be freely articulated because it is dependent upon making links that do not necessarily seek to prove a purity of origins; rather, it is based upon a similarity of life chances and experiences of racism. However, as Gilroy states, "the desire to affirm and celebrate unbroken continuity is clearly a response to racisms that deny any historical currency to black life" (cited in Ugwu 1995, 23). The seriousness of this perspective cannot be overstated, as the alternative claims are derived from an exposure to an Africa before the chattel slave era from which these Africentric, positive self-concepts are generated and expressed in alternative public arenas:

> Me ask them if them ready and them nah talk to me like them no like me. You see when me likkle bit them used to call me everything bad, mock me say you black like ah this. Me no know if ah through the colour. The international blackness. Oonuh no like me? Oonuh like me? If you like me put up you hand. Oonuh know say me love you; the blackness is real!
> (Blackout JA, 2010)

For decades now, many of the most poignant critiques of popular constructions of blackness and black identity have been aired and discussed, as seen in the above extract where the deejay Blackout JA enquired as to whether a London audience "liked" or "disliked" him on the merits of his complexion. Interestingly, he closes with "Oonuh know say me love you; the blackness is real," and similar views are often aired in mainstream arenas. For example, during the summer of 1997 on a radio interview with Bobby Conders (a white Reggae DJ) in New York, the Jamaican, Rastafarian, deejay Capleton explained that what he was promoting was unequivocally blackness for edification and upliftment:

> Cah you done know babylon even try limit I & I as ah nation as ah people
> even pon ah educational level becau them give we O' levels an PhD an
> then them lock we off an seh yow. What I want to know is that you know.
> But the real authentic thing you fi know bout yourself as ah race or ah
> nation or ah people in terms of heritage an culture, an philosophies an
> curriculum, that never taught innah the school, nor the institution or the
> college. So we haffi look pon it pon ah nature-al level so we won't get
> caught innah the disillusion or the fantasy. So this is what life has taught I.
>
> (Capleton, 1997)

Capleton makes known that even though "them give we O' levels and
PhD," the knowledge base which these qualifications represent within the
popular imagination, does not convey a sense of self-worth for those of
African ancestry. Furthermore, Capleton suggests that by the time many of
us have gone through the Babylonian educational system, our notion of
blackness is somewhat distorted, a case of Curtis Mayfield's "educated
fools from uneducated schools." This is because the complex dynamics of
black identity formations that counter the most pernicious manifestations
of whiteness are being played out, negotiated and renegotiated in arenas
that many are not even aware of, much less know how to access. That is
why I stated that "whiteness is the ever present, non presence that moulds
and shapes reality" (Henry 2007), as we are guided by the social, cultural
and political frameworks we find ourselves governed by as subjects of
western/white, hegemonic rule. Therefore it is suggested that:

> We seem to spend so much time talking, to, with, or about white people, or
> posturing for their benefit on matters to do with race and antiracism; the
> whole system has got us caught up in this activity that we begin to assume
> the existence of some sort of consensus amongst ourselves ... based on
> being black.
>
> (John 2006, 95)

John's suggestion is that it is all too convenient to speak of the
historical and, in far too many instances, the contemporary role of white
racists in our unseemly predicament without grounding them in a way that
is palatable to those they impact the most. We therefore cannot continue to
assume that we are of one mind when it comes to dealing with our
situation as black people, without separating the aspects of our oppression
that we can absolutely rid ourselves of once we recognise their historical
role in our oppression.

If whites could "see" themselves as others see them, perhaps they would see others differently too: the white aesthetic is an aesthetic of "the dead" in the eyes of many others.

(Synott & Howes 1996, 149)

Conclusion

In this discussion I have considered how access to an alternative worldview, as provided through the medium of black music, provides a space where the African diaspora can think themselves into being in a more conscious fashion than has been previously recognised. This was demonstrated by describing how there is in the history of deejaying in Britain a "struggle to maintain communities," which not only transcends, but also transforms their racist "host" communities by bringing certain aspects of the struggle to the fore. This is based on a shared sense of oppression/exclusion, because "our imaginations are conditioned by an enduring proximity to regimes of racial terror" (Gilroy 1993, 103). The suggestion is that black music often speaks to the lived experiences of the disenfranchised in a racist society, and thus furnishes a site for various types of inter/intra cultural exchange. For this reason, it is the "moral aspects" of black music that need to be considered, especially with regard to "the ethical value of the music and its status as an ethnic sign" (Gilroy 1993, 36). Thus, in cases like these you automatically identify with those who share your life chances as the black "other" to a white "self," which is why it is logical for the black youth in Britain to recognise our condition in the lyrics we are exposed to via Jamaica and then re-fashion them to fit our social, cultural and political predicament. More importantly, we used this form of "ideological weaponry" (1993, 2000) to express in alternative public spaces our innermost concerns about what it means to be the "other" in the land of our birth, in a language that we could claim as "our" own. Hence, the fact that those who the music speaks to can recognise the message is crucial to my argument about why black youth used the form in Britain to debate and discuss our own "problem" status in a language we belong to. Therefore, how the musical form is validated and authenticated is generated from within the culture and, as Cooper suggests, cannot be geographically bounded because it is a "route of cultural exchange" and an "outernational" voice of the black struggle against white domination. For as Junior Kelly posits:

As musicians, you and I can go out there in any one of these squares with a microphone if they let us and gather a lot of crowd; than Blair or anyone in his office. It's the power of music and the power of what we have to say is

so important to people you understand. Some of the time when we are
trying to teach people about the music and what it have to offer, a lot of
time people shun it, but deep innah them subconscious they know the truth.
This is you, you understand, in the purest essence so some of the time you
have to be the prophet. You have to go out there and show them say this is
what we are talking about. This can liberate a nation. This can liberate you.
This can liberate a community this can liberate the world. Sometimes our
bredrins, brothers and sisters take long enough to realise that but we have
to keep the fire burning and pushing and one day they will realise you
know.

(Junior Kelly, author's interview 2010)

PART III

SYMBOLIC MARRONNAGE

THE CREOLE HIP HOP CULTURE: BETWEEN TRADITION AND MODERNITY, ORALITY AND SCRIPTURALITY

STEVE GADET

At a time when the creative industries in a globalized world seem to compress everything, it makes sense for us to consider the connection between local and global cultures. Many questions are obvious but still need answers. If capitalism is an economic system that facilitates the distribution of mass culture, of a single thought in order to make financial profits, is it reasonable to expect its collaboration in the emancipation of local cultures? What are the consequences when global cultures can reach any given local territory?

In the first part of this chapter, I will trace the emergence of Hip Hop culture in America and in the French West Indian island of Guadeloupe without forgetting that this culture is also present throughout the Caribbean. In Guadeloupe, the oral tradition and transmission are vital Creole cultural elements. Subsequently, I will explore the bond between orality and scripturality, tradition and modernity within Guadeloupean Hip Hop culture.

Creole culture is the collection of information, symbols and behaviours that materialized on the plantations in the West Indies from the seventeenth century until the present. This collection encompasses different branches such as language, food, music, architecture, literature, etc. Hip Hop culture manifested itself in the first half of the 1970s throughout the five boroughs of New York City, beginning in the urban wasteland known as the South Bronx, emerging from the African American, Latino and Caribbean-American communities. It includes four main branches of expression: "deejaying" (the art of combining sounds and songs using two or three turntables), "b-boying" (dancing), aerosol art or graffiti writing (as opposed to vandalism), and the emerging part of the iceberg, "emceeing" (rapping). Hip Hop is a way of life that conditions the way its participants look at the world and the way they interact with people. According to pioneer KRS-One, "Hip Hop is something you live and rap is something you do" ("Get Yourself Up" 2001). The music industry and the media have helped to make the words Hip Hop and Rap synonymous, leaving out the other elements of the culture. When I use the word Hip Hop in this chapter, I will be referring to the culture along with all its elements, and not only rap music.

Hip Hop is a culture that shapes its members' worldview and participates in the making of their social identity. I will describe the emergence of Hip Hop culture in the American french department of Guadeloupe, then I will show that the combination between Hip Hop and local culture is the manifestation of local identity. As a final point, I will explore the link between orality and scripturality within Hip Hop Creole culture in Guadeloupe.

Even though Hip Hop culture arrived in Guadeloupe around 1984, no studies have been written on it, and this is the reason why I had to speak with local people in order to obtain factual information. My principal informant was a composer from Guadeloupe who witnessed the first manifestations of Hip Hop—Christophe Sophy, also known as Exxos, who has been part of Hip Hop culture in Guadeloupe since 1987. Globalization does not hinder a cultural movement from having a local and unique shape. In order to grasp the relationship between music and local and popular culture, the arguments of Australian scholar Andy Bennett exposed in his book, *Popular Music and Youth Culture* (2000) are insightful. He surveys the different concepts that have been used over the years by sociologists and specialists of culture and media to theorize youth culture and popular culture. In the process of cultural identification around the products of popular culture, manufactured and sold by the Euro-American creative industries, there is an interaction between local and global forces. In order to theorize this correlation, Bennett refers to a concept that has been popularized by the English sociologist Roland Robertson called "Glocal culture," referring to the fusion of these two drives.

Hip Hop culture emerged in France then in Guadeloupe thanks to a television show launched in 1984 on the french channel *TF1*. Named *H.I.P. H.O.P.*, the weekly show was hosted by Sydney Duteil, the first black man in France to hold such a position. French television shows were also broadcast in Guadeloupe so *H.I.P. H.O.P.* became pivotal in the involvement of Guadeloupean youth in Hip Hop culture. The appearance of free radio stations such as Kadans FM, Radyo Tambou, Radio Bis (formerly known as Sun FM and known today as Trace FM) facilitated the diffusion of Rap music from France and America. These radio stations provided spaces for local rappers to express themselves firstly in Martinique, another french department located close to Guadeloupe. Since 1989 there were special Hip Hop radio programs devoted to the culture and Rap music in Guadeloupe with a rapper named Trafyk Jam. In Martinique during these gatherings, or *krazé-gòj*[140] in Creole, rappers express themselves freely on the microphone over North-American beats. According to Rodolphe Richefal, aka Nèg Lyrical, one of the first Martiniquan pioneers in Hip Hop Creole culture, the radio programs were listened to in Guadeloupe. The performances of these young Martiniquan rappers hosted in the "Sunshine Mix" by Shakima and DJ Patpo are the first affirmations of the Creolity of Martiniquan Hip Hop. The show lasted for four years from 1990 to 1994. For the very first time, young Hip Hoppers were using Creole, their own language, to paint the pictures of their West Indian reality. The same *modus operandi* was at work at the University of Shoelcher in Martinique on Campus FM between 1995 and 1998. The station inspired Guadeloupian rappers to use Creole as a means of expression. Many rappers in Guadeloupe had chosen to ape their American or French comrades and rapped in French or in English. Creole language became a spontaneous tool to verbalize their way of life and their aspirations. From 1996 to 1999, Radyo Tambou became a vital crossroads for rap music in Guadeloupe. Even though the radio station was known for its nationalistic stance, they never considered the Guadeloupean Hip Hoppers as American-style copycats. The owners considered these artists as young Guadeloupeans articulating the reality of their country with its social, historical and lingusitic complications.

In 1994, the commercialization of the song "Pli Ta Pi Tris,"[141] produced by the group Nèg Ki Pa Ka Fè La Fèt[142] on the compilation *Dancehall Party* is a turning point for Hip Hop culture in Guadeloupe and Martinique. They were influenced by the work of scholars like Aimé Césaire, Frantz Fanon and Cheikh Anta Diop. In 1996, Nèg Lyrical's album *Kimanièoupédimwenbagaykonsapéfèt*[143] was the first Rap album recorded in Creole in Martinique, and was a stepping stone for the movement in Guadeloupe and Maritinique.

During our interview, Exxos confirmed that since he started rapping and producing beats, he always wanted to create a music called "Guadeloupean rap," to paint pictures of his life using the vividness of Creole language. By rapping in their native language, Guadeloupean rappers were clearly showing that they could hold their head high when comparing themselves to rappers from America and France, admitting that Creole is the backbone of their culture and that therefore Hip Hop was being Creolized. The language was playing a role in satisfying the communication needs of these youths.[144]

The first graffiti became visible on the walls in Guadeloupe around the end of the 1980s. Most were painted by Guadeloupean youths based in

France who were home for the vacations, continuing what they had started in Paris. Rival youths would paint their names on walls in order to mark out their territories. The first graffiti artist who gained local attention was Groover, a member of the UBC (Unité Bande de Choc). Meanwhile, small groups like Karukéra Crew, SAM, 2KA, QCP (Que la Couleur te Pénètre), and AEM (Artistes En Mouvement) went from simple tags to more stylish graffiti. Some graffiti seen on walls in Guadeloupe contained colours of a local cloth called Madras (orange, green and yellow). Madras is very popular and strongly associated to Creole culture, and I was able to take representative pictures of this. Other graffiti exposed the cultural patrimony and combined it with Hip Hop culture. Some graffiti displayed Afrocentric symbols influenced by Rastafari, a critical Afro-Caribbean religious movement.

The connection between scripturality and orality is manifested in this visual art because it gives a voice to individuals or to elements that would be speechless were they not able to paint on walls. This pattern is at work in a tag written by the association Groove Art where one can read this statement: "Walls had ears but now they have a voice."

Abymes (courtesy of Steve Gadet)

Pointe-à-Pitre, (courtesy of Steve Gadet)

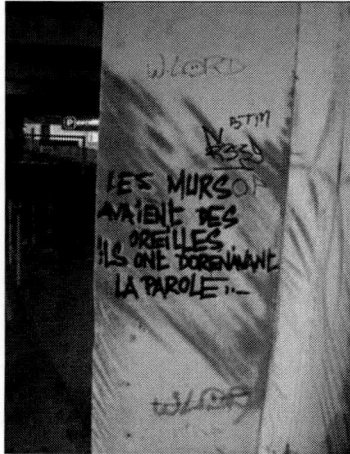

Pointe-à-Pitre, (courtesy of Steve Gadet)

In Guadeloupe, the lyrics of rappers, in this case Nèg Lyrical from Martinique, are transcribed on walls. It clearly traces the continuity between this oral art, graffiti art and scriptural expression.

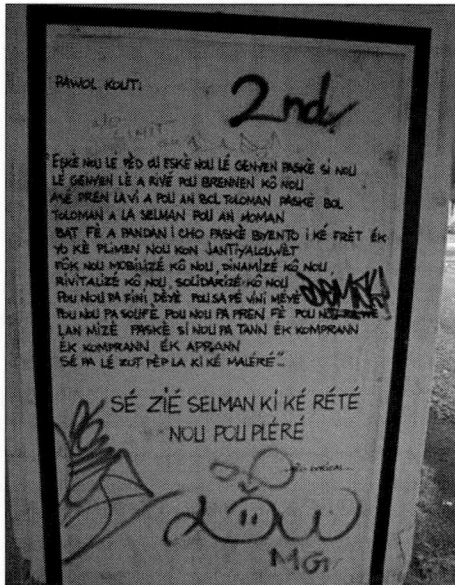

(Courtesy of Steve Gadet)

(Courtesy of Steve Gadet)

The last example represents the proclamation of famous Guadeloupean revolutionnary Louis Delgrès, made on May 10, 1802. During the revolt against the arrival of Napoleon's troops from France, in order to restore slavery, Delgrès pronounced these words: "Resistance to oppression is an inalienable right." At the bottom of the graffiti, there is a signature "Delgrès" and the year "1802" written central behind the main sentence. The history of Guadeloupe here becomes the raw material in the creation process of Guadeloupean graffiti artists.

(Courtesy of Steve Gadet)

According to our informant, Exxos, breakdancing arrived in Guadeloupe at the same time as the other elements of the culture. However, today what is noticeable is its fusion with local dance, with moves from traditional dance also incorporated. A school dance located in Goyave, a local town, invented a new dance style labelled "Hip Hop ka." Another cultural association named Kamodjaka, well known for its defence of local heritage, integrates it into its presentations. Breakdance is not duplicated but is reinvented within a local culture that welcomes it. In this light, it becomes a vehicle for local cultural traditions. Cultural mimetism can have devastating consequences on local cultures. A category of artists that grew up with urban expressions and their own Guadeloupean heritage are inventing an original expression based on their own cultural identity. Through music, a cultural bridge was laid down from the old to the new generations, bringing together *Gwo ka* artists with Hip Hop and Reggae artists. This approach became visible during a show that took place in August 2003 in the economic capital of Guadeloupe, Pointe-a-Pitre and was labeled "Dub-n-Ka."[145]

Cover of "Dub'n'Ka"Album, bringing together Gwo ka and Hip Hop artists

This musical, cultural and generational cross-fertilization is critical for the future of Hip Hop culture in Guadeloupe. Indeed, Star Jee, one of the rappers participating in "Dub-n-Ka" went as far as to say that: "The future of Guadeloupean Hip Hop is bound to *Ka*, if not we will forever be tropicalized copies of the United-States."[146] François Ladrezeau, the drummer and lead singer of Akiyo,[147] a popular *Gwo ka* band, declared: "Their dancehall has to be nurtured by our music which is theirs."

This crossroad of cultures is welcomed and encouraged by both parties; it is an enriching experience for them. For the rappers it is a return to their roots. For the *Gwo ka* singers, their ground-breaking work is being acknowledged as well as projected into modernity. *Gwo ka* and Hip Hop share numerous similarities that have facilitated their connection.

Gwo ka appeared in Guadeloupe during the seventeenth century with the arrival of African slaves who used a wide variety of music and dance from the African continent. From these elements, the slaves forged original expressions reflecting their new way of life. That new culture, over the centuries, became the traditional heritage of Guadeloupe. This new musical expression heavily influenced the lives of the black population, helping them to settle down and to cope. In the same way, the pioneers of Hip Hop culture in New York, originally from the black and Latino communities, invented new expressions with unconnected elements (however, we must also take into account the contribution of technology in the creation of Hip Hop culture in the United States). The similarities between Hip Hop culture and *Gwo ka* are numerous, and they appear even more expressively when taking a closer look at both movements.

Rapper LM Star Jee, 2011

The Central Place of Oral Expression

The evening performances called *lewoz* are the most important spots, in which drums are played without restraint. The *lewoz* started when the black workers, after a week of hard labour in the sugar cane fields, would meet on a Saturday night in order to forget about their living conditions. During these night sessions, participants dance and chant over the rhythm of the drums. These evening celebrations bear a resemblance to those block parties where the first Hip Hoppers would gather in the early 1970s as they still do today in the four corners of the world. These gatherings are quality time for interaction, for expressing oneself and for letting go. The times, the location and the musical elements are different but the backdrops are comparable. One or several artists sing, and a response is given by the audience (Urie 1994, 71), who stand around the drummers. In the middle of a closed circle, the dancers express themselves over the music. The rapper or the MC (Master of Ceremony), the breakdancer and the deejay have the same relationship with the audience in Hip Hop culture. The individual in public is not passive; they become an actor when they respond and dance, and the success of the performances depend on active participation (Béthune 2004, 74). African societies and those founded by their descendants in the Americas have a paradigm centred around oral traditions. Prayers, information, knowledge, stories and genealogy are passed on through oral communication. Orality is a pillar within Hip Hop culture and in *Gwo ka*.

Repetition, Improvisation, Humour and Themes of the Lyrics

In order to establish a relationship, when the singer starts to perform, they engage the audience in a call and response pattern that can be repeated for as long as is wanted. This call and response pattern is always present in Hip Hop and *Gwo ka*. Improvisation is also a central element for both cultures. Many artists (dancers, singers, drummers and rappers) perform using their inspiration in the moment. Nothing is rehearsed; their moves and their lyrics are authentic. Regarding the themes of the lyrics, they can be as varied as life's trials while still remaining focused on the Guadeloupean man or woman. More often than not, the tribulations of the individual at the bottom of the social ladder will be favoured. Rappers and singers act like African *griots*, carrying collective memories in their artistic creation. Sometimes they confront each other verbally or by provoking moves in order to assert their authenticity and their originality.

The Sociocultural Role of the Musical Expressions

Gwo ka and Rap are two musical forms voicing strong identity claims. They have been considered as sub-genres, and the creators and their creations have been despised by the mainstream society. *Gwo ka* was accepted and embraced from the 1960s with the propaganda of the independent movements. As far as Rap is concerned, when it started many observers in the United States, in France and in Guadeloupe predicted its rapid demise. Rap and *Gwo ka* also have in common their function as outlets. Their representation and their commercialization also produce financial profits and economic activity. Lastly, they generate social prestige and help manage individual conflicts.

Predominance of Rhythm

Ka[148] holds a fundamental place in the *lewoz* evening performances and within *Gwo ka* music. The beat holds a similar place in Rap music and Hip Hop culture. The beat can be produced with a drum machine or with the mouth, and in both cultures the mouth can become an instrument to make sounds and create rhythm. The *Boulagyèl* in Creole (mouth drumming) has an equivalent in Hip Hop with the human beatbox. This process is derived from a sound imitation tradition in African and African-American cultures, and can be found at work in those two sociocultural phenomena that emerged in the Americas.

Music Closely Associated to Dance

In the African tradition, dance is always associated with music. Hip Hop and *Gwo ka* dancers usually dance in a circle during their performances, either dancing together or battling against each other, dancing to the rhythm. In *Gwo ka*, the dancer is engaged in a physical conversation with the drummer. In Hip Hop culture, the breakdancer is in harmony with the DJ and the beats played on the turntables.

To make Rap beats, young Guadeloupean beatmakers sample elements from various genres of local and regional music (*zouk*, *Gwo ka*, *quadrille*, *biguine*, dub-poetry, calypso, reggae, compa, etc…). The value of these local elements is reasserted through their productions. To produce their song "Mandé lé Répondè," the martiniquan group Nèg Ki Pa Ka Fè La Fèt sampled a song from the Guadeloupean singer, Guy Conquete. The Guadeloupean group, Gwada Nostra, did the same thing with a local *biguine* song to defend the use of the Creole language. They received a local music award in 2002 for the song "Awogan." One member of the group declared: "As far as I'm concerned this is not for the glory of Gwada Nostra, I see it more like the reward of those who worked before us … This is an exchange from one generation to another."

Guadeloupean and Martiniquan rappers and beatmakers are being creative when they mix Rap music with local musical elements. They are being inventive with Rap and about their own reality in their own language, the language of their ancestors. Two worlds meet, and two generations come together. Exxos, the Guadeloupean beatmaker and rapper, verbalized eloquently what was happening when he said in our interview that "young people sit down in between two cultural chairs but they're doing well."

Hip Hop culture goes back and forth from orality to scripturality, particularly through graffiti and Rap music. The French scholar Christian Béthune acknowledged that "Rap music reinvents words and forces verbal invention to go back and forth from orality to writing" (2004, 11). Therefore, Rap music creates the space for other ways of speaking (like slang or French Creole) that mainstream society does not consider fit for poetic art, in general. If rappers can't "freestyle" their lyrics, more often they write them down first, using complex patterns of rhymes which does not, however, weaken the quality of their oral performance. Using the assistance of technology, orality acquires a new dimension within Rap music (Béthune 2004, 48).

In Tricia Rose's words, an African and African American studies professor, Rap music comes from the African oral tradition but "it is fundamentally literate [and] deeply technological" (1994, 95). The written word does not submit to orality and vice-versa in Hip Hop. Rappers are literate and they write with structures usually reserved for oral debate (Béthune 2004, 51). They are speakers and writers at the same time, doing both naturally. Whereas school separates the two disciplines, rappers reunite them, being both children of school and part of the Hip Hop generation.

To label this school of thought, this new cultural movement connecting tradition and modernity, local and global cultures, Exxos coined the term *Kako*. This artistic approach confirms the motto of Guadeloupean philosopher Lukuber Séjor: "*Tout biten sé on biten pa rapòt a on biten,*" meaning "Everything comes into being via something else." Exxos' motivation was to find a name for that identity before it could be labelled by the media. In Creole, *Kako* usually means "cocoa" or "brown." The colour brown in Creole refers to the term Maroon, the name for fugitive slaves who fled the domination of their white masters. Escaping from the humiliations of life on the plantation made them new individuals, free to invent their own identities. This is also the case for Hip Hop culture in Guadeloupe, as it was able to depart from its originators in order to be empowered by Creole culture. As a matter of fact, when cultural movements coming from capitalist countries, which can spread to anywhere the world, are tailored to satisfy local needs, they can be good vehicles for local cultures that are not completely eradicated by powerful creative industries. Global cultures can be factors of emancipation for local cultures rather than predators. If Hip Hop culture in Guadeloupe is able to reflect the political, the cultural and the social reality of the island, we can objectively acknowledge that Creole Hip Hop is becoming an authentic cultural movement.

WILL THE REAL *NÈG MAWON* PLEASE STAND UP: SUBVERSIVE BODIES IN THE INNER CITIES OF KINGSTON JAMAICA

NATHALIE MONTLOUIS

"My property is my property any lover can trust tight for life. Watch that baby body"

(Patra "Romantic Call," 1993)

Introduction

During the 1990s, Patra, with the album *Queen of the Pack* revealed to the world the Dancehall Queen phenomenon in Jamaica. These women, armed with their "batty riders,"[149] took control over their bodies, challenging the conservative norms of propriety promoted by the Jamaican patriarchal society, in a genuine celebration of their sexuality and fertility (Cooper 2004). The emergence of these women on the Dancehall scene can be considered revolutionary. Indeed, until this period, the discourse of sex, pleasure or consumerism found under the musical genre "slackness"[150] was essentially a masculine prerogative where "respectable" women could not have a voice.

Beyond the notion of sexual liberation, the glitters and the male/female sound clashes, I suggest that the bodies of these women are the physical expression of uneasiness present in the Jamaican mainstream society. With their rather extravagant outfits and accessories on the dancehall floor, these women live on margin of Jamaican society in extremely violent and difficult environments. It has been argued elsewhere that in the poorest neighbourhoods of Kingston, where unemployment, violence and corruption are commonplace, these women capitalise on their bodies in order to win "matey wars,"[151] attract and eventually keep a partner, a "Bad Man," able to assist and defend them where the legislators have failed (Tafari-Ama 2008).

In this context of violence, corruption and poverty, the women of the Rastafari House of Bobo Shanti, also known as the Ethiopian African Black International Congress, are also found on the margin of Jamaican mainstream society. However, the physical expression of this marginality is not translated by wearing a revealing "batty rider" but in long flowing robes and falls. In these attires, they celebrate their fertility and the power of their sexuality in their ability to bring forth life as *Goddesses of Creation*. Numerous are the critics condemning their way of life as obsolete, inappropriate, impracticable and insulting to their femininity (Lake 1998; Yawney 1989; Chevannes 1994).

Coming from the same impoverished neighbourhoods of Kingston, there is a cultural clash between the women involved in Dancehall and those of the EABIC. If they both epitomise the rupture between the Jamaican postcard image and the realities of the ghetto, they clearly do not use the same mode of expression. How can people who come from the same ethnic and social background express the same thing through such different means? In this chapter, I argue that true to the Jamaican tradition of marronnage,[152] Bobo Shanti women express through their bodies the radical ethos of the EABIC counter-culture. Discreet and modest, they are the true Jamaican *Fanm Mawon*[153] of the twenty-first century.

In order to support my claims, I am firstly going establish the historical context from which the Jamaican conception of the African body emerged. I will then define what I mean by marronnage and attempt to demonstrate that the members of the EABIC have engaged in what one may call an aesthetic of marronnage.

Linguistic Clarification

In this chapter, the term marronnage is used to define the action of rebelling, of escaping from an oppressive system. In the French-speaking Caribbean, the term comes directly from the Kréyol expression *Nèg Mawon,* which was attributed to runaway slaves (*Nèg* meaning nigger and *mawon* referring to the fact that he or she was a runaway). The expression *Nèg Mawon* has remained in the French speaking Caribbean to define people living on the margin of mainstream society, challenging the established norms. *Mawon* or marronnage does not therefore necessarily refer to the communities of Maroons found in Jamaica from which the actual word may derive.

Jamaica is indeed a country well known for its tradition of social rebellion. In 1655, the island passed from Spanish to British rule. The Africans who remained on the island after the demise of Spanish rule refused to be enslaved and fought the British authorities to preserve their freedom, lands and culture. Queen Nanny of the Maroons, a woman born in the Ashanti Kingdom in what is now modern Ghana, was one of the fearless strategists and spiritual leaders of the rebellious community which entered the history books under the name of the Maroons. After numerous wars, treaties and negotiations, this community managed to maintain a relative administrative and economic independence from the colonial powers. This independence allowed them to provide a frame in which the African diasporic people could be socially reborn as human beings instead of slaves (Gotlieb 2000; Campbell 1988).

The following section will explore the complexities of the *marron* notion in the twenty-first century.

Dominant Jamaican Culture: Biases and Prejudice

Before going any further, it is essential to define in what social paradigms the women mentioned in the introduction are located. Marx declared that:

> The class which has the means of material production at its disposal, has control at the same time, over the means of mental production ... the ideas of those who lack the means of mental production are subject to it ... they do it in a whole range, hence among other things rule also as thinkers, as producers of ideas, and regulate the production and distribution of the ideas of their age.
>
> (1970, 64)

Under colonial rule, social class was closely linked with race and skin colour. In this context, the class that had the control over the means of mental production was that of the planters, European settlers who controlled the economy of the island, and they formed the dominant culture (Clarke et al. 2006, 6). It is within this paradigm that Wilson elaborated his theory about "respectability and reputation" (1979). He demonstrated in his work that Jamaica and the Caribbean at large revolved around two different systems of values. One was European, thus "respectable," while the other was African diasporic and belonged to "reputation." The former inferred power, classicism and hierarchy while the latter conferred respect, equality and popular notoriety (Burton 1997).

In this dual system, the African body was merely a physical envelope, whose purpose was to generate profit. Between the sixteenth and nineteenth centuries, the dehumanisation of the African diasporic people was institutionalised and systematised in order to justify the horrors of the slave trade (Amelioration Act 1798). This degrading process was at the time warmly supported by the Anglican Church, which admits today its preponderant role in the legitimisation of this organization, both in the colonies and the mainland.

This process of dehumanisation produced a society where race, skin colour, gender and social class were tightly intertwined to materially and cultural profit for Europeans or those with European phenotypes. Cress (1976), Frankenberg (1984) and Henry (2007) called this system "Whiteness." The latter concept is a socio-cultural construction which promotes a European mode of social and material production. Most of the beneficiaries of this system tend not to be fully aware of their privileges. Their ethnic and social background can be considered to be functioning as a true "social capital," allowing them to evolve "naturally" in society. The "other," usually non-white, who is denied the comfort of normality, remains at the margin of mainstream society at different levels of integration. Feeding the controversy, Henry explains that:

> I am fully aware that their behaviour is a necessary consequence of our collective socialisation. For these types, it is natural to be white; it is natural for them to be white and oppress blacks; and it will remain so until the day they are slapped with the black truth of their condition. This is why black folk are the best witnessed to whiteness, because white folk don't seem to get what is at stake when merely trying to "live," whilst being black, in their world.
>
> (Henry 2007, 13)

From these points, one may suggest that it was in the planters' best financial interests to deny the humanity of the African body. In order to achieve their purposes, African diasporic beliefs and worldviews were ridiculed and demonised as they were assessed by the partial lenses of whiteness.[154] Since then, the African body could never achieve respectability, as they could never be considered as equal to their masters. This is the reason why counter values had to be elaborated in the parallel sphere of reputation.

Creating a Subculture: Reputation

The African-Jamaicans oppressed by the colonial system are not to be regarded as passive and subdued figures. Countless people were engaged in active rebellion, while many endeavoured to resist the dehumanising process through their spirituality, dance or sense of aesthetic (Burton 1997; Austin-Broos 1997; Mathurin Mair 2006). Indeed, those who did not physically escape created what one may call a subculture.

According to Gelder (2007), subcultures have their own values, norms and rituals, yet they define themselves against the main culture that can easily absorb them. Indeed, subcultures are not necessarily in conflict with the mainstream culture. For instance, although the games, music and beliefs of the enslaved allowed them to exist as social beings in a hostile milieu, their own system of value could only be defined through the lenses of the dominant culture, which often found them to be deficient or abnormal. This can be illustrated through the necessity of the process of syncretism for the survival of African religious rituals and practices in the Caribbean.

Chevannes explains that at the end of the eighteenth century, the Baptist Church served as a receptacle for the African diasporic religion Myal.[155] The latter was indeed incorporated in an authorised form of Christianity, allowing for the sustenance of African spirituality with its characteristic features such as possession or miraculous healing, both present in modern Caribbean Revivalism (1998, 7–9). These practices were undeniably tools that enabled the creation of a space where serious rebellions could be fomented. One cannot bypass the fact that Daddy Sharpe, to quote only one name, instigator of the rebellion of Christmas 1831, was a pastor of the syncretised Jamaican Baptist Church (Kennedy 2008). This surreptitious incorporation of African values within a "respectable" institution was the foundation of the African-Jamaican subculture, creating the sphere of "reputation" with its elements of popularity and play (stick-fighting *Jonkonnu* or the set girls, for instance), still extremely important in contemporary Jamaica (Burton 1997). Though subversive, the mores of the Jamaican subcultures were not strong enough to overthrow the colonial cultural hegemony. Indeed, even if the slaves managed to conduct successful rebellions, wearing down the system of slavery and leading to its abolition, and sustain African traditions that are now an important component of Jamaican culture, "respectability" has never shifted from its European standards.

Colourism: From "Reputable" to "Respectable"?

In the microcosm of the plantation, three main social and ethnic groups could be observed: the slave (dark-skinned with African phenotypes), mixed race or "coloured" people (brown skin with more European traits, especially in the length and texture of the hair), often manumitted and involved in trade and politics, and the white people, mostly rich, and who, due to their ethnic background, were considered better than non-white people (Knights, in Headley 1984, 215). If the "coloured" people were certainly not considered the equals of the white caste, they managed to constitute a brown middle class without threatening the financial hegemony of the whites as characteristic of the dominant cultures (Mathurin-Mair 2006, 292).

In this context, hostile to people presenting a majority of African phenotypes, the mulattoes, the quarterons, the sambos or the negroes (to use the nomenclature of the time) transmitted to their children what Austin-Broos (1994) calls heritable identity; linking skin complexion with social expectations, which are still present in the Jamaican society of the twenty-first century. Indeed, it has been argued elsewhere that the popularity of the *brownin,* the Jamaican mixed race[156] woman praised in many Dancehall songs, was not merely a matter of personal sexual preference, but also related to the deeply rooted race/class dynamic. A *brownin* is usually associated with the middle to upper middle class strata of Jamaican society. Having a relationship with a *brownin* is therefore somehow to move up the social ladder (Mohammed 2000).

As direct heirs of this colourist society, numerous are those who employ elaborate strategies worthy of the mythical trickster Anansy[157] in order to gain what nature and society has refused them (Cooper 2004, 137). In fact, if social limitation cannot be avoided in these destitute parts of Kingston, the appearance of the body can be altered to at least look like success. For instance, a dark complexion can easily be lightened with the help of bleaching creams. If some claim that it is the easiest way to obtain better paid jobs, others maintain that they use those creams to look glamorous, attractive and trendy (Charles 2003, 715) Arguably, these creams are a popular product among the African-Jamaican population, as the images of success vectored by the media portray a majority of mixed-raced and white people.[158] I am also tempted to suggest that the practice is slowly being absorbed by the dominant culture.

The popular Dancehall deejay Vybz Kartel openly bleaches his skin. Kartel does not hesitate in blaming the colonial past of the island to justify his behaviour, yet he claims to have reinvented the meaning of the practice, turning it into a trend that all fashionable people, regardless of their social class, should follow. Grounding his argument on the importance of appearance in consumerist society, he readily associates skin bleaching with the trendy, the sophisticated, and the festive realm of the Dancehall scene. Through his absurd rhetoric[159] it is clear that the prejudice against African phenotypes is acknowledged, yet the practice is becoming politically correct, following the argument of fashionable trends, as it is slowly absorbed by the dominant culture.

It was argued that this eagerness to depart from natural African endowments was a survival strategy in a milieu where the body was the surest means to gain social and material security (Tafari-Ama 2006, 69). One may also suggest that this desire to remain so far away from their natural bodies might also be derived from the ingrained notion of the worthlessness of the African body, widely spread by the dominant culture. If African phenotypes were linked to slaves and later the world of the "sufferers," of the lower working class, departing from these physical characteristics may be regarded as a way to be seen and heard by the dominant culture.

Although vibrantly creative and resourceful, the Jamaican subculture and its counter-values did not and still do not seriously threaten the established "respectable" order generated by the colonial past of the island. Arguably, Jamaica is now an independent country where slavery and colonialism are officially relics of the past. However, the system instituted by the white minority of the planter class has not quite been abolished. Indeed, the education, the spirituality, and the economic activities of the Jamaicans were grounded on neo-colonial "respectable" or "white" values that the African-Jamaicans did not necessarily benefit from. Chinweizu explains that:

> Even if Ariel were to overcome his ingrained awe and turn on his creator, his conditioning would likewise conspire to defeat his purpose. For as long as Ariel leads the third world, Prospero's old world order—whether economic, cultural, political or informal—will be safe ... Such veneration to Alien cultures leaves the African Ariel susceptible to foreign domination.
>
> (Chinweizu 1987, 2–3)

Even if one cannot accuse the Jamaican government of purposefully elaborating policies that would systematically disadvantage the lower or dark-skinned classes, the people crammed in the ghettos of Kingston are living testimonies to the failure of its social and cultural vision. It would appear that the spirit of Ariel still lingers in the legislators. Nevertheless, to be true to Shakespeare's tale, whenever there is an Ariel, there is also a Caliban, a rebel who refuses the rule, the culture, the beliefs, the norms of Prospero: the *Nèg Mawon*.

Marronnage, a Counter-Culture

If the vast majority of the enslaved chose to culturally resist the system of whiteness by insidiously mixing their African identity with colonial institutions and values, many decidedly chose a spatial rupture with the world of the plantation. These individuals, often united in small communities, where therefore engaged in marronnage. In his definition of the term, Karam (2011) insists that: "Marronnage cannot be regarded as an ordinary form of rebellion. It suggests the open contestation of a social, economic and political system.[160]"

As already mentioned, Jamaica is the home of the Maroons, an African diasporic group similar to the Bushinengés of French Guyana, who to some extent may be regarded as what Clarke et al. call a counter-culture. By definition, a counter-culture is in confrontation with the dominant culture and seeks to modify and overthrow its hegemony (Clarke et al. 2006, 45). In this chapter, I will argue that the counter-culture can be an equivalent to the notion of marronnage. Indeed, in both cases, the rebellious units have separated from the dominant culture and established their own social order and, most importantly, openly and constantly challenged the system from which they have departed. This definition of marronnage can be tested through the communities of Maroons in Jamaica.

In fact, applied to the Maroons, the notion of marronnage does not appear to be a perfect fit. If the former managed to win and negotiate a space where they could be free as Africans, the Jamaican maroons also served the purposes of the very European hegemony that they rejected. Indeed, they were known to be involved in the capture of runaway slaves (Dourmec 2003, 29), an activity that reinforced the power of the dominant culture. It is also important to note that during the second Maroon war, only the village of Accompong, which had remained neutral in the struggle, was able to survive the colonial repression as they were not attacked (Campbell 1988). The abolition of slavery was precipitated by the *Anansi* resistance and countless rebellions of the plantation slaves, rather than by the Maroons.

From the example of the Maroons, one can suggest that living independently on the margin of mainstream society is not enough to be regarded as counter-cultural or to be in marronnage. The Maroons saw their faith as separated from that of the slave and were ready to collaborate with the colonial power in order to defend their lands and independence. From the point that they could no longer be considered as a threat to the dominant culture and ideology, they cannot really be regarded as having established a counter-culture.

Marronnage in Twenty-First Century Jamaica: Rastafari

In the twenty-first century, at a time when African-Caribbeans no longer physically endured the pains and humiliation of slavery on their flesh, the *Blès*,[161] occasioned by the colonial system, still haunts the minds and the bodies of the people of this region. If the evidence of the *Blès* can be witnessed at all levels of Jamaican society, the urban space where the "have nots" survive, the poorest strata of the society, is where it is the most flagrant. It is from this impoverished urban context that Rastafari was born, a radical worldview to which the Ethiopian African Black International Congress (EABIC) belongs.

Rastafari can in fact be regarded as the radical expression of African-Jamaican spiritual resistance, seeking to overthrow the established notion of Christianity promoted by the system of "whiteness." Instead of adopting the generalised *Anansy* methods used by the other African diasporic denominations, Rastafari epistemology openly defies the symbolism and the aesthetic of European Christianity. This bold attitude has been described by McFarlane as that of the "lion," assertive and brave, breaking away from the cunning methods of *Anansy*, but not a serious threat to the dominant culture (McFarlane 1998.)

EABIC: Establishing a Counter-Culture

From the same destitute inner cities, where men and women reproduce the destructive canons of beauty, alien to their own nature, EABIC members, also called Bobo Shanti people, have organised what one may call a counter-culture, a *mawon* community in the twenty-first century. Inherent to Rastafari, the EABIC was founded in 1958 by the Honourable King Emmanuel Charles Edward. The latter was most probably one of the earliest adepts of the Rastafari movement along with elders such as Robert Hinds, Leonard Howell or Archibald Dunkley.

Known as Bongo Eddy or Prince Emmanuel at the time, King Emmanuel was eager to bring a monastic colour to Rastafari and went on to create the *Priesthood Order* of the Ethiopian African Black International Congress (Van Dijk 1993, 117). As such, the Bobo Shanti Rastas, armed with their particular *Livity*, resist, challenge and constantly seek to overthrow the norms of the dominant culture.

Currently established on the heights of Bull's Bay, in the parish of St Andrews, the Bobo Shanti community was born in the inner city of Kingston. From Spanish Road to Back a Wall, the community never ceased to strive and proclaim their understanding of Black Supremacy, in spite of the acerbic persecution of the police (the Honourable Mama Rachel, in conversation with the author 2011). In fact, one of the main characteristics of the EABIC, and of Rastafari in general, is the belief that as the first inhabitants of the planet, Africans ought to be respected and honoured as the parents of humanity. This deference is to be shown by the universal acknowledgement of the importance of: repatriation, the return of the diaspora to the African soil; reparation, pecuniary compensation for the looting of Africa by Europe, and; love, as when all the mismanagement and corruption from the African and European sides ceases, all races would finally be able to love each other as equals. According to the theory of Black Supremacy, solving the cultural and economic problems of the African continent and its diaspora would lead to world peace (The Honourable Priest Wayne, in conversation with the author 2009). The numerous chapters of the EABIC in Europe and in South America are there to demonstrate that the Black Supremacy theory is not about the superiority of an ethnic group, but is a vital matter of social justice.

Repatriation with reparation for all the members of the African diaspora desiring to return to the continent is the admitted objective of the EABIC. Working around these two themes, the congress[162] is in constant *pourparler* with national and international bodies. The EABIC was the first organisation of Rastafari to send a telegram to the UNO in 1967, demanding the organised return of the displaced population on the grounds that "Everyone has the right to a nationality. No one shall be arbitrarily deprived of his nationality nor denied the right to change his nationality" (article 15 of the Universal Declaration of Human Rights). The EABIC is also the only organisation of Rastafari that sued the Jamaican Government for denying them their right to a nationality that they believed was taken away from them. This happened in 1984 with the Honourable Empress Esther representing the Bobo Shanti, but they did not get the opportunity to have a trial as the case was dismissed as frivolous (The honourable Empress Esther, in conversation with the author 2008).

Subversive, militant and organised, the EABIC was able to identify the influences of the colonial norms on the dominant culture of modern Jamaican society. Aware of its perverse effects, this community was able to elaborate African-centred counter values where the African body is normal. It has been argued that through their radical spiritual, educational and economic system, the Bobo Shanti Rastas have not only negotiated a physical space for their community,[163] but haver also sought to overthrow the dominant culture (Montlouis 2011). One can therefore regard the EABIC as a counter-culture, a community of *Nèg Mawon*.

The Body/Temple: Praxis of the Counter Values

Unlike the "respectable" canons of beauty insidiously promoted by the dominant culture, EABIC members valorize the dark skin complexion. In fact, in EABIC cosmogony, the Holy Trinity is composed of four black historical figures: Marcus Garvey as the prophet preparing the way for the dyad HIM Haile Selassie and Empress Menen Asfaw, representing the father and mother, and King Emmanuel in the position of the Priest. From this African, and African diasporic, representation of the divine, there is no stigma attached to the colour black or to the woman. Indeed, the original sin for the members of the EABIC was committed by both men and women when they agreed to marry Europeans, an action forbidden by God.[164] This particular ethos greatly affected the EABIC conception of the body.

Indeed, through the concept of "I and I," the body becomes taboo, sacred and divine. "I and I" is the conviction that the creating force, the divine, that which is usually understood by the word God, lives within one's flesh. United in this manner, people therefore form "one" through their divinity, as the "I" recognises the divine "I" of the other (The Honourable Priest Wayne, in conversation with the author 2011; McFarlane 1998). The body is therefore considered as a temple through which the agency of God is manifested. As a result, with such meaningful bodies, EABIC members seek to maintain their "temples" in the best state of health and as close to nature as possible. I suggest that as a counter-culture, the conception of the body is the praxis of the counter values that the EABIC has elaborated. As a result, the physical appearance of its members will be radically different to that of the Dancehall subculture.

EABIC Body/Temple: A Few Characteristics

The most controversial physical taboo inherent to the EABIC is the ritual of the twenty-one days of purification that women have to conduct every month. Indeed, for twenty-one days, a Bobo Shanti woman is expected to separate herself from the rest of the community, and from her family, in order to conduct the sacrifice of the goddess of creation: returning her menses to the earth. This practice is usually regarded as misogynistic by most observers (Lake 1998). Nevertheless, I will argue that despite the bias of the original sin placed on women, the EABIC is not a strategy to subdue the Empresses but a genuine ritual to emphasise the link between the fertility of the earth and that of the woman. As a Goddess of Creation, rituals are necessary to reinforce the sacralisation of the bodies. Men are also expected to remain secluded for the same purification purposes, as all bodily secretions other than sweat or urine are regarded as pollution.

In the same line of thought, men and women have to cover their hair in public. Like the biblical character of Samson, whose supernatural strength was derived from his hair (Judges 13–16), Bobo Shanti Rastas also consider their locks to be the symbol of their spiritual powers. They have made the Nazarite vow, which requires among other things that the hair of the devotee be left in its natural state, unshaved and uncut. The Nazarite vow therefore acts as an argument of authority as this requirement is a divine command. Their hair is therefore a symbol of their particular understanding of the divine and devotion. The woolly texture of African hair also gains a spiritual dimension. Indeed, its spiral structure is associated with the shape of the human DNA, linking once again the African phenotypes to the mystical origins of life (The honourable Empress Nyah, in conversation with the author 2009). According to the importance placed on their hair, wearing a wig, a weave or any artificial hairpieces is not an option in EABIC fashion.

The EABIC diet is also meaningful. A Bobo Shanti eats *Ital*, just like most Rastafarians. If the word *Ital* is often associated with a vegan diet (Barrett 1997), it becomes in EABIC epistemology another manifestation of their ethos. With their sacred respect for life, *Ital* means a living diet for living temples. Meat and processed food are banished from the kitchens. The food is cooked in order to preserve a maximum of nutrients, allowing their body/temple to benefit from a wholesome diet, protecting them from diseases that may trouble their connection with God within.

If Bobo Shanti Rastas are meticulous about their diets, they are also careful about the type of music that they listen to. In order to remain connected with the divine, EABIC members favour the binary rhythm of the *Nyabinghi*, which is said to replicate a healthy heartbeat and prepare them for meditation. *Nyabinghi* is played on three drums: the *Kette*, *Fundhe* and *Base* drum, which plays a major cultural and spiritual role in Jamaican traditions (Reckford 1998). Though from the same roots, Reggae[165] and its industry is regarded as evil. Beyond the criticism of "slackness" and its ultra-sexualised and materialistic discourse, EABIC members question the very rhythm of this music and its impact on African-Jamaican minds.

To serve the purposes of a European capitalistic system, African bodies in Jamaica were rationalised as sub-human entities whose culture and appearance was not "respectable." Through its radical approach of the divine, the EABIC has shifted the "respectable" from European fantasy to an African-Jamaican reality, creating a vibrant counter-culture with clear ideological guidelines. From the Kingston inner cities, they stand as real *Nèg Mawon.*

Conclusion

The aim of this article was to deal with the question of body perception and conception in the Kingston inner city. The problem was articulated around the very different means used by this population in order to signify the rupture between their living condition and the norms imposed by the dominant culture. Two types of people have been singled out: the followers of the Dancehall movement and the devotees of the Ethiopian African International congress. I have suggested that the expression of this rupture was so dissimilar because of the distinctive ethos of their structure: the former is a subculture and the latter a counter-culture.

On one hand, the Dancehall queens are defying the conservative norms of the dominant culture with their counter values, yet they are not threatening its foundations. Moreover, their distinctive physical characteristics are slowly being absorbed by the same dominant culture. The EABIC on the other hand is of the ethos of marronnage. Aware of the negative impacts that the norms of "whiteness" have on the Jamaican society, Bobo Shanti Rastas have refused to define their persons through the prejudiced lenses of the dominant culture. They were able to create a social frame where African phenotypes are praised, desired, and normal. In order to fight the *Blès*, and regain their dignity, they transformed the black body into a wondrous and sacred temple through its rituals and obligations.

If their worldview has been heavily criticised by public opinion, the EABIC has undeniably identified the prejudice against African phenotypes diluted in the Jamaican dominant culture, and offers another option. Beyond the sound clashes and far away from the cameras, the Bobo Shanti people can be dubbed the *Nèg Mawon* of the twenty-first century.

WALKING THE PATHS OF MARRONNAGE TO THE CREATION OF DANCEHALL AND RAP MUSIC: INTERVIEWS WITH FRENCH-SPEAKING, WEST INDIAN ARTISTS FROM GUADELOUPE AND MARTINIQUE

STÉPHANIE MELYON-REINETTE

Questioning the phenomenon of marronnage implies the questioning of its origins and meanings. Undoubtedly, marronnage is a Caribbean concept, present throughout the histories of the colonial islands and the sociological profiles of the ensuing societies that have emerged and resulted from them. Within the behaviours and social movements in the Caribbean societies it is observable that marronnage induced certain comportments into the populations that are similar or approximately comparable to, or in the mindset of, this old phenomenon. In this article, which gathers interviews I have done with prominent, well-known French-speaking, Creole Reggae-Dancehall artists, I want to highlight that the concept of "marronnage" is rooted by the interviewees in the same historical source, slavery, but that their manifestation of marronnage is different.

Why choose Reggae-Dancehall and Rap artists? First of all, the apparently biased choice is determined and justified by the fact that their practicing of a music which is foreign to their native backgrounds is already a path of marronnage they have walked and sung. Secondly, I wanted to observe and encounter their personal trajectories toward the choice of performing music that is alien to their original cultural environment. In fact, it is a study of the socializing processes that have led them into those artistic and sociocultural spheres; singing Rap or Reggae-Dancehall is not only interpreting songs and melodies that belong to a certain repertory, it's also specifically incorporating, embodying, and adopting codes, gestures, mentalities, philosophies and sometimes beliefs. It is about identifying fully with one's innermost feelings and flesh with a culture.

Rap and Dancehall are by essence "marooned" cultures. I mean that these genres are grounded and founded in the soil of revolts and anticonformism. They appeared as counter-cultures in their natural environment—the United States and in Jamaica respectively—when the epicentres of those trends first appeared. Rappers and Reggae singers were chroniclers of marginalized societies: through their lyrics they depicted the severe conditions of living which minorities—whether cultural, religious, or ethnic—endured on certain fringes of societies, the territories which favoured their emergence. From somatic artistic experiences translating the uneasiness and existential angst of the minorities to generalized sociocultural phenomena, on the margins to the cores of the societies, Reggae-Dancehall and Rap have turned into universalized trends. They are been played everywhere and have crossbred with other music and cultures. They became the means of expression of all the oppressed, the poor, the marginalized and those empathetic to impoverishment or injustices.

Interviewing those French-speaking, Creole artists was an investigation into how they had met with these cultures. Because they were born in the Caribbean, and because their respective native islands are close to Jamaica or the United States, it is possible that Reggae music spread progressively through the French islands, but this does not take into account the fact that Guadeloupe and Martinique were colonized by France and were still dominated by its culture and language. Consequently, growing up and living under French culture and then adopting cultural expressions created in English-speaking countries induces various channels of acculturation. What networks have they have integrated? What codes have they absorbed? Why do they identify with the music? I suggest the following answer: the inadequacies between the slaves' descendants and the French culture imposed on them by their former colonizers is tangible in the numerous social upheavals which have completely destroyed the relationships between certain categories of the populations (Melyon-Reinette et al. 2009), becoming politicized during the 1960s. It is evident that there are still whiffs of the colonial period, since it is only two generations since the departmentalization of those colonies in 1946. Those artists, born between the 1970s and 1980s, are natural heirs of those political and social conflicts that remained in the public mindset as rumours or ghosts, palpable in the insular atmospheres. In addition, their African roots, which are not so distant in the previous generations (for instance, Asaliah's mother is second-generation Afro-Guadeloupean, or Tiwony's father is an African artist who emigrated to France), are claimed and bind them to this history even more than the ancient stories, which most people are oblivious to and have been deliberately forgotten.

Through their interviews, we discover that their links to Rap music and Reggae-Dancehall are both inherited from the unrevealed history of slavery, the psychological wound that the black Caribbean man has inherited, and from their lineages. Thus, their sources of inspiration and the leaders who aroused them from this ontological latency are Caribbean, but above all African Americans. Therefore, their trajectories are antipodes to the colonizing cultures and on a triangular scheme: the United States, English-Caribbean/French-Caribbean and Africa. Marronnage is the stance that they have chosen.

Asaliah Gad, Reggae artist (Guadeloupe)

"Spread Righteousness is I mission! Can't get stop by no one! Burn!!!
Workers of Sheitan!!! See them try to put a stick ina mi wheel!
Don't want people to know who open the 7 seals!
Haile Selassie I 1st! To them I reveal!
So they shall know the truth, What is fake from what is real!!!
Even if they try to buy me with millions euros or dollar bills!
In I integrity shall never accept them deal!
Never eat them meal!!!
What I pretend! I do, I defend!
Expand! Holy incantations towards Jah infants!
Inform them to make up the mind! From the tricks of the heathen
Cause! They know how to control our brain!
Disinformation condition & maintain Us!
But no one can't stop the spirit from rising!
Truth! Haffe revolute when injustice proclaim!!!!

What is your definition of marronnage ?

Greetings in thy Holy name Qadamawi Haile Selassie Power of the Trinity!!! Christafari, Selah

I see in this so-called "escape" of our ancestors from the servile colonial lands, a way of "self-preservation" in order to be able to maintain a historical and cultural patrimony by returning to a natural state, to preserve "the integrity of the origins," throughout time, up until today!! Thus, naturally, I would say that I & I recognize itself, because I perceive the "Rastaman!!" The *Neg Kongo*!!

Can you give me some examples of marronnage?

Marronnage is the fact of escaping from the Babylonian mindset because of receiving a "revelation" in the Christ Haile Selassie I—which means "power of the Holy Trinity" and referring theocratically to RAS TAFARI embodied on earth. He is an example for any fervent man.

By simply analyzing His life, we have learnt the true meaning of "intelligent revolution!" The only way of struggling against any kind of oppressions and negativity with the spirit is by affirming our faith through the Nazarite vow, and by succeeding the integration of our own society into the dominant society. Through education in general, but particularly the one which enables the return to the original identity as well as that valuing life which leads to spiritual elevation!!!

That is why I have chosen music as form of expression because it transcends the verb! Reggae is the music closest to this resonance and this way of living: I have always been surrounded by jazz musicians, dancers and painters, since my childhood. My music style is quite eclectic because I am inspired and aspire to write in accordance with the vibration which emanates from my environment!

My history begins in 1992 in my native town, Basse-Terre (Guadeloupe) with the live band Colt Sweat 4 Cold Sweat, with the pioneer artists of the movement of that time. In 1993, I founded the JAHLAWA Foundation Sound-System with old pals where we span vinyl and played dubplates recorded specially, characterized by cultural and conscious themes.

When I turned eighteen years-old, this is my first trip to Jamaica. I recorded my first disc on vinyl, Divine Guidance, in three languages (English, French and Creole) with SIMBA production at Music Works studio. The well-known Linton "Fatt" Marshall is the sound engineer on Wilrock '68, the standard instrumental of Jamaican music history. That was a feature with Jahju who brought me to his island.

Between 1997 and 2002, I lived in Canada. I could participate in different "mixtapes" (Cut Killer, Dj Phonie, Jah Kingdom, Muzik Medicinal, Arawak Sound, Puppa Sound), collaborate with local artists and perform on stage between Montreal, Guadeloupe and Paris! Then I met the Mellow Mood Band in 2003 with whom I would release one of my most emblematic titles, Let Jah Rise, recorded live on *Ina di Mood* compilation with Mounia Sahara, Dan Fyah Beats and many other local artists from the Caribbean diaspora in North America.

In 2004 was the fabulous meeting with "112 Prod," Stéphane Boutros (guitarist) and the collaboration with Dan Gorgon (bassist of Horace Andy, an emblematic figure in 1970s Jamaica) in Paris. I still work with them up until today.

During this period of time, I performed in many sound systems and on dubplates in Swiss, Belgian and French provinces. I settled back in Guadeloupe in 2004. I participated in the BET Jazz Festival in saint-Lucia sided by Saint-Lucian sax player Luther François, well-known for his collaborations with Peter Tosh, Monty Alexander and many others at the international level. In 2005, I travel back to Jamaica where I have the privilege to be invited to perform at the twelve tribes of Israel Headquarters in Kingston for the celebration of the birth of Rastafari! On July 14, 2008 I performed at the Montreal International Reggae Fest with Midnite, Steel Pulse, Warrior King. Then, I founded the acoustic band Balawak whose music is based on Jazz, Soul and traditional with two bassists as its core. I was the revelation of the off-session of the 2008 Gwadloup Festival! I released a two-title album called *Lily'k Anthem*.

Since that time, I worked on other national and international compilations, performed on various European scenes and began to conceptualize my first album.

I am an artist who demonstrates his spirituality through music and particularly Reggae music because of its revolutionary and rebel character. It is one of the best ways to allow the people on the planet, whatever their nation or ethnic group may be. This music enables me to transcend and touch them and it is a benediction for me as well as for my listeners. Music is a therapy and I try to use it wittingly, as a pedagogical vector.

We live in a world characterized with dominant/dominated relationships. And this has always been a problem for me, since my childhood. That's why, before I became a Rastafarian when I was fourteen years-old, I was close to the "Zulu Nation" and "Black Panthers" movements. It is obviousness for me that I chose to follow this path. Because this is the one in which I discovered Truth and Universal love. One love.

My music is synonymous with Universality and Sincerity, a return to the laws of Our Creator which belong to all of us all around the planet, and of unconditional sharing! So I think that I must fit with my saying, practice what I preach, do what I pretend by living it and defending it whatever the obstacles, because this is a perpetual struggle for the elevation of mankind which begins in the young generations.

Carry Beyond by Asaliah

Dem carry us beyond from Mama Ithiopia in the Caribbean!!!

So far from where we belong!!! Dat's how Jah people lose dem tradition! Dem call it Caribbean! Bcoz dem carry beyond all afreekan! From the Motha Land 2 dem dominions! In exile InI was in captivity! Physically but 2day it is mentally!!! Dem try 2 fool we! Thru brainwash downpression! Manipulated people with money! Try 2 push we in this millenium, style & fashion! So we turn workers of iniquity!!!

Ashaman Jahlawa, Reggae-Dancehall artist (Guadeloupe)

"d'abo yo roté nou Ethiopia,
pou méné nou travail en Caraib' la,
apré yo di pou èt lib' fo nou té blan,
REAL "neg marron" en ba bwa pé pa fè semblan " ASHAMAN.

(First they uprooted us from Ethiopia
To bring us in the Caribbean in bondage
After they said you have to be white to be free
REAL "neg marron" in the wood can't pretend)

What is marronnage?

For me marronnage is, symbolically, the slaves escaping from the plantation. From the master's plantation. This is the symbol. In our population, it's also all the alternatives of moving out of the institutions, whether they are spiritual, social or culinary. It is all the ways of evading from what is already set up. It's being off the beaten tracks. For example, I come from a city called Sainte-Rose which is a former sugar cane plantations area. So it is a bastion of slavery and a place where you can see a lot of rum industry plants, a lot of whiffs of the African culture and of the deported niggers. So I live more specifically at Bonne Mère, a place where the scheme is really clear. There are the plants. Around the plants the government workers—formerly *béké*, the white colonizer—now they are black. Those are little residencies. And the more you climb, the poorer are the people. Middle-class and lower-class. This is a clear vision. Everything is centralized around the sugar cane plants. Even today.

Now marronnage means something else, because it is not simply going out of the master's house. This is really emancipating by any means necessary. It can be linguistically speaking. For me, as a Caribbean man, it can be speaking English and being able to communicate with other Caribbean people who are independent, who have lived histories parallel to ours. It's also a form of marronnage. For example, going away from the Church and the religious system which was imposed on us through the christening of the slaves at that time to question it and return to other forms of spiritualities, are marronnage. Discovering again aliments we had forgotten or little gestures or even little beliefs, superstitions inherited from Africa that our ancestors knew and still know. This is also a form of marronnage. So, as for me, it's really within the way of living. Finally, the marronnage is inside everybody. Every human being. Fleeing! From these boundaries, from a territory... to turn to another identity, toward your very identity, the one which is really yours.

Culturally speaking, it is in music. It can be in classical music that we can divert or in the fundamentally maroon cultures. So, often, this is the urban music very close to the people. Over several generations, we can find the ritual and initiatory music like *Gwo Ka* which really dates back from the maroon period (slavery). This is the path of the slave. Those are pure and raw arts, non-accepted by everything that stands at the core of society. Always something rebellious, wild, raw! Always something strong! Often, it is not accepted in its entirety. Often they take the version which is toned down. Never in its natural state. So always the ones to take it in its natural and raw state are the artists performing urban music. They take it in its initiatory way. In its full shape which brings all the substance. This is the case of *Gwo Ka* which was to be encountered in the wood, in the countryside and now at the core of the city of Pointe-à-Pitre on Sundays. It was played in distant areas instead, far from the cities. Those people had only that so they would cultivate it. For example, in Sainte-Rose, there is the *Léwòz*. Even though you are not fond of *Léwòz*, you hear the *dékatman* from your home. Little by little, this is something that worms into you. Progressively, you are involved in it, and you go to a

Léwòz and you discover something very special. It's initiation. This is a complete art. But *Gwo Ka* is also turned toward the future. That's why even in the new urban music—like Hip Hop or Reggae-Dancehall, and many other modern arts like R 'n' B—can often be found rhythms, topics or philosophies, dances, gestures or roughly speaking manners inspired from that marooned music ...

So, for me there is *Gwo Ka*, Gwada Hip Hop—there a lot of activists who have created that and made an art of it—and then Reggae-Dancehall which has acquired authenticity in Guadeloupe, compared with *Gwo Ka*, our history, rebellions ... and thus, for me marronnage is like waves. Regarding music. Regarding emotion ... There are emersions, and then it calms down, sometimes ... often, when the island is ill, the spirit comes out. Through music, culture, strikes, demonstrations, through everything! There emersions now and then. In the ancient times, it was *Gwo Ka* which was the emersion. Then, it was mostly associated with concrete actions, social or political. It was rather in the thinking of the 1970s to 1980s. In the 1990s, there were new elements. In a country surrounded by water and where people speak French, we heard about Martin Luther King, about Malcolm X, it was fashionable. A whole part of the young generation re-used those new ingredients, but they were again people concerned with marronnage. They helped to enrich our feeling of being maroons. They had lived their own marronnage quite at the same time as we did. So, it appeared in Hip Hop. Plus, in the music of people who had dropped school very early, people living in the ghettos or people who had least financial means, but who had many ideas, talent, and intelligence. They had found an alternative into music, either in Hip Hop, or in *Gwo Ka*, or else in painting! Even by creating arts sometimes! By creating new marooned resources. I think of Gérard Lockel in *Gwo Ka* for instance. In Hip Hop as well, there are people who are really particular. I think about *Kako*. Those are really unique trends! This music or this revolution which were really specific to their feelings were their schools! So those were human forces which, once they manage to federate the whole population it was when art begins to be influential enough, strong enough, visible enough, or when the arguments of a strike become significant enough for a great number of people, they embrace the cause as well ... so marronnage is made of waves, it swells and falls again! Like the sea. It's alive. It's there ... For me, this something which is like an effusion, vapour, a spirit there in the wood and which sometimes takes possession of the people and leaves as suddenly. Depending on those people's interests in those beaten tracks ... or those tracks possess them ... and often, the uneasiness of this people rises through confrontations with authorities. It can be school, this authority that upset their lives. It can be the police on the streets or in the ghettos. It can be the institutions, the judges, the lawyers. When you work it can be your boss …

Why is it authority that finally triggers marronnage?

Because, us, being raised in a society resulting from slavery, we escape from an injustice. And then, we have a new state which could be seen as justice and fairness. But it remains unfair to us. There is still uneasiness. It's progressive. So, we came out from unfair circumstances, but there still exist some unfair prejudices felt by the people. They don't always have the right words to express or synthesize those ideas. So, once they have protagonists who can synthesize them or present them to those Authorities, they become, not opponents, but rather communicants. They are shown what goes really wrong. It is not enough to claim all and everything. It is about showing the very profound feeling of the people and to communicate it to the people who can do something. To be able to get emancipated. To be able to get clothes at one's size, not being too tight or tied. To be free and men of integrity. Well, the authorities are the ones which create the rebellions, but we address them to find solutions. So we can find that in everything we do. There is an authority. This is an everlasting pattern that we have always known. And it is still the pattern that we experience. And sometimes even when it's not there, we create this pattern. Dependency. Sometimes it's hard to overcome the pattern. But as long as it is in force, we have reasons to feel it all around. This is what happens in that music which claims and proclaims in any way possible. And which also bring alternatives. And this is when intelligence appears with understanding of other things, the creation of new arts, of new thought …

What inspired you to choose Reggae-Dancehall?
What paths did you walk?

In fact, as long as I have learnt how to form letters, as long as I can write, I have always written poetry. I have never stopped in fact. To my mother. To the girls. I have always written lines, poems. This is really vital for me. When I turned approximately nine years-old, by hearing of Malcolm X—in fact the tee-shirts with his face on them were fashionable—Mandela, Magic Johnson, Michael Jordan; there was an emergence of black people. We saw other black people. But those were powerful and well-known. So we got interested. And Rap arrived at the same time. So there were the Nèg Ki Pa Ka Fè La Fèt. They had tracks on the airwaves. We were fond of them. There were artists like Tonton David from France. Snap's "I Got the Power!" All those things which were trendy. There was dance as well. The Zulu Nation. The gangs. It was really trendy in the streets as well as in schools. In the books. We were trying to get closer to those movements. So we began to dance and to do beatboxing. And to do freestyles! We did that at school. Outside of school. We were like eleven years-old. So quite early. We did our music. Our little maroon art. After, when we ended middle school, I met other brothers ... including a cousin of mine. My brother as well. We involved more in Reggae music, from Hip Hop to Dancehall, we created more and more. We had more intelligence, understanding and receptivity of Caribbean music, Jamaica, even of France. We really structured our music. Rehearsals on Saturdays, two pm. We tried to do sound systems. And then, there was also a certain period when more Rastafarians arrived. There were already Rastafarians in Guadeloupe, but those arriving had more media coverage on TV. That was *la Famille Jah*. They lived in more severe circumstances. They were with musicians. There was a movement. They were on TV so it created controversies around them. So at that time, we had more interest in them, but also more questions. So a first wave of dreadlocked people. It was fashionable also. Sometimes it was Afrocentricity, and sometimes it was for fashion ... to be a real man, on the streets, a bad man, you had to be dreadlocked. And there were also Rastafarians who would see that in a sacred way, regarding things in the Bible, the Nazarite vow, and so on ...

At that time, there were compilations, and a lot of sound systems. We were involved in that movement. It was our movement. We appropriated something which was ours. We did flyers, we called artists, we called a selector ... we were looking for our sonority. Sometimes we had to go and see the institutions to do our marooned stuff!! But, otherwise, we would do it in some friends' homes. It was about resourcefulness or smartness. It enabled us to structure our music more. To do things. To have things. So I was around fifteen to sixteen years-old. Then, when I began to travel I noticed that it was international! What we believed was so ours was occurring all over the world. And that in France, it existed already in a more developed way! So, I really understood that it was a worldwide discipline. With the same codes almost everywhere: sound systems, dancehalls, and so on ... After graduating, I left Guadeloupe and settled in Canada, and there it was really something universal, that there were Caribbeans all over the world, and that this was their way of living. We had discovered that, but them, they were born in it. The movement developed and increased in our country as well. It got structured and organized. Now, in Guadeloupe, I would say that there are less sound systems like those. But those sound systems really fed everything that happens now. The first school, the first harvest or the first seed. So this all that which get us closer to the marooned arts. Now, I am a Rastafarian. So all those little things made a Rastafarian of me. In my Caribbean sphere, this marronnage led me to identify with Africa.

My spirituality really developed with my music. I was really tied to spirituality through Christianity. I was a Christian. I was more in the Roman and Apostolic church. But through music, I discovered spirituality again. I discovered black history. It's really like a school. *Gwo Ka*, Hip Hop and Dancehall are the very schools of the ghetto. The children who don't go to school can learn the essential knowledge: men, actions, references, everything concrete for our future right away. Nothing that flies away or fills heads uselessly. A lot of ideas, reflections, that can be put in action right away, which impact on us, change us, ourselves or help us to change things around … Definitely, this is what brought me closer to marooned music. This is the idea of being involved in that, of being born where I was born, of seeing that, *Gwo Ka*, Hip Hop, Reggae, of meeting Rastafarians, Africans and black diasporas in the world … I saw that we were not alone! That it was not a matter of islands but a matter of empire, of continents, of the world itself! So this music, this philosophy, this feeling were strengthened. The bark is becoming thicker.

What do you express in your music?
What are the topics you sing about?

My topics? It's life. In all its forms. I think that music nourishes the soul. So, everything that can nourish the soul, the spirit, nourishes everything. So, everything that can feed a man, I try to put it in my music. So it's about thinking, spirituality, rebellion, struggles, work, values, virtue. Sometimes it is about abstractions. But they can become tangible through music with metaphors, actions that put forces in movement. And then, lots of praises because I believe in God. I talk about the unity of the peoples in the world, their cohesion, their maintaining. I wish them to be in welfare. But I think of my own people first. I have done two mixtapes whereof I talk about revolution a lot. That very rebellious feeling which helped us to liberate. And as soon as there is an emersion, a good wave, we understand that it is inside of ourselves. So the artists come to awake and arouse this kind of feeling. Music is feelings through words and chords. I talk about love also those days, because it's life too. One of the most beautiful forms of life. It is something that can lead us to elevation.

Otherwise, I evoke all the sufferings in the world. Mothers suffering, ghettos, youths dying, politics, world conspiracy. That is intangible as well ...

You have lived in Canada, in the West Indies, in France. What place did your music have in those regions? Were they similar? Did those contexts favour its emergence?

Finally, the context gives more or less momentum to our sayings. That's to say that out of a specific context, what we say can seem extreme, or inappropriate. When we get in touch with other ways of thinking, other cultures, we speak different languages, we pray to different Gods, and we have different philosophies. But it is really Guadeloupe—at least for me, the French West Indies or the Caribbean for us, Africa for others—which gives the dimension of truth to our music, to our arts. Afterwards, it intensifies in the world. Foreign people perceive what we are even better than ourselves. When we perform in Canada, the people see who we really are. Even though we sing in Creole, they ask questions. They travel. They understand by feeling the music. They see in it something ancestral, more than our own people. Those dimensions are amplified abroad. I went to Belgium where I met many Congolese. And we are both Guadeloupeans and Congolese, *Neg Kongo*, so there is this direct link. Pure Congo people can be found in our island. When we speak Creole and Lingala we find some similarities. So this is how we see that Africa is far, but it can be found in our traditions, in little gestures and so on. We have our own Africanity. When we encounter altogether in Belgium we encounter also our African dimensions. We are also like those Africans who have lived in France for eight, ten, twelve years. But they remain Africans. Those similarities reinforce our Africanity. Those Arlequin-like patchworked clothes are fine. Crossbreeding or mixing is fine. The "Melting Pot." It's fine. But all this is done with pure ingredients! It's like cooking. Pure coriander! Yam! Dachine! We have to find out the essence in things again! In order to do a better dish, a better mixing. You have to know the ingredients. You have to know where they come from, where they were planted. You have to know it all! So this is the task we have to achieve: find out the right ingredients of the recipe. Me, I have Indian origins as well, there is also Indian blood in Guadeloupe, in the history of slavery, in the triangular trade. Regarding injustice, I have chosen my side, even though, I have a little of everything in my genome. But I try to find out the right ingredients. The real component of history. Know what stands for what. What brought me there. And my future ... even with regards to this discovery, it can be at the people level, or worldwide. Every people needs to know its origins and history. Everyone needs to know as well.

What about women in Reggae-Dancehall?

Well, I take my hat off to them. Because they are activists, those I know at least, whether they are in Hip Hop or Reggae Dancehall. And often, they play the role of mothers. They often have many things to do. Some people would say that they are not many of them around the planet, maybe a smaller proportion than men. They are real forces. Most of them are very active. All those I know are real activists. They take things bodily. They are role models for other women and for me. They could be simply mothers, professionals, but they want more. It's heavy but they are well. I think that they are like some of the women who struggled during slavery. Generally, they are female Maroons. Often they have a strong artistic sensibility. They are creation. What women are by essence. But there is something specific to women in art in general. In our art particularly. Not Reggae itself. But Dancehall is masculine. We come from the Caribbean. Everyone knows it is a milieu of cocks. Mores are changing. In Reggae, it is more structured in the Alpha and Omega pattern. Equity between men and women as we were taught by His Imperial Majesty. And in the Rastafarian Empire, the Nation, in the house, the woman has a very important role. The man as well. Their tasks are complementary.

There is music like *Gwo Ka* wherein people don't accept white people learning to beat the traditional drums, because this is something they want to maintain as exclusively theirs. Do you think Reggae music is the same? Is there another logic which tends toward universality or a reconquering of their roots?

It's like any other arts. In the end, Reggae is universal. It comes from emotions and feelings which are universal, which were circulated by Bob Marley who was half-white, half-black. He talked about Africa where there are essentially black people, and some whites also. So, the white people who do Reggae, I think that they have caught all the aspects—not all of them! But those who have really caught the dimension of Reggae, they have taken it in its entirety. So, there is the spiritual, social aspect. Even if they live in Russia, Germany or Slovenia, it is really the way of living, in their thinking, in the way they feed themselves of everything, in

Dancehall as well as in Reggae. It is an attitude. That's why there are Chinese, Blacks, Arabians, and so on in Reggae. Because it defends universal causes.

Nèg Lyrical, Hip Hop Kreyol Rap (Martinique)

La traite l habitation l esclave et le maitre !
la traite l habitation l esclave et le maitre !
le traite l'être humain traité comme une bête
la traite le maitre qui peut tout se permettre
la délation des traitres
le marronnage qui s entête.

[The Trade, the plantation, the slave, and the master!
The Trade, the plantation, the slave and the master!
The traitor, the human treated like a beast
The traitor, the master who can do anything
The delation of traitors
And marronnage which persists.]

What is marronnage for you?

For me marronnage is the phenomenon of the slave fleeing the master's plantation. The slave fled to go into the Zion, in the mountains, to live a life of freedom instead of living in bondage. It was in the frame of slavery, with a master, a plantation, slaves, and they left to have a more difficult life materially but were at least free.

Do you think that marronnage is always present in our societies today?

Well yes, because the term "marronnage" has become, *in extenso*, representative of escape. Maybe, it can also be considered as contrary to "slavery," finally. So, given that today there are still other forms of slavery, marronnage is still present to counterbalance it, because slavery is not only material or physical. It can be social, economic, or cultural. There so many chains to break, in fact. So …

Is that a word often used in Martinique?

No. No … frankly not. There are still many people who ask me the question, by discovering the title of my last album. And often in the interviews, I am asked the meaning of marronnage. If you say *Nèg Mawon*, they may understand. But marronnage, they won't get the meaning. And this is an opportunity to realize that it was a global phenomenon, and not some single cases, now and then.

Then why did you choose this term?

This is because of the orientation I wanted to take, musically speaking. There were a lot of conscious tracks on this album, lots of tracks dealing with history. It is from this perspective that I wanted to explain the idea of marronnage. In fact, the album is created a scenario, that's to say that the tracks are punctuated by interludes. Between each track, there are kind of scenes which are not instrumentalized or which tell the story of a slave who escaped from the plantation and who, all along the episodes, meets another slave who brings him to other slaves hidden in the mountain. And at the end of the album, he decides to gather and to run down to Saint-Pierre on May 22, 1848 in order to invade the plantations of the colonizer. So, in fact, this is a scenario inspired by real historical facts which have occurred in Martinique. And then the story ends by the fact that they are freed. They have caught their freedom, but they always work for the master, and for basic salaries, and they don't own their lands. So, I open a perspective on the future and the conclusion of their conversation is that they must keep on struggling.

Is your album a way of passing a message over to the audience?

Yes ... not necessarily a message. It is about passing information over to the audience, because most tracks are based on facts. There are certain tracks in which I hardly give my opinion. I expose facts, date by date, as in "a Traite," in which I do a chronological exposé of events around the history of slavery. Like in "Embargo," in which I tell the story of Haiti from Toussaint Louverture to the earthquake. Another track, "Rastafari," is the biography of Haile Selassie, for which I had to do research to match historical facts and my rhymes. In other tracks I give my opinion. Like "Pasé a Prézan" in which the past is present and it results in questioning the maintaining of marronnage. I say that the past influences what we live in the present, and the best medicine to cure all the neurosis resulting from the past is education. This is from this perspective that I did my album: messages; others would say "information." Some would call it "conscious rap" or "activist rap." People qualify it differently, as they feel it. This is the process of informing through Rap which investigates.

You make Rap music. Not so much Dancehall?

There is a little bit of Dancehall. As I have West Indian origins and have contacts with people of the Rastafarian movement and Reggae artists in the studios. I wanted to sing as well. This is a good way to make "listenable" albums. Because in listening to a one-hour Rap album there must be different colours, different tastes, and this is what can be found in the sung parts which differ from the rap parts.

Music is a passion that arrived very early for me, around fifteen or maybe even fourteen years-old. My first passion was writing. I Rapped in French, and then, with people I had met in middle school, I founded the crew Nègkipakafèlafèt. Those meetings were an emulation. We were fond of the same music, had the same passion. Through this passion, we created a concept of Kréyòl Rap. One day, together, we have had an idea of rapping like we talked, in Creole, and those were our first experiences. We began to sing about things happening on the island, about the local reality. This was the very beginning of Kréyòl Rap. It was around the 1990s. The first scene I did was the first part of Kali's concert. My first recording experience was on Don Miguel's compilation with the track "Discipline." Then I also recorded on Don Miguel's second compilation, the track "Pi ta, Pi tris." And then, we went into self-production. We enlarged our horizons. We bought machines to compose instrumentals. A friend of ours had video material and he went into music video realization. We founded an association which was really active at that time, which organized stages at the Centre Frantz Fanon in Martinique. We had greater possibilities and it ended in my first album in 1996 and that of the Nègkipakafèlafèt in 1998. In fact, we were pioneers among the French West Indian crews. Many people recognized that we are really precursors of Kréyòl Rap and recognize that the first time they heard people rapping in Creole, it was the Nègkipakafèlafèt. And then in the 2000s I left Martinique to develop my music business. At that time, I recorded *De A à Z*, and now the freshly-released *Marronnage*.

Why did you choose Rap? What was it about your environment that encourage this choice?

Frankly, what attracted me was the fact that we could have a rather thick discourse in a single track. With pure singing, the flow is less compact. You say tell less. Rap is a good way to have speech with a certain easiness in the talking with music. Contrary to singing, in which syllables are prolonged and the cadence is slower, Rap's cadence is fast and you can really pass more ideas over to the listeners. For someone who has much to say, many opinions to share, messages to transmit, this is a tool, if well used, can be very efficient. So this is what I noticed. By listening to the first Rap crews of that time which were, contrary to today's rap, in a conscious tradition of awareness. I remember the first crews like XClan or Jungle Brothers who bore African necklaces and clothes. They were right in the thick of Afrocentricity and valued Malcolm X's and Fanon's writings. You also had Public Enemy and others … they are the people who inspired me to make Rap music because I noticed, through their works, that there was a political aspect in music.

Why did the Afrocentrist character of this music attract you at that time? What exhorted you to tend toward this movement?

This is the identity quest. Because at that time, in the islands of Zouk, there was a certain tradition that the youths didn't like. We identified more with something more … not aggressive, but rather something more spontaneous, more alive. We recognized ourselves in street life, in the rough reality of what we lived daily in this music, more than anywhere else. So it was really the best way to express frustrations, anger, but also joy. And living in Martinique, in an island, we say overseas department but it is a colony for me. As a youth I had things to say with regards to that reality. I was not interested in getting involved in a political party given that we had a negative image of politicians. And many youths who began Rap with me were in the same mindset. So, we found a way to express our opinions outside of the classical fields.

What do you think of Aimé Césaire, as he was a politician, at least during a certain period of time?

Césaire has different faces. There is the politician and the writer. This is the same person. Anyway, the writer left his mark on the world. And this is pride, except for the Martiniquans, for the West Indian community. He was the precursor of concepts like "negritude," so we had to read his books. It was an obligation to read Cheick Anta Diop, *Nations Nègres et Cultures*, Césaire's *Cahier d'un Retour au pays natal*, or Fanon's *Peaux Noires, Masques Blancs*. All those books were our bedside reading since we were involved in a movement valuing black culture through Rap music.

Not all the youths were in this mood of valuing black culture and thinking!?

It was a reaction to artists like Boogie Flaha or Nèg Madnick, at the time of "Les nouveaux griots." In the end most people were inspired more by Mona than by *La Compagnie Créole*. This is an attitude in which they recognized themselves. For us, Mona was somewhat a rapper. Because we felt his determination, we heard the rage in his voice. We felt the nigger in his singing, and this was rural Martinique and opening up the world all at once. Because Mona liked Blues as well, he also had some songs in this style. In fact, like the American rappers of that time, we picked up elements everywhere in our popular culture to reuse it within our discourse and music.

Did traditional music have a place among your sources of inspiration? You talked about Mona, so what about *Bèlè*, in the musical pantheon of your generation?

It's true. *Bèlè* is the musical vibration. In Guadeloupe, there is Exxòs who created the *Kako* trend. In Martinique, we have Boogie Flaha who developed that. He not only dances *Bèlè*, but also records albums with *Bèlè* singers. You have Nèg Madnik who works in that sense as well. We also participated in the *Bèlè* Boom Bap project in which he invited Max Rancé, Ti Raoul, Gertrude Seinin and many other ancients of Martinique traditional singing, *Biguine* as well as *Bèlè*. Those were collaborations with us, the Creole rappers. So, it resulted in tracks such as "Mizik Sé Travay Ou" or "Bèlè Boom Bap," and so on. It was in the early 2000s. If I I'm not mistaken it was in 2001 or 2002 ... Me, I follow another perspective. Mine is more eclectic. Because on my tracks there is *ti bwa/tanbou* such as the first track of the album *Marronnage*. You also find other sounds, a little bit more American.

Who inspires you among the African American artists?

I must admit that the last few years, and maybe this is a paradox because I make Rap, but I've listened to less and less Rap music. I found was really fed up with most of today's rappers. I could not identify with their discourses. I recognize myself into the music, because musically speaking, it is still precise and efficient. There is still a quest for the right music. I am always impressed by the productions and the flows; the rappers sing well. Regarding the form, it is always perfectly done. I even find that Rap is progressing. We have evolved from sampling other artists music to creating our own. Before we would have taken James Brown's samples, and so on.

Now, the trend is that everybody composes on the keyboard. This is a music which has evolved in the form, but I find that it has severely deteriorated regarding the themes. What first attracted me at the beginning doesn't exist in 2011. I'm exaggerating when I say that it doesn't exist anymore, but this is not what is advertised through the media, so in people's minds, this is real rap. They have Lil' Wayne or 50 Cent in mind, whereas Rap is not that at all; at the beginning this was not the process. This is obviously trade. We are prejudiced, but we have to annihilate prejudices. People who know some music know that there are some rappers who do this work. And then, anyway, in the French and the West Indian Creole spheres, we have, nevertheless, kept a tradition of consciousness. Now, Rap says more things in France and the West Indies than in the United States.

So, my inspirations are varied. I listen to Soul, Erykah Badu's music, Jill Scott. Otherwise, I like Haitian *konpa*. I appreciate some French Rap tracks and Kréyòl Rap. My collection is eclectic. I pick up inspiration almost everywhere. I like World music, Indian music as well. Regarding music, we can tell that there is a form of marronnage because to be able to express myself in music, as I wanted, I couldn't work with big music producers. Today, they don't invest money in projects like that. They follow the formats chosen by the radio stations. They want lightness. They don't want engaged music. And this is not the vocation of my Rap.

So I forcibly chose self-production: learning to release an album by myself, contacting music producers, pressing CDs and distributing them to the shops myself. I learnt by myself. I am a kind of self-made man. At the beginning, I complained about it because I found out that there were not enough people to work with me. But today, I am happy because I realized that this is exactly what permitted me to release albums regularly.

Is there a form of spiritual or cultural marronnage in your music? What marronnage is your music composed of? If there is marronnage, what are you trying to flee? Which model? Which cultural form?

I want to flee from nonsensical music. For me music is an instrument. Music is total, in both form and themes. So, if a kind of music is nonsense, it's not good at all. We can content ourselves with that. Whereas music is a means of passing something over, and there it finds its whole nobility. You use your talent to serve a cause in fact. This gesture is beautiful.

Tiwony, Reggae-Dancehall artists (Guadeloupe)

What is marronnage for you?

For me, marronnage is insubordination to oppression, and in this precise case, slavery. Marronnage is all the people who can escape from colonial bondage, from slavery who, by fleeing to Zion to live in freedom, to live with what they could find. Today, there are some maroon communities in French Guyana or Jamaica.

How did you encounter Reggae-Dancehall?
How did you get into it? What inspired you?

When I was young, we listened to several musical trends, and there was this Reggae movement that we called local Reggae or Ragga. It was national too, because at that time there were Daddy Harry, Don Miguel, Tonton David, Metal Sound and McJanik and all those artists. We were attracted to it, we were a group of friends and brothers who followed this trend. So, we began first with this school of Hip Hop and ended up in this movement since we only knew international music, even though we understood nothing, whether it was Shabba Ranks and many others. It became more significant for us. So we began to seek the origins of the messages. Because it was a way of understanding the politics around us or the system in which we lived, because we were young. We perceived certain things, but what surrounded us was totally unknown. Through those songs we saw that we come from a line of people that have suffered greatly, and we didn't want to suffer any longer. All of this entered into our little world in Guadeloupe, where we lived our lives at our daddy's, at our mummy's without really understanding what was happening on the island. So we tried to deepen the reflection farther. We met brothers who told us about Rastafarianism and who began to explain its origins, the historical movement behind it. From there, we have learnt about the great black men and we saw that it was a humanist movement. We learnt about Malcolm X, Steve Biko, Marcus Garvey, Bob Marley. We understood Bob Marley more in his spiritual dimension, more as a philosophical leader, in addition to the musical dimension that he used as a tool. We began to read and educate ourselves. When we were younger than that, we were wandering about the streets but we didn't have the impulse to read like that, unfortunately. It was school of the ghetto, of the street. So it exhorted us to read more, to be able to talk about serious things in our songs since we had already begun to freestyle a little bit down our blocks, in the projects, to express what was in our heads. We wanted to channel our thoughts, you see, with tools and well-founded information and knowledge. So we read about those great men in order to take a stance within our social circumstances, regarding the experiences they had lived, regarding the battles they had fought. We wanted to understand who we were. We were told that those great men and women sacrificed themselves for our freedom. This was such a strong concept that we had to keep on studying, to find out what sacrifices they made.

Today, we have the impression that everything is alright, but now bondage is on the mental level. The struggle continues. At that moment, I decided to embrace the musical concept of Reggae. I grew up within the Akiyo movement. I was in the group. I played drums. I was also influenced by *Gwo Ka*. I have people in my family who were UPLG members and part of the nationalist movement as well. I found that all that was converging in a movement of liberation of the people. So, we would say, because we wanted to bring something a wider level to this movement, that we had to create something too. So, we were looked at as aliens, because as long as people heard those messages in English it was far from them. It was a little more toned down in French, with Tonton David and all those who had big producers backing them. We had to fight to show that this was not commercial for us, it was not about shining brightly or being stars or making money. We wanted to feel good thanks to our music, to express things that were rotting and becoming gangrenous and corrupt, to resolve a crisis with our own words. And the more we studied, the more we were able to talk about those things, thanks to our literary experiences and the various travels we have done, and meetings with different people. I realized that this is really what I felt when I had the first spark, when I discovered I wanted to do Reggae music. I really feel today I haven't been mistaken. Not only because of the emulation around me, but also because of the people listening. Today I really feel an osmosis with what I wanted to be and my vision of Reggae. Because today, I have always thought that strong words must be spoken as well as acted on. The problem is that we are a "Saint-Thomas" kind of people; we need to see to believe. If you don't show palpable actions, they won't believe … You talk about Africa, but this is a redundant topic in Reggae music. You talk about repatriation, unity, live, peace, justice … all those big words, those social movements and so on. We all talk about the same things, but there are no actions behind it. So the people can't subscribe to the movement. There are some small actions, but, well … it's superficial. Today, I realize that my music is considered with regards to the fact that there are now actions which can illustrate my lyrics, and those are examples we have seen in our big brothers like Bob Marley, who really worked on the fields. He sang "Zimbabwe," and he went over there. He sang "Africa Unite," and he went there and created movements; he committed personally, materially. Those are significative examples for me which show that this music is not only a music, like others, because in Reggae there is something of all the other music (you can find some classical music, some traditional *Gwo Ka*, some R'n'B, some Soul). This is the force of Reggae. A kind of force, at the music level, that federates all the other kinds of music; but even at the spiritual level it is able to unites all the people in the world. I think that this music should have more media coverage, because unfortunately we don't understand why there are so many messages exhorting people to destruction or self-destruction, to debauchery. There should be a balance, at least for the people to make a choice. We think that this is hard, but the fruit of this work is not material. We feel much more gratified with this than with millions of Euros. Because being able to travel, to meet people and sing with them, to go in the ghettos and live with the people whom I address my music to, to see that you are accepted with much love; that is real wealth. This is the force of Reggae. It speaks to all social classes and without distinction of race. For me, regarding my vision of life, this is why Reggae called me.

Concerning your music, what are the topics you develop? Is there a form of marronnage in your music?

Obviously, there is marronnage in the way I express myself and in the way I develop my music. I am an independent. We have our own label. That's to say that there is nobody to tell me what to sing or what not to sing. This is a form of marronnage, in the sense and the structure which enables us to diffuse our works as we want to, without censorship, without wondering if it would be problematic. Because we try to circulate a universal message, there should not be censorship anyway. We often talk about Selassie I. So people would tell you "well, try not to talk about Selassie I." So it already creates a frontier. They already want to put you in jail. That's why lots of youths ask me "how long have you been there? You have already done this and that. How come you never signed with a major label?" Well, this is because of all of that. And I do well, because I managed to mix with the greatest artists of the world and, thank you Lord, I don't feel ridiculous with our little indie label and finances. Because the human means are so unlimited, so that we manage to be in some places, if we had to calculate and think with official majors, we would have never seen. This is marronnage: it is telling yourself that we do things with the strength God gave us and not leaving people to shut us down into some kind of virtual jail. Before we had chains on our ankles, now they are in our heads. For me it is harder to solve. So I sing about what is left unsaid, what is not highlighted, what they have taught us at school. I often illustrate my songs with sayings which are guidelines for mankind, for human thinking, in terms of evolution and emancipation. At last, I speak about Africa under all its forms, my being bound to it, my inner vision.

See how we can do things together. Let's really do things. Let's do something concrete! I take a stance in my songs. I am some kind of chronicler, but without censorship.

Are there artists who inspired you?
What about circumstances, or events?

Of course, there are artists who inspire me, all the time, artists who are more or less experienced than I am. Sometimes, it can just be a song. It is quite global. There are some great names: obviously Bob, incontrovertible. Peter Tosh, Jacob Miller. The great names of Reggae that I have known lately, but progressively as I learnt through life experiences, I began to better understand their lyrics. There I really caught the dimension of the messages, of their commitment. Also, closer to us, Kassav, Akiyo, Jean-Michel Rotin. Various influences, you see. Artists like Soft. I try to get inspired by everything that surrounds me, because it is a great family. Hip Hop artists as well. The Wu Tang Klan inspired me as well because they are very spiritual behind the violence of their music. It's really a two-faced phenomenon, because if you listen well, between the lines, there is spirituality. Public Enemy as well and many others …

What is a crew? What is a dancehall? The space
where your music is heard? Is it welcomed in Guadeloupe
and Martinique?

Roughly speaking, yes. There are specificities regarding the characteristics of the islands. Martinique has its own reality, as does Guadeloupe. But, fundamentally we are brothers and sisters regarding Reggae music because we were inspired by the Martiniquan scene. The first big official Reggae projects to be covered by the media, except for Freedom Sound that we organized with MB et Dalton, were from Martinique. So with people like Don Miguel, Daddy Harry, Ruffneg there was a machine behind them. We were inspired by them. We observed one another a lot. I have learnt a lot on sound systems with brothers like GuilMC, Jah Mike, Straika. Brothers like Brother Jimmy, at that time we still used cassettes, were listened to. We listened to their cassettes in the sound systems. Our first sound system really resulted from the influence of those sound systems. That's why we called it Influence Sound. It was really the place where Reggae-Dancehall was performed. This is just labelling. It can be in a house, in a club, in a stadium, in the ghetto. I mean, as long as there are two turntables, CD or vinyl mixing desks, microphones, and a Master of Ceremony (emcee) who presents and livens it up, who explains the instrumentals, and then one or two artists, or more, who come and sing their titles, or improve on the instrumentals, then that is a sound system. And this happens all the more in Martinique as in Guadeloupe, in metropolitan France, in Jamaica, as in any other country where Reggae is really active. Then there are various forms. Sometimes it's more impersonal or in clubbing atmospheres. Plus, there are two formulas: the first is semi-live, with a Disc-Jokey (called a "selecta" in Reggae) who spins the instrumentals for the artist to sing over. In the second formula, there are musicians too, with keyboards, drums, instrumentalists. I do both. The force of Reggae stands in the fact that it can be exported to all milieus.

Dancehall is found in Guadeloupe and in Metropolitan France?

What happens is that Reggae is a black culture that comes from the black ghettos of Jamaica and which has circulated everywhere afterwards. So, the strangers—because there are not only white people who do Reggae, there are Japanese people, Russians—embrace this culture. They adapt to the culture. But they present and live it up as black people do. They do sound systems with them, in the same spirit. That's to say that they are already committed in the culture, it's a family. As Bob Marley sang, "One Love." This idea is present in Reggae music. We have artists such as Gentleman, who is German-born, but who performs internationally. He is accepted by Jamaicans and has worked with Sizzla, Capleton, Junior Kelly, with other big artists and great names of Reggae music. Same for Alborosie, who is Italian and who evolves in the milieu. But they all speak Reggae language. They come with the codes of the ghetto and they are accepted as such. Because it's "one heart." History says that a minority of people considered us evil, as animals. But I today, mentalities have changed. Bob Marley was able, through his message, to lead people to question their beliefs, to increase the public awareness of the sense of Reggae all over the world, by saying that we are ONE. One people. And this was his message to eliminate all the racist and denigrating clichés discriminating against one race or another. Because we are not the only ones to have suffered atrocities. Today, what is weird is that the white brothers seem to have grown up in the ghetto. In their attitude, their talking, their gestures, the way they dress. They are really involved. They are connoisseurs of Reggae music. Sometimes they even know the music better than us or the Jamaicans. Sometimes, we meet in the ghetto in Jamaica together. The guys are welcomed and appreciated. Protected. But in the spirit of Reggae, when we are in Reggae spheres, in what we call *passa passa* (a kind of outdoor live show), you see all kinds of people! Chinese, Japanese, Canadians, and so on. Everybody enjoys it.

What about women in Reggae?

Yes, there are some. Unfortunately, there are few. In Guadeloupe, there are some as well. The first time I took the microphone it was at Sista Tchad's birthday, who is one of the big sisters of the movement. She was an inspiration for me, with regards to her attitude and determination. There are Sista Slaid, Sweetie, Flyah, Maiky Jah from Réunion, Sista Jahan. On the international scene, there was Patra. At the cultural level, Lady G, Queen Ifrica, Queen Omegah. There is Allen. Because in Reggae, there are variants. There is the "lover" style, the "entertainment" style, and also the "cultural" style. Inside those items, there are many artists who perform. It's a big family. There are some women!

Is the Rastafarian faith communicated through music?

Rastafari is life. In the sense that by defining the word etymologically: *Ras* means "chief," *Tafari* means "creator." We are all the children of the Creator. Those are labels which are of the origins. So, people often tend to mystify when they hear this word. They see a cast in Rastafari. In Selassie I, they see a man. But if you seek inside, deeper, it's the same as "the Creator" in the divine sense. But in Guesde, which is one of the first languages in which the Bible was written, it means "chief creator" which is the label for God. "Haile Selassie" means "power of the Holy Trinity." The same Father, Son and Holy Spirit that people name whether they are protestant, catholic, or else … so for me, that is Rastafari. It's celebrating creation. Paying homage to creation. Compose life with the other elements of creation. Whether they are human, animals … well all the land and heavenly beings. This is a new name for God. An ancient name which resurfaces. That God children have found out again. It is a kind of spiritual quest. We recognize ourselves into it. It livens and invigorates our daily lives. This is a visible force. An inner force. Omniscience. We call it as we want: divinity, providence, Rastafari, Allah, Krishna, Buddha. Those are the same principles but in different circumstances, different frames … this is a matter of gratitude, identity, personal choices … religion is a personal affair, the nation is everybody's. All fervent believers can sit at a table together and work for the nation. When we see all those religious wars, we know that religion doesn't say that. This is also the struggle of Rastafari.

Returning to simple foundations. No dogmas. No doctrines. Well, except the dogma and doctrine of universality. Federating dogma founded on original, historical, well-founded and palpable bases.

Conclusions

Through those interviews, the idea of marronnage is clearly exposed as a counter-culture developed through various philosophical, religious and cultural spheres and a stance inside and in opposition to societies they seem to reject. The four of them, born in the French Caribbean islands of Guadeloupe and Martinique, whose societies were stamped by colonization, have operated a backlash movement toward an original and African rooted culture. Rastafarianism seems to be one of the shelters in which those Creole-speaking artists take refuge in, against postcolonial stigmas and the so-called neo-colonial influence. In fact, they find a refuge not because they feel weak in those societies, but rather underestimated by their environments, from the spiritual, cultural and social invasion of the French universal model. France had definitely developed a project of civilizing and assimilating the populations it colonized. In Guadeloupe and Martinique, the so-called *Neg Mawon* spirit, the spirit of the maroon, is the mentality which has emerged from the germ of revolt which was seeded in the slaves' hearts. It has really flourished in the Caribbean. Here, those young people have recognized their African roots, since there are close links. It is an immediate origin for two of them as their own parents are African (Tiwony's father) or mixed, second-generation African (Asaliah's mother). For the other two, it is a form of recessive origin. They are naturally attracted by Africannesses as they reckoned they experienced a kind of discrepancy between their nature and that of the society they evolved in. Moreover, those African roots they claim are a source of strength and empowerment. Through the radicalization of their stances, they find a new root in a soil they have chosen, literally and metaphorically rejecting the "artificial" culture France would have imposed upon them.

The second point is that, irremediably, the African-American civil rights movement has affected other black populations in the world. So even though it may seem displaced, 1980s and 1990s Guadeloupe and Martinique were affected by the Civil Rights movement because this generation followed the previous one of the 1960s to 1970. In addition, the protagonists of the period became icons, almost "pop" icons, as their identifying with the music trends which circulated the Civil Rights and Black Power discourses resulted in their politicization—or should I say their non-politicization—in the postcolonial system. However, couldn't we say that their taking a stance is a form of politicization, as their claiming of Africanness, Rastafari or counter-cultures are also inheritances of slavery, or at least avatars, alterations, tribulations ensuing from it?

From the Great Island to the African Continent through the Western World: Itineraries of a "Return to the Origins" through Hip Hop Music in Madagascar (2000–2011)

Klara Boyer-Rossol*

*Translated by Stéphanie Melyon-Reinette

A cultural and artistic trend[166] which appeared in the early 1970s in the United States, and now one of the major music industries in the world, Hip Hop is often presented as a movement "imported" from the Western world. And yet, far from being isolated from external influences, this diasporic music[167] was born within the Atlantic Ocean at the crossroads of artists' itineraries, such as New York deejay Kool Herc, of Jamaican origins, seen as the father of Hip Hop, or Afrika Bambaataa, leader of Zulu Nation.[168] The origin of Hip Hop is the reference to Africa. Furthermore, popular interpretations have given to Rap, the form of vocal expression which belongs to the Hip Hop cultural movement, an African origin (the emcee's rhythmic flow recalling the *griot* or traditional storyteller, or African percussion). Hip Hop "returning" to Africa is a phenomenon which is still unstudied. Emerging in the mid-1980s in French-speaking West Africa, with crews such as Positive Black Soul in Senegal,[169] Hip Hop seems still to be used as a privileged means of expression in African youngsters.[170] Often politically aware and conscious, the African Hip Hop artists help to circulate strong messages denouncing the government's failures and claiming more social equality[171] through their art. In South Africa, The Prophets of Da City crew released a Rap album in 1990 which is committed to the struggle against Apartheid. Hip Hop's reappropriation by the musical movement of the African continent seems to breathe new life into the original Hip Hop spirit, based on non-violence, tolerance and positive affirmation values.

This Hip Hop "back to Africa" movement is not circular. Instead, this music trend developed on the continent by implying incessant and continuous back-and-forth movements, constantly renewing itself. Hip Hop is exported, and finally mutates, through the radio airwaves, cable TV channels, and the internet (which upset the music industry), but also through artistic collaborations, tours or else through festivals. Thus, there are back-and-forth movements between Africa, the Americas and Europe,[172] through the very paths that formerly led to the emergence of the black diaspora. Like triangular trade and slavery, the Hip Hop movement is by far better known in the Atlantic region than in the Indian region. Yet, Hip Hop has experienced an important spread in Eastern African countries[173] such as Kenya (with female singer Amani and rapper Nameless among others), but also in the islands of the western part of the Indian Ocean.

In Madagascar, Hip Hop appeared quite late, but has imposed itself rapidly in a decade onto the national music landscape. In the 1990s, in the capital Antananarivo, the Hip Hop pioneers (breakdancers, graffiti artists, rappers) paved the way for this music trend which gained momentum in the 2000s. An urban phenomenon, the Hip Hop movement weaves networks between the artists of the big cities of the island, who gather into "crews" or bands. Impregnated by the "battle" mindset, those various Hip Hop groups confront one another with their lyrics or steps. In 2000, rappers from the cities of Majunga and Antsiranana (located in the north-western coast of Madagascar) gathered into a "Makoa" association, with a notable underground album which announced the emergence of a "coast" Hip Hop and Ragga-Dancehall[174] in Madagascar. Young rappers from Madagascar bound themselves to an eastern African diasporic identity or to a "Makoa" identity. The Makoa are the descendent of East African enslaved prisoners deported during the nineteenth century to the Great Island, and mainly settled on Madagascar's eastern coast. The representations of the Makoa, including the so-called deep darkness of their skins, are re-used by those young rappers claiming an "Afro-Malagasy" identity. In the early 2000s, opposed to the Merina rappers from the high lands, the "coast" rappers of the Makoa crew introduced themselves as the legitimate heirs of Madagascan Hip Hop. The battles or duels moved from the music sphere into politics where the Merina/Coast opposition can also be encountered (the constructions being inherited from colonial policy), and where the Makoa origin is also reintroduced. The ancient presence of the Makoa in western Madagascar proves the African origin of the inhabitants of the coast who look like the true natives,[175] in opposition to the Merina, renowned for their Asian (hence foreign) origins. Those discourses aim at establishing the anteriority of one group before the other, so as to legitimate the maintaining of its power or music movement. In particularly tensed political circumstances,[176] the Ragga-Hip Hop movement in Madagascar, premised on regionalism to a great extent, will manage to overcome those splits in a decade, as the various crews will federate around a single message of unity, and by diffusing Malagasy Hip Hop onto the international scene.

In the frame of field research, I have travelled to Madagascar twice, in 2004 and 2008, and during those stays observed the Hip Hop/Reggae-Dancehall phenomenon and measured its evolution in the 2000s. Through the analysis of Rap lyrics, music videos, press articles, artist interviews, and collected data, we will show how those Malagasy artists have taken Hip Hop and Reggae-dancehall music over by reinterpreting their history of slavery.

Secondly, interest will be focused on the itineraries of this Hip Hop movement in binding the Great Island to the "French Overseas Department."

Finally, we will emphasize the claiming of a real Hip Hop stance in Madagascar.

Taking over a Diasporic Music:
Return to African Origins and a Remembrance of Slavery

How they see their links with Africa and the revival of slavery in Madagascar

For Hip Hop to be incorporated in the musical landscape of the Great Island, it had to first cross the seas. On the one hand, the movement appears to be imported from the Western world, as the first Malagasy rappers wrote their lyrics in French or in English. Malagasy-style Hip Hop began in the 2000s. On the other hand, the young east coast rappers' taking over of Hip Hop passed through a symbolic return to Africa, the motherland (the Madagascans' "Africanity"), and to a reminiscence of slavery. This identity and memorial return movement remains a marginal phenomenon in Madagascar, wherein evoking slavery publicly is still troublesome, or even taboo,[177] and wherein the relationships with the African continent are complicated.[178] If, from the geopolitical viewpoint, Madagascar is often related to Africa,[179] it is not really the case in the population's mindset. Certain Malagasy people would ignore or even have overtly racist attitudes toward Africans, whereas others would show solidarity with them even if they still had differentialist behaviours. These manifestations of identity tension or the maintaining of a certain ambiguity regarding African people cannot be solely analyzed through the prism of

insularity, but must also be placed into the history of their representations
of slavery. In Madagascar, servitude is stamped on the social and
mercantile relationships, or even on the field of political representativeness.[180]
The relationships of domination inherited from the former enslaving
institutions, and much more the representations of the slaves' descendancy,
are still relevant. In Madagascar, as mentioned by anthropologist M.
Rakotomalala:

> the popular interpretation still tries to distinguish between the descendants
> of the freed slaves by the color of their skins, without taking into account
> the fact that the qualitative *mainty*, which means literally "black", (in
> opposition to *fotsy*, meaning "white"), is not a physical complexion but a
> social color.[181]

The association black/slave partakes in the stigmatization of the Makoa.
They are represented as dark-skinned, wooly-haired people with somatic
traits which would prove that their ancestors lived in bondage.[182] The
enslavement-linked social exclusion of the Makoa is reinforced by their
extra-insular origins.[183] In the nineteenth century, the Makoa appeared as a
group belonging to the East African diaspora in the western Indian
Ocean.[184] This African diasporic identity resulting from slavery could also
be shared by Madagascan descendants who have settled in the Creole
Mascarene Islands or in the Americas.[185] By reviewing the souvenir of
slavery, other origins can be found for some Hip Hop expressions whose
roots should be in Madagascar.

The Traditional Origins of Malagasy Rap:
The *Jijy*

Popular interpretation gives to Rap music a Madagascan traditional
origin, the *jijy*. The *jijy* is singing characterized by a rhythmic and
throbbing flow practiced in Madagascar during traditional ceremonies.
Accompanied by a vivid and cadenced music, *jijy* serves to awake the
spirits.[186] Chants composed in a ritual frame, *jijy* lyrics were improvised
according to the ceremony.[187] During the contemporary period, *jijy* was
taken up by the Malagasy musicians and lapsed into the secular sphere. In
the 1970s, *saova* (the name for *jijy* in the high planes) re-used the vocal
and rhythmic traits of the ritual chants, and was part of the popular music
of the Great Island with the specific trait of bearing social claims.[188] More
recently, the band *Tarika B-Jijy*, founded in 2008, uses the *jijy* to compose
a new kind of "world" music resulting from a mix of Malagasy
instruments (such as the *valiha*[189]) and so-called "modern" instruments

(bass, guitar). According to the group's vision, *jijy* was diffused worldwide by slaves deported from Madagascar and might be one of the origins of Rap music. This traditional origin of Rap is transmitted by Reggae-Hip Hop artists from the Madagascan western coast,[190] re-using this diasporic music.

"Makoa" Identity or the "Afro" Identity Reinterpreted by the Young Rappers of the West Coast of Madagascar

The Makoa's presence on the West coast of Madagascar appeared as one of the manifestations of the links woven by the slavery networks between Madagascar and Africa.[191] The Makoa are named after the term *Makhuwa* which designates the most important sociocultural group of today's Republic of Mozambique.[192] The foreign origins and those of servitude given to the Makoa resulted in their maintaining a kind of marginality, with the consequence that many of their descendants have changed their names. This progressive disappearance of the Makoa collective identity seems to have sped up at the turning point of Madagascar independence (1960), concurrent with the progressive abandonment of Makoa cultural practices such as the practice of the *emakhuwa* language (of Bantu origin) or the chants and dances imported from North Mozambique. However, the name Makoa still resonates in the stories, and the representations associated with it are still vivid. Today, the term Makoa is used to define a very dark-skinned, wooly-haired, person or else a strong, hard-working man, with many terms being stamped with the stigma of bondage.[193] More recently, a phenomenon has appeared and this stigma is reinterpreted by young rappers from the Madagascan west coast. The Makoa music crew released a self-produced and locally broadcast underground album in the early 2000s, of which is extracted the Rap piece entitled "Jaly Makoa" ("Makoa Wound"). The analysis of this piece makes interesting research regarding the emergence of a "coastal Hip Hop" in the early 2000s, whose spokespersons are the Makoa crew. The lyrics of this piece are written in the *sakalava* dialect (the most used in western Madagascar). One of the singers, Kazambo,[194] seems to rap in a somewhat "Malagasized" African language, and it isn't really possible to determine if it was an *emakuwa*[195] language or not. The Makoa identity or Afro-identity is clearly claimed by those "coast" rappers who seem to confront the rappers of the high lands through their lyrics. The battle or duel spirit is conceptualized through a chess game in which the black pawns (coast rappers) confront the white pawns (the rappers of the high lands), in a struggle whose winner would dominate the Malagasy Hip Hop scene.

Concerning the musical composition of the "Makoa" album, the US Hip Hop influence is noticeable through the choice of instrumentals.[196] We will focus particularly on the topic broached in the track "Jaly Makoa" or "Makoa pain," whose title seems to refer to the ancient Makoa's bondage and to the marginalization of their descendants. The Makoa rappers introduce themselves as "crazy," "thugz" and "Rough guyz," re-using the American Gangsta Rap bad boy imaginary and ego trip mindset.[197] The former stigmas of bondage associated to the Makoa are used positively and reclaimed by the young "coast" rappers.[198] They make a claim to being black people, colour demonstrating their Makoa identity, opposed to the "whites" who lose face in front of their vocal virtuosity. Redundant in this Rap text, the white/black dichotomy, the traditional groups in opposition, opposes in this case Rap crews from different regions of Madagascar: the west coast versus high lands. The term *mainty* (the colour black in Malagasy) is also used for artist pseudonyms by the high lands Hip Hop artists. Thus, we can see a positive claiming of the black complexion through the Hip Hop phenomenon. The stereotypes linked to black complexion are re-used by the rappers of the west coast who claim an identity linked to slavery (even when they themselves are of noble or royal origins).

"Bondage we have forgotten, this is the door that we have reached,"[199] sings one of the rappers of the Makoa crew. In the meantime, the coast rappers frequently use the expression *Makoa lahy* or *Makoa man*, employed to speak about a strong, virile man (the Makoa were known for being hard-working or good farmers), or to speak about a very dark-skinned man. The Makoa image of robustness and masculinity is an illustration of an offensive and virulent kind of Rap. The stigma of bondage is reversed, and the Makoa rappers state: "we are lazy, this is a kind of struggle."[200] It must be emphasized that, in the *sakalava* ideology of the Madagascan west coast, agriculture was seen as a slave task. Thus, showing a certain laziness or nonchalance in work appears as a form of social claiming. The reversal of the Makoa's stereotypes is particularly notable in the following lyrics; "Look in the books, the Makoa history, in fact we are the first one (to arrive), and you are the last one to get there."[201] A full reverse is operated and the former foreign slaves become the new natives. Though the forced migration of the Makoa's ancestors is recent (in the nineteenth century), it is often linked to the settlement history of Madagascar. Deschamps presents the Makoa's migration as "the last wave of African invasions contributing to the peopling of Madagascar."[202] The Makoa reckon that they have ended the long migratory cycle which has led to the ideological construct of an insular indigenousness linked to the African continent. The African origin of the Makoa is here instrumentalized anew in order to confirm their alleged anteriority over the Merina of the high lands. So the Makoa can be drawn closer to the Vazimba, known to be the first inhabitants of Madagascar, presented either as being of Austronesian origin, or of African origin.[203] The debate around the Vazimba's origin brings to the fore an extremely simplified historical reading distinguishing two large migratory flows, one from the west, the other from the east, risking the creation of a national duality, based on a "native-versus-foreign" opposition.[204] This discourse echoes the false debate in the confrontation of the Merina to the coast populations (an artificial opposition constructed during the colonial period). Recently, in Madagascar a political indigenousness based on non-natives (the Merina) against natives (the "others") was invented. Inherited from the race-based colonial policy, a dichotomy based on phenotype. Each group may be recognizable by the colour of their skin or of their hair texture.[205] Such representations have fed the strong social and ethnic tensions linked to the political crisis which upset the country in the early 2000s.[206] This political territorializing echoes an apparent regionalization of Hip Hop in Madagascar.

The Hip Hop Makoa Crews of the West Coast

In the early 2000s, the rappers from Madagascar's west coast presented themselves as the pioneers of "coast Hip Hop," opposed to the Hip Hop movement centred on the central high lands.[207] The apparent regionalization of this Hip Hop movement must not obliterate the fact that it emerged in the early 1990s, resulting from the meeting of artists of various regions of the island in Antananarivo, the capital city located in the High Lands. Among them was Shao Boana, one of the members of the Makoa Crew from Majunga who settled in the capital in the early 1990s where he collaborated with other artists such as Dj Momo who spun in night clubs. Together, they created in 2002 the independent label One Lova, and introduced Reggae-Dancehall on the Malagasy scene. Shao Boana is also presented as one of the pioneers of Hip Hop in Madagascar,[208] and was a fervent supporter of coast Hip Hop. The west coast/high lands duality in Madagascar echoes the famous east coast/west coast opposition which appeared in the United States in the early 1980s, when the Hip Hop movement took momentum. Thus, the Rap crews seem to be linked to a strong territorial identity. The formation of the Rap crews, firstly in the great cities, then at the regional level with their networking, draws a map of national Hip Hop movements. A Rap crew can also gather artists from

various cities, but located in the same area. In the 2000s, we can see Rap
cews emerging and presenting themselves as Makoa Crews or at least as
heirs of the Makoa or Afro identities. Those crews multiply in the various
big cities of the coast: in Mahajunga, Antsiranana or else Sambava. The
music video phenomenon is in full expansion allowing for the diffusion
and the accessibility of many Makoa Rap tracks, broadcast on a large scale
on youtube.com or dailymotion. Most of the time, those amateur videos,
often realized with small budgets, feature very young artists. In a
Dackman and Sil J video, entitled "Makoa Misoma Makoa,"[209] we can see
youngsters swimming in the sea surrounded by young women, singing a
nonchalant rap on a slow beat recalling west coast American Rap. The
image participates in fixing the representations, as shown by Dj Knife's
Rap video entitled "Makoa l'Or."[210] The title of this Rap track, shot by
Nosy-Be, is named after the neon sign of an "Afro" hairdressing salon.
These young Makoa rappers claim an "Afro-Malagasy" identity.

Claiming of an Afro Identity and Malagasy "Back-to-the-Roots" Movements

The claiming of an "Afro-malagasy" identity is also conveyed through
music from Jamaica such as Reggae, Ragga and Dancehall, which also
coexist in the Madagascan Hip Hop movement. Those diasporic musical
forms often convey the message of a return to the roots, implicitly the
return to Africa. In Madagascar, this return is subjectivized as a
reinterpretation of the links with the African continent, or else as a
symbolic return to the roots, that's to say to the "Malagasy sources." This
"return" is translated through music with purist Reggae sounds and beats,
seen as "classical" instrumentals on which the singers record their songs.
If certain Ragga-Dancehall artists are known for their "hardcore" texts, the
majority of the Reggae-Rap lyrics come from a peaceful but also
enlightened "roots" spirit. The phenomenon may be related to the "new
roots" wave, which appeared in 1995 in Jamaican Reggae with the renewal
of the Rastafarian influence, a return to conscious texts and to a less
digital, more acoustic sound. The "Malagasy-stylizing" of this imported
music is realized through the use of the Malagasy language, the
introduction of instruments from traditional music or through the
collaborations with bands of local popular music. This Malagasy "back-to-
the-roots" movement is undoubtedly prefigured by the reggae movement
in Madagascar. The fathers of this movement, such as Sammy
Rastafanahy,[211] are still very influenced by the Jamaican reggae of the
1970s, and regularly perform English recreations of Bob Marley. In 2004,

in a concert given at the famous cabaret Le Glacier in Antananarivo, Sammy Rastafanahy shared the stage with a band from the south of Madagascar. The realization of this "back-to-the-Malagasy-roots" idea can be seen through their clothes (on the one hand the *Exodus* tee-shirt and on the other a South-Malagasy traditional costume) and also by the artistic duet itself.

Courtesy of Sammy Rastafanahy (left), next to a musician from the South of Madagascar. Concert at Le Glacier cabaret, Antananarivo. August 2004.

While Reggae is already well implanted in the Madagascan musical landscape, in the early 2000s, a new trend emerged, that of Reggae-Dancehall, with shows scheduled in the cultural centres of the capital,[212] and the organizations of the first sound systems.[213] This trend spread very quickly and many Ragga-Dancehall crews were created, such as Afro-Janga (a contraction of "afro" and the name of the west coast city Mahajanga[214]). In the same vein, other "afro" crews appeared affiliated to the Hip Hop/Ragga-Dancehall movement, gathering artists from the coast in crews such as Afro-Sambava (named after the city Sambava) or Afro-Diego. Jahfro, one of the members of Afro-Janga, explains the appearance of those clans: "those clans do different music styles (rap, reggae or ragga) but all of them are Afro. We are all Afro. Those who do not recognize that their *razana* [ancestors] come from Africa have not understood history well enough."[215] We find the idea according to which the *raza be* (the first ancestors) or the natives of Madagascar are of African origin. The symbolic return to Africa finally leads to re-rooting in the Malagasy *tanindrazana* (ancestral land). The rastafari philosophy, based on the idea of a (symbolic or real) return to Africa (and particularly to Ethiopia) is re-used in the Malagasy model. Thus, Jah, the supreme Almighty being for the Rastafarians, is translated by the Malagasy artists through the equivalent of "Zanahary" (God, the Creator). The artist Jahfro (a contraction of "Jah" and "Afro") identifies with Rasta and bears, like many Malagasy Reggae and Ragga-Hip Hop artists, dreadlocks.[216] Paradoxically, those distinctive signs of a so-called "roots" attitude, close to the ancestral roots and values, stigmatize those reggae artists seen by the Madagascans as eccentric depositaries of an imported culture and a foreign music. On the other hand, those artists often come from urban (we must remember that Madagascar is mainly a rural country), and lower-class milieus; they are educated, speak several languages and are in touch with the foreign tourists. Thus, they are forced to make incessant back and forth movements between the various influential trends they try to reconcile. This is proved by their reinterpreting and re-using of the Rastafarian philosophy in Madagascar, country of the zebu *par excellence*, where it is difficult, even impossible, to be vegetarian, beef being not only prized in culinary practices but also intimately associated with the Malagasy culture (the sacrifice of zebu is part of the ancestral rites). Thus, the Malagasy Rastafarians explain that they cannot abide by this, because it would infringe their Malagasy ancestors' culture. Malagasy traditions are evoked by maintaining and even by giving new life to the Rasta-roots spirit. Inside the music trends themselves, new styles emerge: one is called "Rap-Roots" with which artists like M'Tsat, who raps in the *sakalava* dialect and sings about the land of his ancestors from Menabe (the western region), claim affiliation. Mika Killah's[217] album, *Killahmanjaro*, released in 2008 in Madagascar by Malaland Records, is classified as "Roots-Rap-Reggae."[218] It is under the Reggae influence that Hip Hop pioneers have enlarged their musical panel (by also integrating Ragga-Dancehall). The album *Killahmanjaro* (the title refers to the highest peak of the African mountains) suggests a Rastafarian belonging, and also uses symbols such as the red/gold/green colours of the Rastafarian flag or the crowned lion king, standing for the sovereignty of Africa.

The "back-to-the-roots" movement is expressed by the titles of the tracks themselves, often composed in Malagasy. Inspired by this "roots" spirit, the new generation of Reggae singers in Madagascar return to the source of this musical trend. The group *Bi.Ba*, founded in 2000 by the singer Kazy, reinterpret the 1970s Jamaican Reggae style by introducing Malagasy sonorities. During the 2000s, the phenomenon became more pronounced with the "Gasy Reggae" (or "Malagasy Reggae"), its most prominent ambassador being the singer Abdou Day. His album *Tous égaux* ("All Equal"), released in 2009 in France, is thus classified under the term "Reggasy." Amongst the characteristics of this Reggae, we can note the use of the Malagasy language (which coexists with the use of French, Réunionese Creole and English) and the introduction of rhythms belonging to the *salegy*, the most widespread music in western Madagascar. Madagascar is a source of inspiration for artists like Abdou Day, who come from the Great Island, and who have done the greatest part of their career in "Andafy" which means "abroad." The youngsters from the Malagasy community that settled abroad, and more particularly in France, seem to play a determining role in the development and the diffusion of Malagasy Reggae-Hip Hop. Part of the Creole population in Réunion or in the African diaspora in France, those young artists of Malagasy origins are all the more linked to the Afro identity. Thus, outside Madagascar, the regional disparities seem to be erased behind the claiming of an Afro-Malagasy identity.

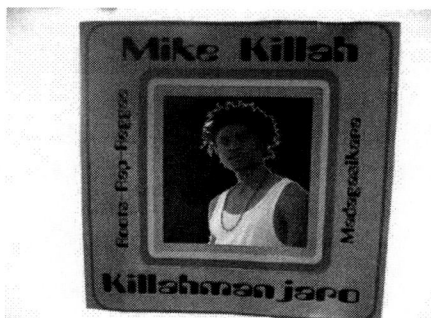

Mike Killah's album (2008), classified in the « Roots-Rap-Reggae » item. The colors and symbols (lion with royal attributes) which appear on the cover refer to the representations of the Rastafarisn philosophy.

From Madagascar to Mozambique, Partitions of the Remembrance of Slavery

One of the artistic collaborations between Madagascar and Mozambique, the duet composed of a Malagasy female pianist and singer Môta[219] and the Mozambique rapper Simba gave birth to the wonderful track "Last Hope."[220] During an artistic residency in Maputo (Mozambique) in February 2009, Môta met the rapper Simba on the scene of the French-Mozambican Cultural Centre. Within two days, they had composed and recorded "Last Hope," a trilingual song (Môta sings in Malagasy and Simba sings both in Portuguese and English), which evokes the struggle against human trafficking. This is how the duet reinterpreted the links woven by the ancient slave trade networks which unified Madagascar and Mozambique.[221] A poetry full of hope is vibrant in the Malagasy chorus sang by Môta:

Mitsiky aho, kanefa ny afon'ny fanantenako madiva hipiaka izao
Mitolona aho, miezaka mafy ny foko sy fanahiko mba tsy hiviaka dieny izao.

[I smile, and yet, the fire of my hope is about to extinguish
I struggle, my heart and soul struggle so as not to get alienated now.]

Môta explains that she has chosen to sing in her mother tongue in order to be closer to her feelings, and thus to touch the listeners with the emotion transmitted though the music.[222] Simba sings his rap in Portuguese by punctuating it with English words over a piano melody played by Môta. Formed from an improvised duet, the result is breath taking. The song creates a universal language: music, a bridge between Madagascar and the rest of the world.

From the Great Island to "the French West Indies": Itineraries of the Hip Hop Movement in Madagascar

An Imported and Re-exported Culture

In Madagdascar, Hip Hop was imported from *Andafy*, ("abroad/beyond the seas"), the term being mostly understood as a reference to the Western world.[223] The urban culture of the "Overseas Departement," Hip Hop appeared in the capital Antananarivo in the 1990s, where artists from various provinces met. Among those Malagasy Hip Hop artists, some emigrated abroad in the frame of their studies, and developed their art in the islands of the Indian Ocean or in the Western World.[224] Youngsters from the Malagasy community settled abroad, and more particularly in France, which seems to play a determining role in the development and the diffusion of Malagasy Reggae-Hip Hop. At the crossroads of multiple influences, informed by the latest trends in music (Ragga-Hip Hop), using the very latest technologies (the internet to compose and broadcast their music), and performing on various scenes and multiplying their (often polyglottal) collaborations, those Malagasy artists, through their music, create a network and develop an expanding Hip Hop movement rooted in Madagascar. These trajectories allow for a return to the native land, either symbolically (through their lyrics) or actually (through performances, festivals or albums distributed in Madagascar). Still connected with Malagasy Reggae-Hip Hop through social networks, blogs and specialized websites,[225] these artists in the Western world diaspora continue to influence the Hip Hop movement in Madagascar.

An Example of an Artist's Trajectory

Rapper Don Smokilla's[226] trajectory is a good illustration of this phenomenon. In the early 1990s, he was part of Urbann Jamm, one of the very first Rap crews in Madagascar (the first to rap in French at that time). In 1996, he left to continue his studies in Réunion, where he participated in the first Hip Hop mixtapes and festivals on the island. Since settling in France in 2001, he performs on several scenes (sound systems, Parisian theatres, concert halls, and so on) and works on several artistic collaborations. He encountered Réunionese or Malagasy rappers in France at the time of Urbann Jamm and during his stay in Réunion. With these Indo-oceanic networks, Don Smokilla sings on many mixtapes, net-tapes[227] and street albums,[228] participates in the creation of new music bands (like 974 with l'Armada) and in running an independent label, Sékel Prod, specializing in urban culture. The collaborations with Reggae-Dancehall artists enlarge the rapper's music panel, also influenced by American Hip Hop.[229] Don Smokilla is one of the rare Malagasy rappers to export his art beyond the Atlantic Ocean. He appears with a Bostonian rapper on the music video of the Rap track "Were we From," in which he rhymes in Malagasy.[230] The Malagasy rapper also alternates French with Réunionese Creole, reaching a larger audience. Considered as an underground rapper, the numerous self-produced tracks by Don Smokilla are often offered to download for free on the internet. His news can be read on websites, blogs and Hip Hop forums, but also through his personal pages such as MySpace or Facebook.[231] Finally, the artist takes part in the development of Hip Hop in Madagascar through the organization of events like the L'Héry-Thier Tour, held on august 12, 2011 in Antananarivo, starring many Rap bands, among whom are certain pioneers of the Hip Hop movement in Madagascar.[232]

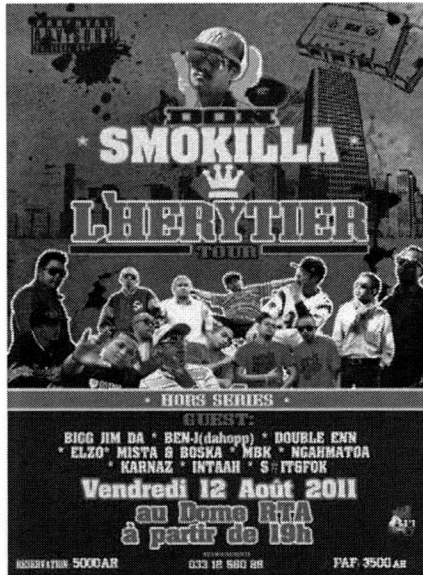

L'Herytier Tour poster held on august 12, 2011, Antatanarivo

A Hip Hop Scene in the Indian Ocean Area

In the year 2000, the capital Antananarivo welcomed numerous
national Hip Hop festivals. In 2005, the second edition of the HH for Life
festival confirmed the talent of the best rappers such as those of Doubln'
or Da Hopp, but also the emergence of a feminine rap, represented by
bands like Zazavavindrap, Kilo Watt or Farah and Bamb's. Ragga-
Dancehall is also incorporated in the national music landscape through
new scenes dedicated to emerging music in Madagascar.[233] Finally,
Madagascar also appears as an international Ragga/Hip Hop scene, and
welcomes stars such as Admiral T (2008) or the female rapper Diam's
(2010), whose concert was inaugurated by Raboussa and Farah. On the
international Hip Hop scene, the young Malagasy rappers gather around a
message of unity.

Toward Unity in the late 2000s;
The Claiming of a Malagasy Hip Hop

Toward a national movement:
collaboration between different crews

In the early 2000s, Hip Hop appeared in Madagascar as a somewhat regionalized movement. Many Rap clans were created, weaving networks between artists from the same city (the Afro-Janga clan for instance) or coming from different cities belonging to the same region (the Makoa crews from the west coast region for instance). Little by little, the members were recruited from larger areas; from the central eastern coast region (the Bogota clan, for example, which includes secondary clans in Antananarivo, Fianarantsoa, Antsirabe and Toamasina), or else the central north-western region (for example the Akkadia'n Crew that included members from 2001 to 2004 who were from Antananarivo, Fianarantsoa, Majunga, and Antsiranana). In 2008, a Hip Hop scene was dedicated to those clans who performed in Antananarivo.[234] During the national Hip Hop festivals (HH for Life,[235] Afondasy, Rap'n'Dago Festivals) which occur each year in Antananarivo since 2004, a certain cohesion shows between those different crews. Their common point is the claiming of a "gasy hip hop" which links those different crews to the young rappers of the Malagasy diaspora established in France. Even more outside the Great Island, the artists seem to overcome the regional competitions and differences in order to unite around a common cause: the defence of the Hip Hop culture and its Malagasy identity. In 2009, during the Afondasy festival, the different groups sang the national anthem in chorus with the audience. This call for national cohesion is also interpreted by the Reggae-Dancehall artists preaching for a "return" to the Malagasy sources.

Thus, in 2008, during the Ragga-Hip Hop New Scene held on April 7 in Ankorondrano (Antananarivo), Malagasy groups of artists residing in France (such as TRS) or from different regions of Madagascar (the 201 crew from Antsiranana, or Mataram from Toamasina) passed a message of brotherhood and tolerance over to the audience. When Madagascar was about to celebrate the fiftieth anniversary of its independence (in 2010), the different crews and music trends from the Hip Hop movement gathered around a message of unity.

A Message of Unity

The title of the solo album of Shao Boana, *Unity*, released in 2007, undoubtedly prefigured the orientation taken by the Malagasy Hip Hop movement. In 2010, when Madagascar celebrated the fiftieth anniversary of its independence, the album *Independaza* was released, gathering Malagasy artists of all musical styles, including Hip Hop. The same year, the Rap'n'Dago festival united the artists who created the Hip Hop movement in the year 2000, featuring Shao, Mt'Sta, Kaz T. Matik, Farah and X-Crew. It resulted in an eponymous track (Rap'n'Dago) of high quality. The spirit is resolutely Hip Hop oriented, that is to say, resolutely positive. The breakdancers performed their moves and steps on the place of independence in the Rap music of many crews from all the Madagascan provinces. They united around the same language: Malagasy. As emphasized by female rapper Bam's: "If Rap gave birth to a new language, it has also valued the national language. Some Rap texts turn to be very rich in Malagasy vocabulary."[236] Exported to the French Overseas Department, Malagasy Rap is still performed in the mother tongue. The youths of the diaspora in the Western world, and particularly in France, play an important role in the claiming of Malagasy Hip Hop. In the late 2000s, groups of Malagasy artists, or groups of French of Malagasy origin, emerged in Andafy ("beyond the seas"). There was an appearance of We Malagasy in 2009, and afterwards the release by Dago'sy Mouv, created by the rappers Tekillah and Mams, with the title "Firaisan-kina Unité," the video of which was shot in Paris.[237] *"Un jour, j'irai là-bas"* ("one day, I'll go there") is the chorus of the track. *"Un jour, j'irai là-bas"* sing the youths of the diaspora who relate with Madagascar through their music. In this track, certain rappers also allude to the political crisis in which Madagascar is mired. The message of unity, relayed by the rappers in Madagascar and abroad, is extremely significant in troubled times. Since 2009, Madagascar has experienced serious political instability and a bankrupt economy. Rap tracks such as MTM's crew's "Politika" denunciate the government's shortcomings. But these youths want to be optimistic. They look to the future of the country: "Mada se lève" ("Mada stands up") is another of Don Smokilla's song titles.

A Return to the Origins of Hip Hop Culture?

Finally, we can speculate on whether Hip Hop has come back to its native culture by returning to Madagascar: a moving art (with dancers and street artists, very *en vogue* in the Great island) adapting to modern shapes without ever submitting to them, but also an art which remains fully independent (self-production though independent labels), showing solidarity (networks between the artists of Madagascar and its diaspora) and federative (its message of unity). In ten years, in a particularly tense political and economic climate, Hip Hop in Madagascar has experienced an astonishing development, passing from the cassette to the MP3 format, and keeping its identity and its beloved language at the same time. Imported and reinterpreted culture, and exported again by the diaspora, Malagasy Hip Hop shows that one can walk the worldwide paths of a globalized culture without losing oneself. The Malagasy Hip Hop artists may have succeeded where politicians over the last ten years have failed; they can exceed the regionalisms and internal differences to gather around a message of unity and thus create a national movement, recognized and supported abroad.

On stage, in a battle, after each duel and confrontation, the Rap crews shake hands, since what is important is, above all, to excel oneself. The Hip Hop spirit is undoubtedly tangible here. As some people think, the future of Hip Hop is perhaps in Africa and in Madagascar,[238] and after witnessing the talented youths of this region, that could well be the case.[239]

BIBLIOGRAPHY

The Evolution of *Gwo Ka*, from the Twentieth century to the Present Day
Marie-Line Dahomay

Ageg. *Rapport Culturel.* Paris, 1977

Cyrille, D. *A la rèpriz Une étude des quadrilles de la Guadeloupe.* Edition Nestor, 2008.

Dahomay, C. *Metod-Ka.* 1997

Diop, Cheickh. A. *Nations Nègres et Culture I.* Paris: Présence Africaine, 1979

Fonds Boissel, C. P. COLLECTION GERRIT VAN DEN BOOM , 1905 et 1935

Gadet, S. "Le 'blues de la canne et du coton': étude comparative des fonctions socioculturelles du gwo-ka et du blues." *Etudes Caribéennes* (August 2012). http://etudescaribeennes.revues.org/4675. DOI : 10.4000/etudescaribeennes.4675 (accessed August, 2011).

Lafontaine, M.-C. "Le Carnaval de l''autre'." *les Temps Modernes N° 441–442*: 126–217. April–May, 1983.

—. "Terminologie musicale en Guadeloupe: ce que le créole nous dit de la musique." *Langage et société N° 32* (June 1985). http://www.lameca.org/dossiers/lafontaine_terminologie/p2.htm (accessed August 29, 2011).

—. "Unité et diversité des musiques traditionnelles guadeloupéennes." In *Les Musiques Guadeloupéennes dans le Champs Culturel Afro-Américain, au sein des Musiques du Monde*, 71. Pointe à Pitre: Editions Caribéennes, 1988.

Laumuneau, M.-H. *Gwo ka et politique en Guadeloupe.* Paris: L'Harmattan, 2011.

—. *Gwo ka et politique en Guadeloupe.* Paris: L'Harmattan, 2011.

Laviso, C. *Timoun a Lafrik*, 2008.

Leauva, H. *Je refuse la pensée unique.* Gourbeyre: Editions Nestor, 2008.

LKP. *Pawol LKP*, 2009.

Lockel, G. "Lolo Camphrin un des derniers grands danseurs de gwo-ka." *Jakata.*

Lulu. P'Iti Papa les effets du tam-tam "Honni soit qui mal y pense." *Le Colonial*, 1912.

Mérovil, A. Bamboula. *Le Colonial*, 1918.

Négrit, F. *Musique et Immigration dans la Société Antillaise*, 2004.

—. *Musique et Immigration dans la Société antillaise*, 2004.

Pichette, M.-H. "Comprendre le *Gwo ka* guadeloupéen par la performance." In *Territoires Musicaux mis en scène* (2011): 311. La presse de l'Université de Montréal.

Plougastel, Y. "Jacques Schwartz-Bart jazzman caribéen." *Le Monde* (2010): 92.

Uri, A. E. *Musique et Musiciens de la Guadeloupe*. 1991.

Bèlè in Martinique: The Foundation of Resistance and Existence
Edmond Mondésir

Le Père du Tertre. *Histoire générale des Antilles, habitées par les Français. Réed*. Editions des Horizons Caraïbes. Fort de France, 1973.

Le R.P Labat. *Nouveau Voyage aux Isles de l'Amérique*. Réédition Editions des Horizons Caraïbes. Fort de France 1972.

Pinckard, G. *Notes on the West Indies*. London 1806.

Tambor de Crioula and the question of Afrodescendants
Marie Cousin

Câmara Cascudo, L. *Dicionario do folclore brasileira*. São Paulo: Global Editora, 1999.

Da Costa Eduardo, O. *The Negro in Northern Brazil. A Study in Acculturation*, New York: J. J. Augustin Publisher, 1948.

Daher, Andrea. *Les Singularités de la France Équinoxiale, Histoire de la Mission des Pères Capucins au Brésil (1612–1615)*. Paris: Honoré Champion, 2002.

De Azevedo Nunes, I. (Ed.) *Olhar, Memoria e Reflexões Sobre a Gente do Maranhão*. São Luis: CMF, 2003.

D'Évreux, Y. *Voyage au nord du Brésil fait en 1613 et 1614*. Paris: Payot, 1985.

Dorigny, M. and Bernard Gainot. *Atlas des Esclavages. Traites, Sociétés Coloniales, Abolitions de l'Antiquité à Nos Jours*. Collection Atlas/Mémoires. Paris: Autrement, 2007.

Ferretti, Sergio F. « O negro e o catolicismo popular ». In *Sincretismo religioso : o ritual afro*, eied by Organization Tânia Lima, Fundaçao Joaquim Nabuco, vol. 4, Congresso afro-brasileiro, Recife, 1996.

—. "Tradiçao religiosa de origem africana no Maranhão." In *Nossos ancestrais e o terreiro*, edited by Organization Elbein dos Santos, Juana. Salvador : SECNEB, EGBA, 113–119, 1997.

—. *Tambor de crioula, ritual e espetaculo.* São Luis: Comissão Maranhense de Folclore, 2002.

Figueiredo, J. *Folclore do Maranhão.* Maranhão: Senac, 2003.

Ribamar Souza dos Reis, J. *Folclore Maranhense.* São Luis, 2004.

Soares, Firmino Antônio F. *Festejos de Sao Benedito.* São Luis: Lithograf, 2003.

Vieira Filho, D. *Os cultos fetichistas no Maranhao.* São Luis: Folclore Sempre, 9–10, 1955.

—. *Maranhao, Foclore brasileiro.* Rio de Janeiro: Funarte, 1977.

Maloya and Dance
Florence Latappy

Samson, G., Benjamin Lagarde and Carpanin Marimoutou. *L'univers du maloya, Histoire, ethnographie, littérature.* Saint André, Ile de la Réunion: Editions de la DREOI, September 2008.

La Selve, J.-P. *Musiques traditionnelles de la Réunion.* Saint-Denis, Ile de la Réunion: Azalées Editions, 1995.

Freedom in the Mas:
Marronnage in Trinidad's Carnival
Michelle Bermiss-Smith

Harris, Wilson. *History, Fable & Myth in the Caribbean and Guianas.* Wellesley, MA: Calaloux Publications, 1995. Print.

Jazz Music and Amiri Baraka's Continuum:
A Perpetual Marronnage?
Stéphanie Melyon-Reinette

Crouch S. "The Genres: Stanley Crouch on Mainstream." In *Jazztimes*, September 2000. http://jazztimes.com/articles/20295-the-genres-stanley-crouch-on-mainstream (accessed November 20, 2011).

—. "Four-Letter Words: Rap & Fusion." In *Jazztimes*, March 2002.

http://jazztimes.com/articles/20011-four-letter-words-rap-fusion (accessed November 20, 2011).
—. "The Negro Aesthetic of Jazz." In *Jazztimes*, October 2002. http://jazztimes.com/articles/19772-the-negro-aesthetic-of-jazz (accessed November 20, 2011).
Friedwald, Will and Yuval Taylor, eds. *The Future of Jazz*. Chicago, Illinois: A Capella Books, 2002.
Isoardi, Steven L. *The Dark Tree: Jazz and the Community Arts in Los Angeles*. Berkeley and Los Angeles, California and London: University of California Press, 2006.
Jazziz. "*Jazziz* Celebrates Twenty Years." 20 (1) January 2003.
—. "The World on Edge." 20 (5) May 2003.
Jones, Leroi (Baraka Amiri). *Blues People: Negro Music in White America*. N.Y., William Morrow, 1963.
Lewis, Robert J. "Bass Note and Drum and the Moon Goes Crazy." In *The Spectator*, February 3, 2001. http://montrealserai.com/_archives/2001_Volume_14/14_1/Article_11.htm (accessed November 20, 2011).
Lowe, Jacques, B. Blumenthal and Cliff Preiss. *Jazz, Portraits des Maîtres*. Paris: Cliff Preiss Copyright, 1995.
McDavid, Henderson. "Where is the black audience?" In *Jazztimes*, January/February 2003. http://jazztimes.com/articles/14163-where-s-the-black-audience (accessed November 20, 2011).
Springer, Robert. *Le Blues Authentique, Son Histoire et ses Thèmes*. Robert Springer, Filipacchi, 1985.
Wagner, Jean. *Guide du Jazz, Initiation à l'Histoire et à l'Esthétique du Jazz*. Paris : 4ème édition, Syros/Alternatives, 1992.

Discography

Adams, Yolanda. *Moutain High ... Valley Low*. Elektra Entertainement, 1999.
B.B. King. *Lucille & Friends*. MCA Records Inc., 1995.
Benson, Georges. *Absolute Benson*. The Verve Music Groupe, 2000.
Carter, Betty. *It's Not About the Melody*. Polygram Records Inc., 1992.
Coleman Steve (and Five Element). *Def Trance (Modalities of Rhythm)*, BMG Music, 1995
DJ Logic. *Project Logic*. Ropeadoe Music Entertainment, 2001
—. *The Anomaly*. Ropeadope Music Entertainment, 2001
Dominguez, Chano. *Hecho a Mano*. Nuba Records, 1996.
Ferrell, Rachelle. *First Instrument*. Somethin'Else Records, Blue Note

(Capitol), 1990, 1995.

—. *Live in Montreux 91-97*. Blue Note (Capitol), 2002.

Freelon, Nnenna. *Soulcall*. Concord Records, 2000.

Hancock, Herbie. *Head Hunters*. CBS Inc., C Inc., 1974.

Hargrove, Roy. *Family*. Polygram Records, Inc., 1995.

Horn, Shirley. *You Won't Forget Me*. Polygram records, Inc., 1991.

Jamal Ahmad. *A Live at the Alhambra*. Chen Records, 1960. Vogue, 1989.

Jobim, Antonio Carlos. *The Composer of "Desafinado" plays recorded in 1963*. Polygram Records, 1997.

Jones, Norah. *Come Away With Me*. Blue Note (Capitol Records), 2002.

Kenny G. *Kenny Greatest Hits*. Arista Records, Inc., 1998.

Krall, Diana. *The Look of Love*. The Verve Music Group, 2001.

Marsalis , Wynton. *Blue Interlude*. Sony Music Entertainment Inc., 1992.

McBride, Christians. *Getting' To It*. Polygram Records, Inc., 1995.

McLaughlin, John. *The Promise*. Polydor/Polygram S.A. France 1996.

Miller, Marcus. *Marcus Miller*. Warner Bros, 1984.

Monheit, Jane. *In the Sun*. Sony Music Entertainment, 2002.

—. *Never, Never Land*. N-Coded music, 2000.

Perez, Danilo. *Motherland*. The Verve Music Group, 2000.

Reeves, Dianne. *Celebrating Sarah Vaughan*. Blue note (Capitol Records), 2001.

Sanchez, David. *Obesiòn*. Sony Music Entertainement Inc., 1998.

—. *Travesia* (produced by P. Sanchez). Sony Music Entertainment Inc., 2001.

Shorter, Wayne. *Alegria*. The Verve music group, 2003.

Weather Report. *Heavy Weather*. Sony Music Entertainment, Inc. Columbia, 1991.

Weston, Randy. *Spirit! The Power of Music*. Universal Music SA France, 2000.

Wilson, Cassandra. *New Moon Daughter*. Blue Note (Capitol Records) 1989, fantsay, Inc. Prestige records, 1995.

Workman, Reggie. *Summit Conference*. Postcards Inc., New York, 1994.

Yellowjackets. *Live Wire*. GRP Records, Inc., 1992.

Zawinul, Joe. *Faces and Places*. Cream Records, 2002.

Mizik Kont Pwofitasyon:
The Sociological Relevance of Guadeloupean Music
Steve Gadet

Braflan-Trobo, P. *Conflit sociaux en Guadeloupe*. Paris: L'Harmattan, 2007.

Catalan, S. *Sa moun ka di*. Cayenne: Ibis Rouge, 1997.

Eyerman, R and Andrew Jamison. *Music and Social Movements: Mobilizing Traditions in the Twentieth Century*. London: Cambridge University Press, 1998.

Lafontaine, M.-C. "Terminologie Musicale en Guadeloupe: Ce que le Créole nous dit de la Musique." In *Langage et société 32*, June 1985.

Le Monde. "Guadeloupe: La Situation a peu Évoluée Depuis la Decolonization." 13 Février, 2009.

Longhurst, B. *Popular Music and Society*. Cambridge: Polity Press, 1995.

Macionnis, J. and Ken Plummer, ed. *Sociology: A Global Introduction*, 2002.

Sept Magazine N° 1,542. "Mizik Gwadeloup: 50 Ans de Conditionnement à la Lutte.

Traini, C. *La Musique en Colère*. Paris: Science Po, Les presses, 2008.

Discography

Karukéra Sound System. *L'Album*. Guadeloupe: Don's Music, 1998.

Fuckly. *L'indiscipliné*. Guadeloupe: Riko Records, 2001.

Star Jee et Exxos. *Wòch goumé a vié nèg*. Guadeloupe: Fwi Sons Records, 2002.

Soft. *Kadans a péyi la*, Créon Music, 2006.

Robert Loyson. *Nostalgie Caraïbes*. Guadeloupe: Disques Celini, 2007.

Will the Real *Nèg Mawon* Please Stand Up:
Subversive Bodies in the Inner Cities of Kingston Jamaica
Nathalie Montlouis

Austen -Broos, Diane. "Race/Class: The Discourse of Heritable Identity". New West Indian Guide. http://www.kitlv-journals.nl/index.php/nwig/article/viewFile/3287/4048 (accessed March 27, 2011).

Campbell, Mavis C. *The Maroons of Jamaica, 1655–1796: A History of Resistance, Collaboration & Betrayal*. Granby: Bergin & Garvey. 1988.

Chamoiseau, Patrick. *Biblique des Derniers Gestes*. Paris: Gallimard. 2001.

Chevannes, Barry. *Rastafari Roots and Ideology*. USA: Syracuse University Press. 1994.

—. "Introducing the Native Religions of Jamaica." In *Rastafari and Other African-Caribbean Worldviews*. New Jersey: Rutgers University Press. 1998.

Chinweizu. *Decolonizing the African Mind*. Lagos Nigeria: Pero Press. 1987.

Clarke John et al. "Subcultures, Cultures and Class". In *Resistance through Rituals: Youth Subcultures in Post-War Britain*. Edited by Stuart Hall and Tony Jefferson. London: Routledge. 2003.

Cooper, Carolyn. *Sound Clash: Jamaican Dancehall Culture at Large*. New York: Palgrave Macmillan. 2004.

Cress Welsing, Frances. *The Isis Papers: The Key to the Colors*. USA: Third World Press. 1992.

Donatien-Yssa, Patricia. *Vaincre la Souffrance dans Autobiographie de ma mère de Jamaica Kincaid*. Paris: Le Manuscrit. 2007.

Dourmec, Eric. *Caribbean Civilisation: The English Speaking Caribbean since independence*. Toulouse: Press de l'Université du Mirail. 2003.

EABIC. *Deliver us From Evil*. Nantes: EABIC Press. 2008.

Frankenberg, Ruth. *White Women, Race Matters: The Social Construction of Whiteness*. Minneapolis: University of Minnesota Press. 1993.

Gelder, Ken. *Subcultures: Cultural Histories and Social Practice*. New York: Routledge. 2007.

Henry, William "Lez." *Whiteness Made Simple: Stepping into the Grey Zone*. London: Nubeyond Ltd.2007.

Karam, Antoine. Preface. Region Guyane. *Le Marronnage ou la Resistance á l'Esclavage*. http://www.cr-guyane.fr/ressources/File/jan10/livret-Marronnage-V8.pdf (accessed March 16 2011).

Kennedy, Fred W. *A Narrative of the Life and Adventures of Samuel Sharpe, A West Indian Slave Written by Himself, 1832*. Kingston: Ian Randle Publishers. 2008.

Lake, Obiagele. *Rastafari Women: Subordination in the Midst of Liberation Theology*. Durham: Carolina Academic Press. 1998.

Mathurin Mair, Lucille. A Historical Study of Women in Jamaica, 1655–1844. Jamaica: University of the West Indies Press. 2006.

McFarlane, Adian, A. "The epistemological Significance of 'I-and I'." In *Chanting Down Babylon*, edited by N. Murrell, D. Spencer, and A. McFarlane. Philadelphia: Temple University Press. 1998.

Montlouis, Nathalie. *Bobo Shanti Empresses In and Out of Babylon: A Radical community and the Gender Debate in the Caribbean*. Diss. School of Oriental and African Studies. 2011.

Price, Richard. *Maroons Societies: Rebel Slave Communities in the Americas*. USA: JHU Press. 1996.

Reckford, Verena. "From Burru Drums to Reggae Riddims: The Evolution of Rasta Music." In *Chanting Down Babylon*, edited by N. Murrell, D. Spencer, and A. McFarlane. Philadelphia: Temple University Press. 1998.

Tafari-Ama, Imani. *Blood Bullets and Bodies: Sexual Politics Below Jamaica's Poverty Line*. USA: Multi Media Communications. 2006.

Van Dijk, Frank J. *Jahmaica*. New York: One Drop Books. 1993.

Yawney, Carole. "To Grow a Daughter: Cultural Liberation and the Dynamics of Oppression in Jamaica." *Feminism from Pressure to Politics*, edited by A. Milesand G. Finn. Quebec: Black Rose Books. 1989.

The Creole Hip Hop Culture: Between Tradition and Modernity, Orality and Scripturality
Steve Gadet

Bennett A. *Popular Music and Youth Culture: Music, Identity and Place*. London: Palgrave Mac Millan, 2000.

Béthune C. *Pour une Esthétique du Rap*. France: Klincksieck, 2004.

Rose T. *Black Noise: Rap Music and Black Culture in Contemporary America*. USA: Wesleyan, 1994.

Uri F., Uri A. *Musique et musiciens de la Guadeloupe: Le chant de Karukéra*. Paris: L'Harmattan, 1991.

Interview with Christophe Sophy alias "Exxos" in 2005, Guadeloupe.

Internet sources

Raphael CONFIANT. Conference given on May 7, 2004 at the headquarters of DDE to address the new French executives that were transferred to Martinique.

http://www.potomitan.info/atelier/culture.php
http://www.rfimusique.com/musiquefr/articles/060/article_15060.asp
www.rfimusique.com/musiquefr/articles/060/article_15060.asp - 38k -
http://www.nastycrew.online.fr

Reggae, Rasta and the Transcendental Use of Alternative Public Spaces in the UK by Dancehall Deejays William "Lez" Henry

Alleyne, M. *Roots of Jamaican Culture*. London: Pluto Press, 1988.

Back, L. *New Ethnicities and Urban Culture*, London: UCL, 1996.

Barrett, L. *The Rastafarians*. Boston, USA: Beacon press, 1988.

Beckford, R. *Jesus Is Dread: Black Theology and Black Culture in Britain*. London: Darton, Longman and Todd, 1998.

—. *Jesus Dub*, London: Routledge, 2006.

Benston, K, W. *Performing Blackness: Enactments of African American Modernism*. London: Routledge, 2000.

Brathwaite, E. *History Of The Voice: The Development of Nation Language in Anglophone Caribbean Poetry*. London: New Beacon Books, 1984.

Cooper, C. *Noises in the Blood: Orality, Gender and the "Vulgar" Body of Jamaican Popular Culture*. London and Basingstoke: Macmillan Education Ltd, 1993.

Cooper, C. "'Rhythms of Resistance': Jamaican Dancehall Culture and the Politics of Survival." Paper received via email, May 2000.

—. *Sound Clash: Jamaican Dancehall Culture At Large*. New York: Palgrave Macmillan, 2004.

Foster, C. *Roots Rock Reggae: An Oral History of Reggae Music from Ska to Dancehall*. New York City: Billboard Books, 1999.

Gabriel, D. *Layers of Blackness: Colourism in the African Diaspora*. London: Imani Media Ltd, 2007.

Garvey. A. J. *The Philosophies & Opinions of Marcus Garvey: Or Africa For The Africans*. Mass USA: The Majority Press, 1986.

Gilroy, P. *Between Camps: Nations, Cultures and the Allure of Race*. London: Penguin Group, 2000.

—. *There Ain't no Black in the Union Jack: The Cultural Politics of Race and Nation*. London: Hutchinson Education, 1987.

—. *The Black Atlantic: Modernity and Double Consciousness*. London: Verso, 1993.

Hebdige, D. *Subculture: The Meaning of Style*. London: Methuen, 1979.

Henry, W 'Lez'. *Whiteness Made Simple: Stepping into the GREY zone*. London: Learning By Choice Publications, 2007.

—. *What The Deejay Said: A Critique From The Street!* London: Learning By Choice Publications, 2006.

John, G. *Taking a Stand: Gus John Speaks on Education, Race, Social Action & Civil Unrest 1980–2005*. Manchester: Gus John Partnership

Ltd, 2006.

Jones, S. *White Youth And Popular Jamaican Culture*, PhD thesis for Centre for Community and Urban Studies, Faculty of Arts, University of Birmingham, 1986.

Martin, T. *Race First*. Dover, Massachusetts, USA: The Majority Press, 1986.

Mintz. S. W. *Caribbean Transformations*. New York: Columbia University Press, 1989.

Noble, D. "Ragga Music: Dis/respecting Black Women and Dis/reputable Sexualities." In *Un/settled Multiculturalisms: Diasporas, Entanglements, Transruptions*, edited by Hesse B. London, New York: Zed, 2000.

Pickering, M. "Racial Stereotypes". In *Social Identities: Multidisciplinary Approaches*, edited by Taylor, G. & Spencer, S. London: Routledge, 2004.

Pieterse, J. N. *White on Black : Images of Africa and Blacks in Western Popular Culture*. London: Yale University Press in association with Cosmic Illusion Productions, Amsterdam, 1992.

Pryce, K. *Endless Pressure: A Study of West Indian Lifestyles in Bristol*. Harmondsworth: Penguin, 1979.

Spencer, J. M. *The Rhythms of Black Folk: Race, Religion and Pan-Africanism*. Trenton, NJ: Africa World Press, Inc, 1995.

Sutcliffe, D. and Wong, A., eds. *The Language of the Black Experience*. Oxford: Basil Blackwell Ltd, 1986.

Synnott, A. & Howes, D. "Canada's Visible Minorities: identity and Representation". In *Re-Situating Identities: The Politics of Race Ethnicity Culture*, edited by Amit-Talai, V. & Knowles, C. Ontario: Broadview Press, 1996.

Ture, K. and Charles Hamilton. *Black power: The Politics of Liberation in America*. USA: Vintage Books, 1992.

Ugwu, C., ed. *Let's Get It On: The Politics of Black Performance*. Seattle: Baypress, 1995.

Author's interviews

Blacker Dread, Carolyn Cooper & Junior Kelly all feature on the documentary *Resisting the system: Reggae in the 21st century*, London: Nu-Beyond, 2010

Macka B. October 24, London, England, 2001.

Discography

Blackout JA. *Live session*. Albany Theatre, London, 2010.
Buju Banton. *Love me Browning*. Jamaica: Penthouse Record Label, 1992.
Capleton. Interview Hot 97 FM, New York: Audio tape, 1997.
Lezlee Lyrix. *Sound System Recording*. 1991.
Macka B. "African Slavery," "Global Messenger Album," London: Ariwa Records, 2000.
Nardo Ranks. "Them a Bleach," Jamaica: Dancehall Classics Label, 1992.
Vibz Kartel. "Look pon we" Jamaica: Reggae Promo copy, 2011.

On the Paths of Marronnage to the Creation of French Speaking Dancehall and Rap Music: Interviews with West Indian Artists from Guadeloupe and Martinique
Stéphanie Melyon-Reinette

Melyon-Reinette et al. *La Révolution antillaise: quelle place pour l'outre-mer dans la République?* Paris: Eyrolles, 2009.

From the Great Island to the African Continent through the Western World: Itineraries of a "Return to the Origins" through Hip Hop Music in Madagascar (2000–2011)
Klara Boyer-Rossol

Bayart, J.-F., Peter Geschiere and Francis Nyamnjoh. "Autochtonie, démocratie et citoyenneté en Afrique." In *Critique internationale* 10, 177–194, January 2011.
Bazin H. *La Culture Hip-Hop*. Paris, Desclée De Brouwer, 1995.
Boyer-Rossol K. "Les Makoa en Pays Sakalava : Une Ancestralité Entre Deux Rives. Ouest de Madagascar, XIXe-XXe siècles." In *Les traites et *les esclavages. Perspectives historiques et contemporaines*, edited by M. Cottias, E. Cunin, A. de Almeida Mendes, 189–199. Paris, Karthala, collection Esclavages, 2010.
—. "La stigmatisation des *Makoa* ou *Masombika* : les séquelles de l'esclavage à Madagascar (XIXe -XXe siècles)." In *Kaf*, edited by L. Medea, 31–38, Zarlor Editions, 2009.
—. De Morima à Morondava : itinéraires d'ancêtres venus « de l'au-delà des mers. Contribution à l'étude de la formation du groupe makoa (côte ouest de Madagascar au XIXe siècle) ». In *Madagascar et*

l'Afrique, edited by D. Nativel, F. Rajaonah, 183–217. Paris, Karthala, 2007.

Campbell G. "The origins and Demography of Slaves in Nineteenth Century Madagascar: A chapter in the history of the African ancestry of the Malagasy." In F. Rajaoson, I. Rakoto, *Fanandevozana ou Esclavage. Colloque International sur l'esclavage à Madagascar, Antananarivo, 24–28 sept. 1996*, Antananarivo, Musée d'Art et d'Archéologie, vol. I, 1996.

Guedj J. and Antoine Heimann. "Sociologie Politique du rap Français : Nouvelle Approche du Mouvement Rap."http://heimann.antoine.free.fr/ (accessed September 26, 2007).

Nativel D. and Rajaonah F. *Madagascar et l'Afrique. Entre Identité Insulaire et Appartenances Historiques*. Paris, Karthala, 2007.

Ntarangwi M. *East African Hip-Hop: Youth Culture and Globalization*. Urbana, University of Illinois Press, 2009.

Rafidinarivo C. *Empreintes de la Servitude dans les Sociétés de l'Océan Indien*, Paris, Karthala, 2009.

Internet Sources

Vidéoclips de rap malgache consultables sur dailymotion et youtube (2000–2011)
http://www.donsmokilla.com/
www.hhdago.com
www.madahiphop.com
www.myspace.motamd
www.myspace.com/sekelblock
www.rap-gasy.com

CONTRIBUTORS

Michelle, Bermiss-Smith (PhD)
Assistant professor
Literature, Cultural Studies, Carnival. James Madison University, Harrisonburg (Virginia)

An assistant professor in James Madison University's English department, she was awarded the Woodrow Wilson National Fellowship Foundation Junior Faculty Career Enhancement Fellowhip (2007) for the book project Carnival of the Spirit, a study of the Trinidad Carnival's aspects of freedom in music and fiction.

Her research generally focuses on the formation of the black diaspora identity through Caribbean, African and black American fiction and popular culture. Other scholarly interests include American and French-language Rap music; and the intersections of Hip Hop cultural formations and politics.

Dr. Smith-Bermiss is an alumna of Queens College, City University of New York (BA), and completed a CUNY Study Abroad Year at Université de Paris VIII: St-Denis. She is also a graduate of the University of Virginia (MA, PhD). She has held a Social Science Research Council/Mellon Dissertation Fellowship, the Patricia Roberte Harris Graduate Fellowship at the University of Virginia and an Andrew W. Mellon Minority Undergraduate Fellowship. She currently teaches courses in Caribbean Literature and Culture, African American Literature, Oral Lit.: Evolution of Hip Hop and American Studies.

Klara Boyer-Rossol
Postgraduate student in African History

A postgraduate student in Africa History at the Université Paris 7, she is a member the SEDET and CIRESC (GDRI du CNRS) research laboratories, and is preparing her PhD dissertation dealing with "Les Makoa à l'Ouest de Madagascar, une ancestralité entre deux rives. XIXe-XXe s." Her main research topics essentially concern illegal human trafficking, the oral memory of slavery, the African diaspora, and the history of representations. She participates and heads projects such as the training of teachers in the new national school programs, the presentation of "Regards sur l'Afrique" for the Creteil Academy (2010), the organization of the first commemoration day of the Makoa in Western Madagascar,

2008, and the UNESCO Route de l'esclave mission. She has published "De Morima à Morondava: itinéraires d'ancêtres venus "d'au-delà les mers. Contribution à l'étude de la formation du groupe makoa (côte ouest de Madagascar. XXe siècle)," in *Madagascar et l'Afrique*, by Khartala Editions, 2007.

Marie Cousin
Postgraduate student in ethnomusicology
Marie Cousin is continuing her doctorate at the Nice Sophia Antipolis University, tutored by ethnomusicologist, researcher and Professor Luc Charles-Dominique, writing thesis in ethnomusicology on the *tambor-de-crioulas*. She is interested in themes such as ritual, performance, rhythm, dance, Creole identity and memory. She is part of the French Ethnomusicology Society (SFE) and gives music classes at Paris-Est Marne La Vallée University. She wrote an article on *Bumba-meu*-boi's ritual published in the "Cahiers d'ethnomusicologie" (2011–23).

Marie-Line Dahomay
Traditional Gwo Ka singer
Curator at the Caribbean Heritage Multimedia Center, Guadeloupe.
A traditional artist, D.U. in Ethnomusicology, world dances and rhythms at Sophia Antipolis University in Nice (2002), she is curator at the Caribbean Heritage Multimedia Centre of Guadeloupe's *Conseil Général* (the local assembly in charge of the department). As a singer, she is part of a female traditional music band, composed of women only, called Kalindi Ka.

Steve Gadet
PhD in English Language and Literature
Lecturer, English Department, UAG
Steve Gadet lectures at the University of the French West Indies (Université des Antilles et de la Guyane, UAG). Before being appointed in 2011, Steve GADET monitored English classes at the Guadeloupe Campus in Saint-Claude. He is also a Radio broadcaster. He is the author of *La fusion de la culture Hip-Hop et du mouvement rastafari* (March 2010) and *La culture hip-hop dans tous ses états* (September 2010). His work was awarded the Prix de Thèse 2009 of the Institut Des Amériques.

William "Lez" Henry
Social Anthropologist, Visiting Research Fellow.

Dr. William "Lez" Henry is a social anthropologist, born in Lewisham, London of Jamaican parents and is the British deejay Lezlee Lyrix. He lectured in the Department of Sociology, Goldsmiths College and is now a visiting research fellow. He is a researcher, consultant and staff trainer for Nu-Beyond Ltd: Learning by Choice!

Dr. Henry delivers various educational and training programmes, specialising in race, ethnicity, diversity, equality, education and black history and is presently delivering his "Goal Models: striving for self excellence" and "guns, gangs families & communities" empowerment programmes in secondary schools in Lewisham and other boroughs. He is a founder member of the National Independent Education Coalition and The Lewisham Black Fathers Support Group and in summer 2010 led his second successful study tour to Egypt.

Dr. Henry's commitment to educational excellence, especially for African and African Caribbean children, has resulted in Positive Mental Attitude Community College and Nu Beyond Ltd applying to open an Independent Free Secondary School, the Positive Mental Attitude Community School, under the UK Government's Free School initiative.

Dr. Henry has a keen interest in the counter-cultures of the African diaspora and whiteness studies, and his research in these areas have led to several publications including two sole-authored books : *Whiteness Made Simple: Stepping into the Grey Zone!* (2007) and *What the Deejay Said: A Critique from the Street!* (2006), published by Learning By Choice Publications.

He has featured on numerous documentaries, TV and radio programmes and his latest publications is "Conceptualisation and effects of Social Exclusion, Racism and Discrimination and Coping Strategies of Individuals and Families," in *Black Families in Britain as the Site of Struggle*, Manchester University Press 2010.

Florence Latappy
Réunionese Dancer and choreographer

Florence has been dancing Réunionese traditional dance since her early childhood. She started ballet when she was eight years-old, first at the "Centre Culturel de Neuilly Plaisance," then at the "Conservatoire de Neuilly Sur Marne," and the "Ecole Goubé" in Paris. She has taken classes and workshops in African dance in France, Belgium and Africa, respectively with Norma Claire, Eneida Castro, Vincent Harisbo, Chryzogone Diangouaya, Irène Tassembedo, Alphonse Tiérou, Elsa Wolliaston, George

Momboye and Chantal Loial. She trained at Free Dance Song. She also attended classes for professionals at Micadanses, Ménagerie de Verre and the CND (Serge Ricci, Lola Keraly, Frederic Lescure, Martin Kravitz, Nina Dipla). After collaborations in Paris with Christelle François, among others, in 2004 she created the Compagnie Maloya Metiss, seeking her Creole roots and taking African and Réunion musicians as an example. Florence gets most of her inspiration from traditional and modern (Hip Hop) Réunion Creole culture, but also practices other body techniques such as Tai Chi. She works from improvisation, but is also interested in the social role of *maloya* and *moring*. In 2006, she moved back to Réunion. She continued to practice *moring* and took percussion classes. She met Didier Filo, a Hip Hop dancer with whom she has been working with since, and continues her work with amateurs (classes, internships, interventions in schools). Florence is mostly interested in ethnic dances, non-Western techniques, especially African contemporary dance, and contemporary dance in all its diversity. She seeks her Metis identity and respect for the body. Florence teaches traditional Réunion dance and a very personal contemporary Afro-Creole dance.

Stéphanie Melyon-Reinette, (PhD)
Postgraduate student in Political Science
PhD in American Sociology/Civilization
    Stéphanie Melyon-Reinette is from Guadeloupe (FWI). As a researcher (PhD in US Civilization), she graduated from the University of the French West Indies in 2008. She gained her doctorate with the highest award, A+, with congratulations of the whole jury. In her PhD, she was interested in the integration of the Haitian population. She has published two books extracted from her PhD dissertation. The first one is entitled *Haïtiens à New York City; Entre Amérique Noire et Amérique Multiculturelle* (L'Harmattan, Coll. Minorités & Sociétés, 2009). She deals with the issue of integration of the Haitian community in New York City through the migratory process, the strategies adopted by the protagonists, between a segregated black America and a dominant "mainstream," and from the first-generation to the others. A crossroad of factors and cultural spheres giving birth to varying identity and cultural patterns, rhizome-wise. She has just got released a second book entitled *Mémoires de Jaspora; Voix intimes d'Haïtiens enracinés en Amérique du Nord* (Editions Persée, 2011), focussing her research on Haitin integration in France. She has published numerous articles and organizes conferences (via her association Agoraculture). Among her other publications are: "Afro-Américanisation: D'Haïti à New York City," In *Cahiers Sens Public n°10, Un Monde en*

Noir et Blanc. Amitiés Postcoloniales (2009); "De la dédiasporisation des jeunes Haïtiens à New-York," in *Études caribéennes*; "Haïti, Une lépreuse parmi les Nations: Essai sur l'antihaïtianisme caribo/nord-américain," in L.-A; Joint et J. Merion (coord.) and *L'Immigration haïtienne dans la Caraïbe: quel défis pour l'unité des peuples?* (Editions Nestor, 2011).

Edmond Mondesir
Bèlè (Martinique Traditional music) singer

Edmond Mondésir, born in Fort-de-France in 1948, is a professor of philosophy and Martinican politician. He is also known as a *bèlè* singer and composer. He is a pillar of traditional music in Martinique. He is a real activist in the defence of this music. Since the 1970s, he has fought and advocated for the maintaining of *bèlè* authenticity and integrity of the *bèlè* spirit, even in the modern trends.

He founded the band Bèlènou with Léon Bertide in 1980 and recorded the first traditional album, releasing a second in 1983. Between 1980 and 2002, Edmond Mondésir realized nine recordings of traditional and modern *bèlè*.

In 2003, he was awarded the Martinique Sacem Prize for his whole body of art, among which are the recordings: *Emosion Bèlè: Les chants du Père, la musique du fils* (2006), *Emosion Bèlè 2: Hommage à Ti Emile* (2008), *Nou Pa Pè* (2009) and *Emosion Bèlè* (2011).

Nathalie Montlouis
PhD student, SOAS, London.

Born in Martinique, Nathalie Montlouis has always been attracted by Caribbean culture. After graduating with a Literature Baccalauréat at the Lycée polyvalent de Sainte-Marie, she attained a Bachelor of Art in English at the Caribbean Union College, Trinidad. Back in Martinique, she gained a DEA in English-speaking Caribbean Civilization. She is presently a postgraduate student at the School of Oriental and African Studies in London. Fond of Caribbean culture and gender studies, her PhD dissertation deals with the concept of submission of women in the Bobo Shantie's Rastafari House. Nathalie is also particularly interested in the universe of *bèlè* and African history in Creole traditions.

Ronnie "Tiwony" Moukoko-Edimo
Reggae Dancehall artist, Guadeloupe

Influenced by local and national artists such as Féfé Typical, Nbee, Janik and Nuttea, he began music in Guadeloupe by founding the famous Influence Sound in 1993. Two years later, he returned to Paris to make a career in music. He features on the compilation *BIG UP* in a duet with Boubou entitled "JAH est l'honneur" and many others. It was the original soundtrack to the movie *Ma 6-té va craquer* which made him widely known, with the track "Pas de Timinik." He was awarded a gold disc for this song. His open-mindedness enables him to participate in Hip Hop projects like 2Bal2Neg, Manu Key, Rohff and Lady Laistee. His album *BENI YO* saw him awarded his first Guadeloupe Sacem Prize in 2000. A second album *Double Trouble Express* in 2002 won a second SACEM prize in 2003. His personal sound system Blackwarellsound released a mixtape "Mon Itinéraire," compiling more than fifty tracks. In 2007 he recorded the album *Fly* with Influences Music. In 2009 he recorded *Viv la Vi* and *Cite Soleil*.

Rodolphe "Neg Lyrical" Richefal
Creole Hip Hop emcee, Martinique

Neg Lyrical was born in 1974 in Fort-de-France. Through literature and history he recognised the complexity of the West Indian identity and the importance of Creole that he would use in the future. In the 1980s, a new trend broke out in Europe and the whole Caribbean area, US Rap music, with its icons Public Enemy, Run DMC, KRS One and Gangstarr. For Neg Lyrical, it was a revelation. He took to the mic at fourteen years-old, working on his musical style, a hybrid of local influences and a flow inspired by the greatest US emcees. The rapper founded a crew Negkipakafélafet in 1989 with Boogie Flaha, Neg Madnick, MP, Duduss, Steel, Kool Saze, and deejay Spécial Mark. His lyrics are politically conscious. He is recognized as the natural pioneer of Martiniquan Rap music and the spearhead of the urban movement. He has recorded for various compilations and singles (Plitaplitris, Discipline, Manmay lev) and works with different artists in the US and Caribbean, such as New-Yorker Erick Prad, Wu Tang Clan member Buddha Monk, Straïka D, Mc Janik, Guy Al MC, King Kalabash, Baron Black, and Féfé Typical. His latest album was *Marronnage* in 2011.

Joel "Ashaman" Valandy
Reggae artist, Guadeloupe

Ashaman Jahlawa aka Joël Valandy, was born in 1980 in Sainte Rose, Guadeloupe (FWI). He undertook, in parallel with his musical projects, pharmaceutics and chemistry in Canada and then in Belgium. He then focused on music anew, with recordings on compilations: *Ti Moun Soley* ("Béni Mwen"), *Hold Up* ("Gwada World"), and *Lalin Riddim* ("I Don't Know").

NOTES

[1] In this article, this will be focussed on Guadeloupe. Indeed, because of the various migration movements, especially the massive waves of the Bumidom, *Gwo ka* evolved differently in Paris. This particular topic is analysed by the musicologist Frédéric Négrit in his work: *Musique et Immigration dans la Société Antillaise (2004)*.

[2] In the Collection Gerrit Van Den Boom, In the collection of Boissel, Candalen, Petit et Phos (1905 and 1935).

[3] At the beginning of slavery, Labat describes drums called *baboula* and *grand tambour* ("big drum") by the enslaved (Labat, 1704).

[4] Gosier is the name of a coastal village in Guadeloupe.

[5] *Gros tambour* in French.

[6] This *santimanka*, difficult to define, is in the choice of intervals and harmonies.

[7] *Makè* is the name given to the drummer who plays the solo on the *make* drum.

[8] The Creole word *bigidi* comes from the onomatopoeia *bigidi*, used when someone or something has fallen.

[9] Swaré Léwòz can be translated by Léwòz Party. Léwòz is the name of one of the seven rhythms of Ka and also the name given to this type of parties. A more thorough description of the Swaré Léwòz is available in Lafontaine, (1988, p. 71)

[10] *Kout' Tanbou* can literally mean "a piece of drumming." It is a shorter performance than the *Swaré léwòz. Kout'tanbou* are organised on markets, usually during local fairs. Nowadays, the *kout' tanbou* on such occasions has been replaced by the *Swaré-léwòz*.

[11] *Bamboula anba mawché* : Gwo ka demonstrations during local fairs.

[12] Groups such as : La Brisquante, Les Acacias, Le Cercle Culturel Ansois, Emeraude.

[13] Doudouistic is a neologism created for the purpose of this article's translation. It comes from the French concept *Doudouism*, which defines all art forms presenting Caribbean clichés as the cultural reality. The tour operators selling the Caribbean as paradise with white sand beaches and smiling, non-intrusive locals can be said to use a doudouistic approach to commodify these islands.

[14] In 1946, the French Caribbean islands received a new status. They were no longer French colonies, but French departments and regions with the same rights and duties as those on the continent.

[15] Bureau des Migration des Départements d'Outre Mer (années 60). The migrants from the Bumidom can be compared to the Empire Windrush generation in the UK.

[16] (Négrit, Musique et Immigration dans la Société Antillaise, 2004).

[17] The record *Vélo et son Gros ka* was the first to which notorious drummers such as Vélo, Brabant and Napo contributed. In 1962, the ethnologist Alan Lomax made *Gwo ka* audio tapes, which only became accessible to the Guadeloupean public in

2007 thanks to a donation made to the Médiathèque Caraïbe de Basse-Terre that allowed a CD to be released.

[18] A Rhythm made with the mouth that can be loosely compared to beat box performances.

[19] Many of them were already performing with folkloric groups.

[20] Schools of Bébé Rospart, Teddy Pelissier, Foubap, Latilyé Vélo.

[21] Sony Troupé, Arnaud Dolmen.

[22] Kamodjaka, l'Akadémiduka, Akiyo.

[23] The drum or *tanbouka* is covered with goat skin.

[24] A *djembe* is a West African Drum, from Mali.

[25] This can be translated by an Artisan Master.

[26] Kamodjaka, Akadémiduka, Sa Ki Ta'w.

[27] A Prominent *Gwo ka* dancer and teacher, and founder of l'Akadémiduka dance school.

[28] This centre, internationally known, promotes a dance technique based on the *bigidi* posture, or the art of remaining on the verge of balance and instability in *Gwo ka*.

[29] François Ladreseau, Aurel, Chibon, Rozan Monza

[30] The work of Gwosiwo, of the Big Band Ka, of Lizin Tanbou.

[31] Société des auteurs, compositeurs et éditeurs de musique. A French professional association collecting payments of artists' rights and distributing the rights to the original authors, composers and publishers.

[32] Among the most famous are Josélita Jacques, Jacqueline Etienne and Evelyne Zenon.

[33] Women sing the classics of *Gwo ka*.

[34] *Group a po* or *Mas a Po* is a Creole expression defining carnival groups using drums covered with an animal's skin. The *group a po* is different from the *group á caisse Claire,* which are synthetic materials.

[35] Senjan is the characteristic rythm of the *group a po*.

[36] Kafé Ka Lévé, Gwakasonné, Les Libératè, Katouré, Milflè, Héritage.

[37] "Creole Project," 1998 Label Justin time.

[38] "Liyannaj," 1999, Déclic Production.

[39] David Murray, Kenny Garrett, Chris Joris, Archie Cheep.

[40] "My objective is not to restore something that exists, *Gwo ka*, the *Swaré*, or the jazz from the Blue Note label. My objective was to define a full toned space that cannot be found elsewhere because I have created its parameters according to my own emotional needs. What I have sought was the opening of a window from one music to another. *Gwo ka* is essentially rhythm and voice. Its collaboration with Jazz enriches it with harmony, orchestration, and melodic improvisation. This allows the creation of colours that are not usually found in Jazz. It's a happy marriage" (Schwartz-Barth in Dicale, 2006). Interview de Jacques Schwarz-Barth, *Le Figaro*, August 29, 2006, Bertrand Dicale.

[41] The album *Invitation* from the Modern *Gwo ka* group Kimbol, produced under the artistic direction of Sonny Troupé in 2009 symbolises a new conception of "*Ka* modernity" by the group.

---

[42] Dominique Coco, Soft, Ka Koustik, Kassav

[43] Zouk is a French Caribbean musical genre.

[44] Patrick Saint Eloi, Jocelyne Labylle, Tanya Saint-Val.

[45] Principally in their first album *Kadans a Péyi La* (2005).

[46] Admiral T, Chris, Daly, Ka and Y, Ines Kay, Exxos.

[47] Carole Venutolo et Marie-Line Dahomay (Opéra Ka, Opéra Soleil), Marie-Claude Buffon (album *Sé Nou Dé* 2011).

[48] Author of *Métod-Ka* (1997) a method for *ka*.

[49] Online magazine *Parallèle*, Jazz and *Gwo ka*, la belle Alliance, March 10, 2005.

[50] Negro music.

[51] http://www.citizenjazz.com/Jacques-Schwarz-Bart.html

[52] LKP Lyannaj Kont Pwofitasyon (alliance against exploitation) is a social movement instigated by the trade union UGTG in Guadeloupe, denouncing the imbalance between the cost of life and the standard income per household in the island. The general strike, which lasted for at least forty days, was massively supported by the Guadeloupean people.

[53] Article 2 of the *Convention Pour la sauvegarde du patrimoine immatériel*. http://www.unesco.org (accessed September 2011).

[54] Article 13 de la *Convention Pour la sauvegarde du patrimoine immatériel*. http://www.unesco.org (accessed September 2011).

[55] This could be translated in Creole as *vié nèg*, literally meaning "old nigger." "Nigger" practices were usually those associated with the African cultural heritage of the island. "Acceptable" practices were European or what was regarded as such.

[56] Creole translation: *An Lot Chimen Pou la Jénès*.

[57] Granier de Cassagnac. Voyage aux Antilles françaises, anglaises, danoises, espagnoles, à Saint Domingue et aux Etats Unis d'Amérique, 2 volumes. Première partie : Les Antilles françaises. Paris, Dauvin et Fontaine Libraires, 1842, p. 211.

[58] *Pour les blancs, la nuit est le moment du repos; pour le nègre qui ne travaille qu'à contre-cœur, la nuit c'est le moment de la danse ... Il oublie qu'il a travaillé aujourd'hui, et qu'il faut dormir en paix et réparer ses forces pour recommencer demain*

[59] Le R.P Labat. Nouveau Voyage aux Isles de l'Amérique. Paris 1742. Réédition Editions des Horizons Caraïbes T 2. p. 401. Fort de France 1972.

[60] *La danse est leur passion favorite, je ne crois pas qu'il y ait peuple au monde qui y soit plus attaché qu'eux. Quand les maîtres ne leur permettent pas de danser dans l'habitation, ils feront trois ou quatre lieux après qu'ils aient quitté leur travail de la sucrerie le samedi à minuit pour se trouver dans quelque lieu où ils savent qu'il y a une danse*

[61] *Ils passent en ces récréations non seulement l'après dinée entière les dimanches, mais continuent quelque fois leur divertissement toute la nuit, ne se séparant les uns des autres pour s'en retourner à leurs habitations que pour se rendre avec les autres à l'heure qu'on les mène au travail. Pendant que les hommes et les femmes dansent et sautent de toute leur force, les petits enfants composent une autre danse à part, où il y a du plaisir à les voir imiter les postures de leurs Pères et Mères, et contrefaire leurs gestes : mais ce qui est étonnant dans ces enfants, c'est qu'ils ne*

s'ennuient pas plus dans ces passe-temps que les grandes personnes, de sorte qu'ils chantent et dansent jusqu'à ce que le sommeil les accable

[62] G. Pinckard. Note on the West Indies, London 1806. p. 263–264.

[63] Le père du Tertre. Histoire générale des Antilles, habitées par les Français. Réed. De l'édition de Th. Jolly de 1667–1671, Ed. des Horizons Caraïbes, Fort de France, 1973 t 2 p. 491

[64] "The events of December 1959" euphemistically refers to the three days of rioting that shook Fort de France in December 1959. It was a riot with nationalistic undertones opposing the French (white) police and the French (Martiniquan) population. It concluded in the death of three teenagers. For more information, see Placide (2009).

[65] In French: *Organisation de la Jeunesse Anticolonialiste Martiniquaise.*

[66] These are the names of several Martiniquan traditional dances and music styles.

[67] Ti-Emile is one of the first *bèlè* artists to have been noticed both locally and internationally.

[68] Arid zone, desertification inside Nordeste.

[69] Bush.

[70] The *quilombos* are large communities constituted by a group of little Maroon villages called *mocambos*.

[71] Alvarenga, Oneyda (1948).

[72] Here, the word Creole is used according to the Réunionese meaning: as a noun, it means any person born in Réunion Island or born outside, but of Réunionese culture and parents. The adjective has the same meaning.

[73] *Sega* is a traditional dance probably from *maloya*. It is thought to be a European interpretation of the original *maloya* of the slaves. *Sega* is generally danced in pairs. It has been rocking Réunion people for generations, just like the *bigine*. There are several different styles, such as romance, the *sega* of the street singers, and more humorous. There are even *segas* with very beautiful lyrics, stating that everything is possible. Some very modern *segas* also exist. The tertiary base is the same as *maloya*. The orchestra, sometimes live, is often composed of a battery, a bass, a guitar or an accordion, sometimes a *kayamb* and a triangle. You cannot miss it if you visit the island. The lyrics will give you an idea of Creole life, the taste of the population and its habits. Everybody knows at least one or more *sega*.

[74] I deliberately refrained from using the term patois, a word that has been rejected by most linguists since structuralism and more especially Saussure's works, because it implies a judgement about a language derived from another language that was politically imposed, like Latin in the Middle Ages in Europe. Today's linguists argue that languages are created through all sorts of influences. Because of their relative youth, it is not possible to say whether or not Creoles are languages. On this subject, I recommend reading specialised linguists on Creoles and pidgins (languages derived from English). I know, thanks to my linguistic studies, that a language builds itself on a reality and a way of thinking and working, and it reflects and transmits this. Its liveliness is an important issue in all cultural policies for this reason.

[75] Moring is a tradition similar to a war dance that has become a sport, first informal like most traditional practices of Réunion. It can be compared to the Brazilian *capoeira* and the Caribbean *damier*. Thanks to pioneers like Mr Jean René Dreinaza and historian Sudel Fuma, *moring* was rehabilitated and enhanced and became a sport with a Réunion Committee for Moring. I have been interested in this tradition for several years. I follow it and practise it, although I do not participate in the competitions.

[76] Réunion traditional wrestling

[77] Harris, Wilson. *History, Fable & Myth in the Caribbean and Guianas.* Wellesley: Calaloux Publications, 1995.

[78] Walcott, Derek. *The Antilles: Fragments of Epic Memory.* Harper Collins Canada, 1993.

[79] Jordan, Winthrop. *White Over Black: American Attitudes Toward the Negro, 1550–1812.* Chapel Hill: University of North Carolina Press, 1968.

[80] Smith, Faith. *Creole Recitations: John Jacob Thomas and Colonial Formation in the Late Nineteenth-Century Caribbean.* Charlottesville: University of Virginia Press, 2002.

[81] Franklin, John Hope & Loren Schweninger. *Runaway Slaves: Rebels on the Plantation.* NY: Oxford University Press, 1999.

[82] Gottlieb, Karla Lewis. *The Mother of Us All: A History of Queen Nanny, Leader of the Windward Jamaican Maroons.* Trenton: Africa World Press, 2000.

[83] Price, Richard. (ed.) *Maroon Societies: Rebel Slave Communities in the Americas.* Baltimore: Johns Hopkins University Press (3rd edition), 1996.

[84] *Caribbean* here is meant to refer in a generic or metonymic sense to the individual(s), as well as to the historic and political shared collective experience.

[85] Identity here describes both a unique individual sense of self, and in the Trinidadian context a shared sense of cosmopolitanism I call a "diversity-identity."

[86] As both key example and foundational text, we may cite Query XIV of Thomas Jefferson's *Notes on the State of Virginia* (1781): "To these objections [to racial integration], which are political, may be added others, which are physical and moral. The first difference which strikes us is that of colour. Whether the black of the negro resides in the reticular membrane between the skin and scarf-skin, or in the scarf-skin itself; whether it proceeds from the colour of the blood, the colour of the bile, or from that of some other secretion, the difference is fixed in nature, and is as real as if its seat and cause were better known to us. And is this difference of no importance? Is it not the foundation of a greater or less share of beauty in the two races?"

[87] Warner, Keith Q. *Kaiso! the Trinidad Calypso: A Study of Calypso As Oral Literature.* Passeggiata Pr, 1999.

[88] Boyce-Davies, Carol. *Black Women, Writing and Identity: Migrations of the Subject.* Routledge, 1994.

[89] "Palance" is a uniquely Trinidadian verb denoting enthusiastic feteing and dancing; in 2010 the artists JW & Blaze won both the Road March and International Power Soca Monarch with a song by that title.

[90] The European "carnivalesque" via Mikhail Bahktin is often misapplied to the New World's carnival traditions; I argue for a Caribbean recentring here.

[91] Robert Nesta Marley, "Them Belly Full (But We Hungry)" on *Natty Dread* (Island Records, 1974).

[92] Mr. Vegas, "Tek Way Yuhself" on *Hot It Up* (Universal Records, 2007).

[93] http://marvel.com/universe/Silver_Surfer, especially "Powers"

[94] Alyn Shipton, A new history of Jazz, Chapter 4.

[95] In 1942, the President of the American Federations of Musicians launched a strike on recordings that lasted until 1944.

[96] This term was invented on June 25, 1949.

[97] Translation: *Music against exploitation.*

[98] "Coalition Against Exploitation."

[99] http://www.lkp-gwa.org/revendications.htm

[100] 13:00 news bulletin presented by Eddy Planté, on Radio Caraïbe Internationale.

[101] Sept Magazine N° 1542, "Mizik Gwadeloup: 50 ans de conditionnement à la lutte" Paul Léo d'Hurville ["These are the ones who call the tune, and poor people work without being able to secure their future"].

[102] "Guadeloupe is choking! My friends, Guadeloupe is choking, she will not make it … We are planting sugar cane for a living, we sell it to the factory, they have closed the St Marthe factory I saw Guadeloupe choking, now, they close the Blanchet Factory and the one in Darboussier, what has Guadeloupe come to? The workers employed in these factories have worked there for years. Today the factory has shut down, where are they going to be employed? Guadeloupe is entangled; quickly remove the rope around her neck. There is no riches, the only riches is the sugar canes of the unfortunates."

[103] "Sugar cane juice from wealth."

[104] "Guadeloupeans, watch over the harvest, if you do not do it, Guadeloupe will go bankrupt."

[105] "Coalition Against Exploitation to untangle Guadeloupe"

[106] Karukera is the pre Colombian name for Guadeloupe.

[107] "The boat."

[108] "What will they do on the day that the boat will no longer moor in Guadeloupe? What will they eat, a piece of building or a piece of breadfruit? I say that it is high time that we wake up, let us fight to prevent the country from further collapse. Stop taking us for fools, stop taking us for Frenchmen, stop making us believe that we must worship money, our cultural heritage is not merely drinking rum and dance, working during the week and watching TV on weekends, while the country agonises, I know that the fishermen and the farmers are determined." From *L'Album* (1998) Don's Music.

[109] "Nowadays, no one wants to plant sugar cane, they do not want to work on the land to eat dasheens and yams. Guadeloupeans only drive Japanese cars, Mitsubishi, Hyundai and Daewoo cars are very popular … they do not want to farm while unemployment rates are soaring, everybody wants to become a lawyer or a doctor, and it is chaos. We have a beautiful country, but economically weak. If you analyse the situation, nothing works. It is not surprising that in such a system,

the tare is growing. Too many people live on benefits. They take us for children. Long ago, we used to produce and export a lot. Nowadays, we do not own anything and keep on buying Hyundai cars. We consume too much, we are the kings of champagne. We consume so much that we do not see the problem. They take our lands and as far as I am concerned, it is not a detail."

[110] Patrick Saint-Eloi, singer of the group Kassav (1958–2010).

[111] A popular *Gwo ka* singer.

[112] "They do not want Saint-Eloi, they do not want Marcel Lollia. In truth, they do not like the melody of their country. La soufrière (the Sulfurer) does not sleep. Just like you and me, she bubbles, one day she will erupt. It is she who carries me, it is she that moves me, she will take me further down the road. One day, the country's sufferings must explode."

[113] "Them."

[114] "Us."

[115] *Béké* is the name given to the descendants of the planters who owned slaves and most of the land available in Guadeloupe.

[116] "I am not better than anyone else, I need your opinion/ when I analyse what is going on, there are people that we should prosecute for crime against Guadeloupe."

[117] "Many want to become mayor at any cost, even if their hearts have turned sour/ They create alliances to sell their brothers and win trophies of longevity. They bequeath town halls to themselves and for the others, there is only unemployment. I do not earn much, I watch the others live large."

[118] "Politics has turned into foolery, scholars are on clouds, they sleep, many enjoy themselves, they flourish while we suffer, our history stagnates …."

[119] "The youth complains of being deprived, but what do they do to improve their situation, they finely plait their hair and criticise the society while looking at it …."

[120] "A young one shot another young one, a negro shot a negro/ What is more criminal is that we stand by and look."

[121] "Tell me, what is freedom when you do not have money to sustain yourself/ I long to see equality, but the children of the poorer families are always in need/ I long to see fraternity, but I see that the negroes never have money."

[122] "I am not better than another, I just need your opinion/when I analyse what is going on, we are those that deserve to be prosecuted for crimes against Guadeloupe."

[123] "I am fed up."

[124] "See how things run this year/ death is sold in small packs, it is an entire generation that is wasted/ cut, distributed and banked, the devil makes you trip. Some deals are profitable, the police is incapable /Men in ties take advantage, the block tries to manage/engaging in illegal businesses has become the only means to resist … The youth is threatened, sawed/sawed off shotgun/There aren't any jobs everyone gets excited over common places/Sitting in their council flats they wait for the flood. These guys stay there without ambitions, they are looking for trouble/ We have reached a level where to survive one must be play hard/Stop talking nonsense, in Guadeloupe one must play hard! / Your father is already tired, your mother gave up, your education has died … I am fed up with violence and

guns, it is high time that all of this stops/ I am fed up with scams and corruption/This gets on everyone's nerves, it is not going to end well."

[125] "A minimum of integration, a maximum of expulsion, a maximum of problems, a minimum of solutions, a maximum of men who cannot perform their paternity/ too many b... sleeping around to get benefits/ Too many employers robbers, scammers, exploiters/Too many trade unions, too many people on strike, too many empty promises for every elections/ Too many misuse of public m oney at the Conseil Regional ... They are all irresponsible, they are the ones responsible/Due to all the misuse of the public money, everyone is going crazy/while we are agonising, they gas tank is full/ They elaborate all sorts of strategies to fool the poor and everyone knows that when the cat is away, the mice will play."

[126] Sept Magazine 1,542. "Mizik Gwadeloup: 50 ans de conditionnement à la lute."

[127] Cité dans Musique en colère, Christophe Traini, 2008.

[128] Rapper from the group Karukera Krew, taken from the title "Lumumba", album: Wòch goumé a vié nèg, 2002, Fwi Sons Records. "I know the function of words when it is question to rekindle the pride of a people."

[129] Sonia Catalan, Sa moun ka di, Ibis Rouge, 1997: 26. "It is with music that the Negroes can be caught."

[130] Deejays are Reggae vocal performers and are akin to MCs or rappers and do not play records like DJs or Disc Jockeys.

[131] Sound systems cannot be reduced to "large mobile discos," as there is an aesthetic value that far transcends any such description. Speaker boxes are generally custom built or even home-made and the "set" amplifiers and other electronic equipment are electronically maintained by at least one member of the sound system family.

[132] Garveyism is a pan African philosophical stance taken from the teachings of the Honourable Marcus Mosiah Garvey.

[133] "Outernational" is a Jamaican term that has been used in Reggae circles for decades and basically suggests that the influence of the music and culture transcends geographical boundaries.

[134] Shadism is the privileging of lighter skinned Africans/blacks over darker skinned.

[135] S.S. Empire Windrush was one of the first ships to bring migrants from the Caribbean which explains why blacks in the UK are generally referred to as the Windrush generation.

[136] Rastafari suggest that the African needs to "overstand" their predicament which literally means to fully comprehend a problem by reasoning and therefore overcoming it, as opposed to being under it as the African has been "under-the-stand" of white supremacy for far too long. The sentiments are much the same in the usage of "downpress" as opposed to oppress, as your oppressor presses you down and not up.

[137] Rastafari say your oppressor presses you down therefore they are "downpressors."

[138] I use Africentric and not Afrocentric as an Afro was a powerful aesthetic, political statement, linked to the poignancy of the Black Power/Panther movement

of the 1960s and 1970s. As such, if we are to challenge the assumptions that an "enemy language" like English is premised upon, then we as Africans must determine how such challenges are made.

[139] For more on this idea of "Seasonal browness" see Cooper, C., *Sound Clash: Jamaican Dancehall Culture at Large,* New York: Palgrave Macmillan, 2004, 136–7.

[140] It literally means "to crush one's throat"; it's a time when rappers can express whatever they have on their mind, holding nothing back.

[141] "Laugh now cry later."

[142] "Niggers with attitude."

[143] "How could something like this happen?"

[144] Raphaël Confiant, Conference given on May 7, 2004, at the headquarters of DDE to address the new french executives that were transferred to Martinique. http://www.potomitan.info/atelier/culture.php

[145] Dub is a genre of music which grew out of Reggae in the 1960s. It's an instrumental version of an existing record.

[146] www.rfimusique.com

[147] Akiyo is a leading carnival band that returned to Guadeloupean culture during the 1970s despite the fact that it was looked down upon by a large majority of Guadeloupeans. They decided to place drums at the centre of their parade. Today, they are leaders and references regarding culture and Guadeloupean heritage.

[148] "The drum in French Creole."

[149] "Batty riders" are micro shorts revealing part of the backside!

[150] In the Reggae world, "slackness" is usually opposed to the "conscious." Slackness would evolve materialistic or sexual topics while conscious would stay closer to the militant Rastafari ethos with African pride or repatriation.

[151] "Matey war" is a Jamaican expression referring to the rivalry between women desiring the same man.

[152] In this article, I am going to use the word marronnage to mean social rebellion. See section 1.1. Linguistic clarification for a further explanation.

[153] *Fanm Mawon* is a Kréyol neologism that can literally be translated as woman-marron. In this article the word is used to translate the agency of women in the rebellion.

[154] Playing drums and worshipping African Gods, for instance, was prohibited. Only the *Burru* drums were tolerated as they were used to cadence the work of the enslaved (Reddock 1998).

[155] Myal is an African-Caribbean religion similar to Vodun in Haiti, or Santeria in Cuba. See the work of Stuart Stewart (2005) on the topic.

[156] Through the expression mixed race, I comprehend people who are visibly of mixed ethnicity. Indeed, because of its particular past, very few can claim to be from only one ethnic group.

[157] Anansy is the name of a very popular hero of Caribbean folk tales. He is usually a spider who compensates for his lack of physical strength with fantastic cunning abilities. Anansy is present in most Caribbean countries. In the French Caribbean, Anansy becomes a rabbit called *Kompè Lapen*.

[158] The images of success that are portrayed in the Jamaican society are of persons who are white, brown, and fair.

[159] Worth of the most epic rum shop arguments, guarantors of one's "reputation." (Burton, 1997).

[160] Original text : *Le Marronnage ne peut être regarde comme une forme ordinaire de rébellion. Il suggère la contestation ouverte d'un ordre social, économique et politique.*

[161] The Kréyol word *Blès* defines a deep physical or psychological injury that needs to be exorcised in order for the subject to heal. The concept is used by Chamoiseau in his monumental work: *Biblique des Derniers Gestes* (2002) where he associates the word with the atrocities of slavery lingering in the flesh of the contemporaneous Caribbean. Donatien Yssa associates it to the "colonial disease" in her work *Vaincre la souffrance dans Autobiographie de ma mère de Jamaica Kincaid* (2007).

[162] The Ethiopian African International Congres sis also known as "Congress."

[163] As the Maroons did before them.

[164] *Deliver us from Evil* is a book written by an unknown Bobo Shanti woman on the commune in the early 1980s. The book endeavours to explain the theological point of view of the EABIC. Complex notions are touched on, such as the reincarnation and the trinity. The book has recently been edited and printed by the Honourable Jah Karl in Nantes.

[165] See the mini documentary from an EABIC production about Reggae: http://www.youtube.com/watch?v=O3Au7AzeLfU&feature=related

[166] "Total art," Hip Hop is not limited to music but includes a multiplicity of artistic practices, such as dancing, street graphic arts, or streetwear. The Hip Hop movement is incessantly renewing, with the appearance of new dances, such as Krump or new rap styles such as Dirty-South or Crunk.

[167] By "diasporic music" I mean known, categorized and lived or experienced as an artistic and cultural expression created by a diaspora, here the black diaspora of the Atlantic region resulting from slavery. In fact, Hip Hop is commonly presented as a contemporaneous black music. However, this statement tends to obliterate the role played by other diasporas in the development of this music, including that of Hispanics in the Bronx. The racial identity of the subculture was confirmed by the policies of the music industry, largely founded on an ethnic classification of musical genres. Paul Gilroy (1993) emphasized the importance of this music in the habitus of the black diaspora through the example of Hip Hop. The distinguished sociologist reminds us that Hip Hop success was grounded on structures of transnational circulation and intercultural exchanges. He underscores the hybridity of this black Atlantic culture.

[168] The Zulu Nation Organization, founded by Bambaataa in the 1970s, had the objective of federating the gangs and to make them evolve positively and in a non-violent way thought the practice of deejaying (DJ), dance or with graffiti. These are all avatars of the Hip Hop movement.

[169] The Positive Black Soul rap in Wolof, one of the main languages used in Senegal, and in French.

[170] In December 2010 emerged a movement of social contestation in Tunisia which announced the Arab Spring revolution. Rap is then presented as the spokesperson of the Tunisian youth (Flora Genoux's article published in the French newspaper *Le Monde*, January 11, 2011). In December 2011, during the events, many rap videos circulated the internet through social networks (Facebook) and sites like Youtube or Dailymotion. The young Tunisian rappers denunciated the tyranny of Ben Ali's regime and called for his removal.

[171] The Y'en a marre movement created in February 2011 by Senegalese rappers bears a peaceful opposition to the Senegalese president Abdoulaye Wade.

[172] We can quote the example of the French-Congolese crew Bisso Na Bisso, created in 1998 by French rapper passy.

[173] See the book of Ntarangwi Mwenda, 2009.

[174] Dancehall was created in Jamaica at the very beginning of the 1980s, following directly from Reggae. This trend has spread rapidly in the Creole islands of the West Indies, of Réunion and Maurice, before it reached the rest of the French-speaking countries.

[175] The first inhabitants of Madagascar, called Cazimba, are often related to an African origin.

[176] In 2002, Madagascar experienced a serious political crisis. The supporters of Marc Ravalomanana, mayor of Antananarivo, who had contested the presidential elections of December 2001, were opposed to the supporters of Didier Ratsiraka, the outgoing president. After Marc Ravalomanana's ambivalent presidency and the increasing impoverishment of the Malagasy population, another political crisis appeared at the beginning of 2009. Ravalomanana's government was overthrown in favor of Rajaoelina, the mayor of Antananarivo, who became president of the Haute Transition without being elected. For almost two years, Rajaoelina has not been recognized by the international community, and the elections promised have so far not been organized.

[177] The term *andevo*, usually translated as "slave," is almost never said publicly.

[178] See D. Nativel and F. Rajaonah, *Madagascar et l'Afrique. Entre identité insulaire et appartenances historiques*, Paris, Karthala, 2007, 485.

[179] Besides, the O.U.A. appears as a mediator at the forefront in the resolution of the political conflict which gets bogged down in Madagascar.

[180] See C. Rafidinarivo, *Empreintes de la servitude dans les sociétés de l'Océan Indien*, Paris, Karthala, 2009, 237.

[181] In fact, during the "Royaume de Madagascar" (Madagascan realm) period in the nineteenth century, the *Maintys* were not slaves, but commoners. Proclaimed in 1896, the definitive abolition of slavery in Madagascar, which became a French colony, leads to a status change and the former *andevo* (slaves) joined the *mainty* rank. Opposed to the Fotsys (literally "white" or nobles), the *Maintys* (literally "black" or commoners) are associated with slavery, and the black complexion becomes synonymous with bondage and servitude. Cf.Rakotomalala M., Razafimbelo C., "Le problème d'intégration sociale chez les Makoa de l'Antsihanaka," in *OSA* 21–22, 1985, 93–115.

[182] The Makoa might have been the most represented in the colonial iconography n Madagascar. See V. Morabito, "L'esclavage à Madagascar à travers des images peu connues inédites," in I. Rakoto, *L'esclavage à Madagascar*, Antananarivo, Institut de Civilisations, Musée d'Art et d'Archéologie, 1997, 169–180.

[183] According to Campbell, the discussion on the origins of the slaves in Madagascar during the nineteenth century, should take into account the two categories of slaves: those coming from the African continent and those of the malagasy slaves. See. G. Campbell, 1988.

[184] On the diasporic issue, see. K. Boyer-Rossol, 2010.

[185] The Malagasy slaves deported, between the eighteenth and nineteenth century, to the Creole Mascarene islands, or the Atlantic region, including Cuba, were often incorporated into the category of servile Africans.

[186] The spirits of the ancestors are invoked during the trance ceremonies or *tromba*, widespread in Madagascar.

[187] We can link the improvisation of the traditional chants and the "freestyle" practiced in Rap music.

[188] The 1970s are marked in Madagascar by the nationalist, social and anti-colonial ideas which dominated the public opinion. The socialist revolution supported D. Ratsiraka's campaign for the presidency of the Madagascan democratic Republic, the political regime set up from 1975 to 1992, a period of time during which Madagascar was considered as a part of "the communist block" in Africa.

[189] The *valiha* is the national malagasy instrument. It is made of bamboo attached with ropes made of bark or metal. The easels are made of dried calabash.

[190] Those traditional origins of Rap music were collected through Reggae-Hip Hop artists from the malagasy west coast. Interview with Jahfro, August 2004, Antananarivo. Interview with Shao Boana, June 2008, Antananarivo.

[191] See K. Boyer-Rossol, 2007.

[192] In this country, they represent approximately four million inhabitants out of a total of nineteen million.

[193] See Boyer-Rossol K., 2009.

[194] Kazambo is a widespread Makoa name in Madagascar.

[195] See Gueunier N., "Documents sur la langue Makhua à Madagascar et aux Comores (fin du XIXe-début du XXe siècles), avec un lexique du makhuwa de Madagascar et des Comores," in *Etudes Océan Indien*, 35–36, 2003, 149–223.

[196] An instrumental (like the beat or the rhythm) is the musical part of a track on which the singers record their voices.

[197] The re-using of such clichés which stick to rappers' images are also re-used by the French Hip Hop artists, as demonstrated by Julien Guedj's and Antoine Heimann's sociological analysis, "Sociologie politique du rap français : nouvelle approche du mouvement rap." http://heimann.antoine.free.fr/ (accessed October 5, 2010).

[198] Most of the rappers who identify as Makoa are not of Makoan descent, but re-appropriate this identify by re-using the associated representations associated to the former West African slaves, including the black complexion.

[199] Lyrics by Shoa Boana. "Jaly Makoa,"from the album *Makoa*, 2000.

[200] Ibid.

[201] Ibid.

[202] Deschamps, *Les migrations intérieures passées et présentes à* Madagascar, Paris, Berger-Levrault, 1959, 150.

[203] For a long time, the debate on the source of the peopling of Madagascar has opposed those who defended the thesis of a first human stock from the south east Asian areas (regarding the linguistic issues, Malagasy being an Austronesian language) to those who supported the anteriority of the bantu source.

[204] Researchers present the generalization of this native/non-native opposition as one of the most worrying political evolutions on the African continent. A continental issue, the political question of indigeneousness also appears through the madagascan example as an insular phenomenon. See Jean-François Bayart, Peter Geschiere and Francis Nyamnjoh, "Autochtonie, démocratie et citoyenneté en Afrique," in *Critique internationale*, 10, January 2001, 177–194.

[205] Interviews of a prominent Sakalava citizen, who had formerly political responsibilities. Morondava, August 2004. Interviews of an *andriana* family (nobles) of royal lineage. Antananarivo, July 2004.

[206] During the political crisis of 2002, ethnicized speeches full of hatred have multiplied and continued to spread for a few years on the internet, where you could still read, in February 2005, on sites advocating for the *andrianité* (the merina nobility), sentences like: "The coast populations are seeds of Makoa, slaves in the making."

[207] Yet, the rappers who come from the high lands seem to claim their regional belonging more than the coast rappers.

[208] The documentary *Backstage Madagascar*, broadcasted on November 21, 2003 on the French TV channel *Arte*, presented Shao Boana as "the number 1 rapper of the island."

[209] Music video posted on Dailymotion, February 12, 2007.

[210] Music video posted on Dailymotion, June 20, 2008.

[211] Sammy Rastafanahy is regularly presented as the ambassador of Reggae in Madagascar.

[212] In 2003, the artists Shao Boana and Mc Crotal performed at the C.C.A.C., Antananarivo.

[213] The sound system, appearing since the early 1950s in Jamaica, are popular parties (street party) organized in the open air or in halls consisting first of all of a deejay and his machines (turntables, speakers). It also defines different syles of Jamaican music produced at that period (for example ska, reggae, raggamuffin).

[214] The group Afro-Janga was created in 2003 in the capital city of Antananarivo, where they met artists from the city of Mahajanga.

[215] Interview with Jahfro, August 2004, Antananarivo.

[216] From the *zokybe* (elder) of Madagascar reggae, Sammy Rastafanahy, through to the singer Abdou Day, but also the rappers Shao Boana or else Mike Killah: all of them have dreadlocks.

[217] The artist Mika Killah founded one of the first Rap crews in 1998 gathering in the capital city of Antananarivo, artists from the Madagascan West Coast, known

under the name of Too Black or *les Blackos*.

[218] See appendix 3.

[219] Môta, her real name being Danielle Raharivola, is one of the rare female pianists-composers-singers of Africa and the Indian Ocean. Discovered by the public during the 2004 Madajazzcar Festival at only nineteen years old, this female singer performs on multiple scenes and artistic collaborations. See www.myspace.motamd.

[220] Video posted on youtube March 30, 2009.

[221] We have to remember that the East African slaves deported during the nineteenth century to Madagascar were mostly of Mozambican origins.

[222] Interview of Môta realized by K. Boyer-Rossol via email between May 25 and 27, 2011.

[223] If, most of the time, the expression refers to the Western world, "Andafy" can also be employed to designate Africa. Comparatively, the term *Vazaha* or "alien/stranger" is most of the time synonymous with "whites," but can also used to talk about African continental people.

[224] The biographies of Malagasy Hip Hop artists indicates that many of them, born in the 1980s, have studied in Antananarivo, or have gone abroad to carry on with their studies. The stigmatization of the rappers, perceived as young eccentrics for a long time, sometimes seems to be distant from the young Malagasy's social reality, as Hip Hop appears to be practiced by a rather well-off youth.

[225] During the 2000s, there is a proliferation of Malagasy music videos (which can be seen on youtube or dailymotion), of blogs or specialized forums. We can name HHDago, the websites www.rap-gasy.com or www.madahiphop.com.

[226] Don Smokilla's biography is on http://rap-gasy.com.

[227] A net-tape is an album or a compilation created and broadcasted exclusively on the internet.

[228] A street album is a format used in the French Hip Hop world. Similar to an album, it does not necessarily have an editing line and is primarily based on performance.

[229] The mixtape *L'Hery-Tier vol.2*, released in 2010, re-uses instrumentals of American Hip Hop.

[230] Don Smokilla Feat. Seek (Radix), "Were We From," extracted from *L'Hery-Tier vol. 3*. Upoloaded to YouTube on May 22, 2011.

[231] www.myspace.com/sekelblock, http://www.donsmokilla.com/, http://www.facebook.com/donsmokilla

[232] Like Ben-J de Da Hopp or rapper Mista.

[233] On April 5, 2008, "New Scene," Studios of the RTA, in Ankorondrano (Antananarivo).

[234] This is the New Scene Spécial clan , organized in collaboration with the Bogota clan, which occurs at the Dôme RTA d'Ankorondrano à Antananarivo.

[235] http://hhdago.wordpress.com/2009/04/02/hh-for-life-2-a-antsahamanitra-le-05-novembre-2005/

[236] Interview with Bam's by Domoina Ratsara, published on June 4, 2010 in the newsaper *l'Express deMadagascar*. Today the female rapper is a journalist-reporter on RTA.

[237] Video realized in 2011. Available on Dalilymotion.

[238] At the Hip Hop Culture Festival, held in 2008 in Marseille (France), many African rap crews were scheduled. The organizers justified this programm saying that the future of Hip Hop was in Africa.

[239] I want to acknowledge the malagasy artists I met during my stays in the Great Island, without whom I would not be able to reach the core of the gasy Reggae-Hip Hop milieu: Jahfro, Sammy Rastafanahy, Mike Killah, Shao Boana. Among the malagasy hip hop crews of France, I want to thank, among others, Rija Randria-Draz, de Dago'sy Mouv. In France, some actors of the Hip Hop culture also pointed me to some highlights of the scene: thanks to Dj Reego, Clovis of "Coqlakour" as well, who participates in developing the Raga-Dancehall Réunionese movement in metropolitan France. Finally, I would like to mention the wonderful work realized by the volunteer Battle Afro team (La Cigale, Paris), that work for the promotion of Hip Hop culture in France, and more largely, the culture of the African diaspora.